DAVID GOLDSTEIN.

Socialism:

The Nation of Fatherless Children

DAVID GOLDSTEIN
AUTHOR

———

EDITED BY
MARTHA MOORE AVERY

———

PUBLISHER
The Union News League (Incorporated)
BOSTON

CONTENTS.

In honor of its work:
In appreciation of its leaders:
In hope for a bright future:
In my love for the wage worker:
I dedicate this book to the
American federation of Labor.

PREFACE

THIS work is presented to the consideration of the public, not as a piece of literature, but as a compendium of socialist data, which it is hoped will be found useful in acquiring the necessary knowledge to meet, and to turn back, the activity of socialist propaganda; which is progressively on the increase. We have altogether refrained from the use of socialist documents printed in foreign languages—Every quotation herein contained is taken from works published in or translated into the English tongue.

This book was begun in the hope that the facts presented in available form may lead to a better understanding of socialism—and thus, by this public service, to make amends, as far as possible, for the error committed in the advocacy, for so many years, of centering the political power of our country into the hands of socialists. It is with due deliberation that the position, outlined in this book, has been taken—And with the aid of Almighty God we shall withstand the shafts of bitterness thrust at us by those our one time comrades, with whom, in season and out of season, we have worked day and night for what we had believed to be the organization destined to give to the oppressed industrial emancipation. We have no apology to make as to the motives which prompted our course, we cheerfully leave judgement upon that score to the Power Above—Knowing that we shall be justly and mercifully dealt with.

The casual reader would, no doubt, reading in the public press the notice of my withdrawal from the socialist party, conclude that that action was prompted by the thought of a day. Such, however, is far from the facts in the case. Having for years been interested in the study of economic principles, rather than in the acquaintance of socialist data, I naturally gave my attention, outside of propaganda proper, to acquiring a knowledge of the economic principles which socialism is alleged to rest upon. I came long ago to a realization that the mouthing of the name of Karl Marx was no guarantee of economic knowledge. Seven years ago, together with a few of the then comrades we organized the Karl Marx class, for the study of his (Marx) work "Capital." Three years ago, having outgrown the work of the socialist master, we changed the name of the class to the Boston School of Political Economy, and took up the study of the original work of the Director, Martha Moore-Avery. I know, now, that this was the point at which I began intellectually to move away from the socialist propaganda.

The parting of the ways, from moral standing ground was more abrupt. The Herron episode furnished the occasion—I resented the attitude taken by the socialist press in regard to George D. Herron's divorce and his "socialist marriage," which had disgusted me—Especially for the reason that it could not be denied that he, Mr. Herron, was a socialist leader who was fast mounting to the very top of the ladder in socialist favor. It was at a public meeting held in Boston at which the then editor of the "Haverhill Social Democrat" was the speaker. After he had finished his address in praise of George D. Herron, whom he had lauded as being in power and virtue second only to Jesus Christ, in the discussion which followed, together with Martha Moore-Avery and one or two others, the author gave voice to strong condemnation of the lecturer's opinions and to the general tone of the socialist movement throughout the country. It was being sharply forced upon me that that which I had so long fondly believed to be socialism was not socialism at all. It was a severe blow to me—I was cut from my moorings—I could not tell for some months to come whether it was but a personal episode or whether I must in fact regard it as the deliberate position, taken in strict accord with socialist philosophy—I had thought my life work would be given to the cause of socialism, consequently the conflict in my mind and heart was great.

There will be found inserted within the pages of this book an article on the State, written in May—1901, which clearly defines my opposition to the position of authoritative socialists on that subject. As I look back upon it I regard it as a point of intellectual revolt from the socialist philosophy.

On the question of religion, I beg leave to say that when I joined the socialist movement I was not a church goer—nor an advocate of any religious creed whatever. Yet I always had an abhorence for the coarseness of atheistical teachings. I well remember the sensations of repugnance which came over me at the assertions of the German members, who at that time controlled the organization, that "you cannot be a socialist without being an atheist." I took this as their personal opinion—not for what it is, the bed rock of socialist philosophy. I know that an atheist political party could not gain the ascendency over an intelligent citizenship— But I assumed that the control of the movement would pass into competent hands— That it would come under American management and so outgrow its foreign atheistic accompaniment. Since those years the membership has changed, but with the influx of English speaking members, there has been a corresponding increase of loyalty to the founders of " international revolutionary scientific socialism," and its atheistic dogmas.

PREFACE.

In the mean time I had taken advantage, so far as I was able, of unexampled opportunities for the study of basic principles, as related to the order of the cosmos, which has led to a clearer understanding of religious principles and their necessary influence in sustaining and advancing human institutions and in preserving and elevating human life—While on the other hand I had gained a clearer understanding of the fact, which is substantiated by the data here presented, that in its very nature socialism preys upon the ambitions and the hopes of workingmen, leading them into the mazes of the materialistic den—where the beast now takes on the modern form of political atheism.

So dazzling are the brilliant pictures which socialists present, so bold and entrancing are they, clothed with a language all their own—that many are led to its door in the hope of finding that elixir to cure the sufferings of the race,—The author is too well acquainted with the demagogic demonstrations of the platform which are met by rounds of applause, by a like set of minds as those which delighted in the bold, the brilliant, the pathetic, the charming, but always irrational utterances of the late Ingersoll, to expect the issuing of a book will stop their farther advance—But it will, I trust, enable those who have not the time nor the inclination to spend the energy required to make a personal investigation into all the literature circulated within the socialist propaganda to find between the covers of a single book sufficient data to get a full glimpse of what a vote for socialism signifies. For it is upon the recruits to socialism that it depends for its progress, for its success—Therefore upon those who are now sympathetically approaching the socialist party devolves the responsibility of aiding and abetting a movement whose express purpose is the disruption of human society. Upon such rests the responsibility of gathering a great force of men and women, who think to aid in righting the wrongs which the working class suffer, under the command of socialist leaders who are fully aware of the real purpose of their movement. Upon socialist sympathizers who shall have read the facts herein contained rests the responsibility of propagating a doctrine which by the votes of the people would enforce upon themselves decrees of disaster and shame—There is no half-way place of rest, after one has been presented with this evidence in the case—Either he stands with law and order—for the advancement of human society—or his hand is red with the purpose of its destruction—To those then who read these testimonies as to what the socialist doctrine is we would say, "Lift up thy eyes and look from the place wherein thou now art, to the north and to the south, to the east and to the west."

It was the accumulation of fact upon fact which at last has left me with the conviction that the atheistic forces, which under the socialist propaganda are taking political form, will compel a closer association of those organizations which stand for the propagation and enforcement of religious law. — The time worn battle between right and wrong is on. The weapons in use are those of modern warfare—The unbiased investigation cannot fail to see that the struggle will determine whether religious institutions are to survive or to perish.—They have withstood the shocks of all these centuries of assault, and I have no fear of the outcome—for if civilization is to survive, religious institutions will stand as they stand now as the bed rock of human society. But the struggle is to be long and bitter. The religious battles will be fought upon political ground—with the upholders of materialism on one side and the lovers of religion on the other—The thousands and tens of thousands upon one side come but to destroy, for their banner is the dense dark sign of uncontrolled passion. While on the other side are the hosts guided by the light of revealed knowledge who once again will lead the nations out of the paths of greed and of lust into those of peace.

It is my personal conviction, which I may say I have arrived at without association or affiliation with the institution—that upon the religious aspects of this great issue the fight now centers around the Catholic Church —which is the first and only church that has boldly taken up the gauntlet thrown down with scorn and defiance by socialism. This church is not only international, or rather universal, and so equipped to meet the power of the international enemy, but it is erected upon a basis—upon religious science—which gives it the strength to cope with the aggressions of the approaching foe. There are I am aware many persons who would rather see hell reign than that the Catholic Church should be the victor in so great, so masterful a struggle—for such I have but sympathy, for they but veil themselves in darkness. They may be assured if this institution fall in the fight (if that were possible) all religions, sects and cults would collapse in its ruins.

There is marked evidence to show that upon economic ground, the battle to sustain the industrial progress made by the race will come to issue between the American Federation of Labor and the socialist propaganda organization. It will no doubt be a long drawn series of hand to hand fights upon the floor of trade unions—and in the halls of trades union conventions, state and national. Having fought desperately in the glare of its false light, at last the truth was revealed to me that socialism is the cause of the damned—not the cause which maketh men free—and now within the strength of reason rather than in the excitement of fanaticism I shall hope to add somewhat to the victories of the American Federation of Labor.

BOSTON, SEPTEMBER 11TH, 1903.

x

INTRODUCTION

"What in me is dark
Illumine, what is low raise and support;
That to the height of this great argument
I may assert eternal Providence
And justify the ways of God to men."
—Milton.

WHEN a movement attracts to itself so large a following as socialism has it is deserving of serious consideration. Does the power of its attraction lie in its analysis or in its condemnation of existing forms or in its promise of establishing a higher order of society?

Careful study of the socialist movement will prove that its centre of attraction is its negative condemnatory attitude rather than in its positive understanding of the underlying causes and conditions which press upon the public conscience for solution; that its attractiveness lies in its promise of a new mould for the whole existing order rather than in its understanding of those principles which make for true progress.

On the destructive side socialism stands for the abolition of the present educational, religious, family, social and economic forms of society. While on the constructive side it declares for the ownership of economic capital by the people organized into a "business administration." The other departments of governmental activity will be abolished. Each and every person will be allowed the free exercise of personal will, without the communities' hand showing itself in legal or other form of authority. "The place of a government over persons is taken by the administration of things" ("Socialism, Utopian and Scientific," by Frederick Engels).

" Under socialism the government will have no other function
but the administration of the public industries. Socialism is
opposed to all interference with the personal liberties of the
people." (Appeal to Reason, July 11th, 1903.)

Socialists complain, and justly so, that many of its opponents quote Spencer, Duehring, Sombart, Boehm Bawerk,
Ely, Flint, Rae, Kirkup and others of kindred schools as
authority on socialism. They argue "you would not quote
Tom Paine or Ingersoll as authorities on the divine inspiration of the Bible—why quote our opponents as authority on
socialism?" This error we shall strictly avoid. We shall
listen to the evidence and take the testimony from the mouth
and pen of the recognized national and international authorities on modern socialism. For our desire is that the socialist
position may be clearly understood by the men who cast their
votes in favor of a socialist political programme: that the
responsibility of this knowledge may rest upon those men
when entering the sacred precincts of the voting booths
should they ask themselves the question, is it to the best
interest of the men, women and children of the present generation and of generations to come, to centralize political
power into the hands of men who are committed to the philosophy of socialism?

One point must be clearly understood by the reader,
which is that it is not our purpose to analyze the evils from
which men suffer owing to unjust economic conditions—or
from otherwise unfavorable causes—neither is it our purpose
to offer a panacea for any of them. But our object rather is
to present unquestionable data which will allow a comprehensive view of the quality of the forces which are gathering for
political expression under the socialist banner.

Certainly men who impartially investigate the economic
unrest which disturbs the whole social fabric will find many
evils justly entitled to severe condemnation by those who seek
a higher standard of industrial life. It is true that we have a

degree of aristocracy in industry which is out of harmony with the fullness of our democracy in government. But, after all is said about the terrible economic conditions that prevail—the deeper—the more important—the vital question, which requires the will of a Moses, the head of an Aaron and the heart of the Nazarene to solve, is what shall be done to soften the human heart, to elevate the human mind, and to discipline the human will, that social harmony may be the possession of man?

The socialist is quick to give his answer, dissolve the present order! Having walled himself within the narrow breastworks of "economic determinism," his concept of the state, the family and the industrial world covers only the distance encompassed by the dim light of atheistic understanding. He fails to see the length, breadth and depth of the present order. The advantages which we enjoy, despite the disadvantages, given as a result of the establishment and development of the state which protects life, liberty and property and guarantees the system of free contract. He fails to realize the divine institution of the family in its monogamic form—fails to distinguish between a family and a collection of persons as the necessary basis of organized society. He fails to see that industry is established upon and is maintained upon the basis of equity. How easy! The state? abolish it. The family? make it free—abolish its legal and ecclesiastical forms. The industries? let the people confiscate the capital and own it in common. Socialists would throw over the inheritance of all the centuries; pull down the experience that has led the race out of darkness. Blinded by the spirit of hatred, they centre the mind on the economic conditions as the fundamental cause of all social evils.

Sane men dealing scientifically with sociological matters examine the phenomenon which presents itself, seeking to correct present abuses—seeking to erect new forms to replace outworn methods. While socialists, in unscientific, irrational manner, seek the complete overthrow of the present form of society, putting forth as a substitute brilliant but speculative conditions, which in the nature of things and from all data extant has experimentally been proven impracticable.

This conclusion is not the thought of a day, but the deliberate judgment of one who has been intoxicated with the socialist vision of a coöperative commonwealth—where equality of industrial opportunity would regulate all human affairs. Substituting this alluring prospect for those supreme religious qualities which shall one day turn spears into ploughshares and swords into pruning hooks.

Painfully recovering from this intellectual debauch, with sober earnest I set to work examining critically the quality of literature and the character of the movement, which resulted in my severing all connection with socialist organizations.

BOSTON, May 23, 1903.

To the Massachusetts State Committee, Socialist Party,

HON. JAMES F. CAREY, Chairman,

MR. SQUIRE E. PUTNEY. Secretary.

GENTLEMEN : —

After a lapse of eight years of active work upon the soap-box, on the lecture platform, in debate and in the press in behalf of what I had understood to be the principles of socialism; after eight years of work as organizer, executive officer and candidate of socialist parties; after eight years of study of the alleged scientific basis of socialism, namely Karl Marx' "Capital," now when I feel competent to expound its doctrinal points, I have come to the point where I desire to terminate my connection with the socialist movement. I am convinced that it is not a bona-fide political and economic effort, that it would gain political power to the end of dis-.

solving the social — religious — civic — economic and family relationship which now exists — which have cost man countless ages in upbuilding. Careful study of the underlying causes of discord and disruption which are of constant recurrence, not only within the socialist parties of the United States but also in every country in which socialism has taken up its propaganda leads me to the conviction that the attitude of negation to all that is fundamental in human affairs — the denial of God — the opposition to the state — the disruption of monogamic marriage — does not nor can it ever lead to a coherent political party with a constructive programme.

The basic reason for the long sustained and persistant attempt to stifle the voice and pen of Martha Moore Avery is that she may not throw the lime light upon the low browed philosophies cherished as socialist sentiment. Even though Mrs. Avery devotes her knowledge and her critical ability, not to speak of her life to the upbuilding of a state wherein workmen may come into a position of industrial equity, but the fact that she is philosophically opposed to those socialists who control the press and the commanding official positions prompts even dishonest methods to be employed in their effort to suppress open discussion. How weak must socialists feel when free speech is denied its membership?

I had long hoped and often expressed the sentiment that the irrational literature and the economic absurdities spread broadcast amongst the people of our country would change in character with the growing power of the organization. But after close application to the doctriniares, their philosophy and their so-called science, I must conclude that the socialism I was preaching had no basis in fact — it was not the kind which the political socialist movement stands for. It is my conviction that were the philosophical doctrines applied to a given country, or to the civilized world in general, as promulgated by the founders of "modern scientific revolutionary international socialism" namely by Karl Marx and Frederick

5

Engels, by Kautsky and Babel of Germany; Guedse and De Ville of France; Hyndman and Bax of England; Vandervelde of Belgium; Ferri of Italy; and many others upon the continent of Europe; by Simmons, Herron, Lee, Unterman and others in the United States that economic justice, even to the degree which exists to-day, would be unknown. — That is to say I am convinced that socialism as organized internationally stands for the entire breaking down of the individual standards of moral responsibility — That the socialist philosophy of "economic determinism" stands for the substitution of religious principles by social standards of ethics set up upon the basis of mere physical satisfactions.

The State —, no; did I say the State?

Socialism, according to the authorities which I have cited, stands for the dissolution of civil law — for the dissolution of political action — in short for the abolition of the state. These socialist authorities declare they "have no respect for the present marriage system," they stand for the abolition of marriage; the children? Yes, there will be children under socialism — but they will not belong to the mothers. The community will be the father and mother of them all — the guardians of all children, "legitimate and illegitimate."

Are these doctrines new in the socialist field? No! You know full well my opposition to them is not new — I would recall the resolution which I presented to the last convention which declares that speakers who attack the theological doctrines or dogmas, who advocate violence, "free love," or other doctrines in opposition to the principles of socialism shall be by the Executive Committee deemed disqualified for the socialist platform. Your hostility to my attitude towards these questions caused you to make strenuous efforts to block my progress on the socialist platform and in the press. I do not forget the deceitful challenge from the floor at the last state convention to produce evidence of my assertions, many were prejudiced by your clamor into thinking it did not exist.

INTRODUCTION.

I may tell you that I have taken up your gage of battle. — I will bring forward my proofs — overwhelming you shall find them. I have for months been engaged in collecting the material for a book which, with the help of Almighty God, I will in the near future give to the public which will prove to the candid mind (if facts count for anything) that a vote cast for socialism is a vote cast for the destruction of those institutions which promote and sustain civilization. Namely, the Church, the State and the Monogamic family.

Citizens will ponder this question ; can society be saved from the present economic injustice, which is a stench in a true man's nostrils, by the general destruction courted by the socialist philosophy in control of the political power? For myself I answer emphatically NO.

Therefore I take my leave of socialist organizations. I have this day tendered my resignation as member of the Highland District Socialist Party Club, and of the Boston Socialist Party Ward and City Committee. — I have too tendered my resignation as representative of the General Committee of Massachusetts Socialist Clubs. I beg leave herewith to resign my membership in the State Committee of the Socialist Party of Massachusetts.

Respectfully,

(Signed)   DAVID GOLDSTEIN,

37 Maywood Street,

Boston.

Materialistic Doctrine of Socialism.

"Could great men thunder
As Jove himself does, Jove would ne'er be quiet,
For every pelting, petty officer,
Would use his heaven for thunder;
Nothing but thunder. Merciful Heaven!
Thou rather, with thy sharp and sulphurous bolt,
Splitt'st the unwedgeable and gnarl-ed oak,
Than the soft myrtle: but man, proud man!
Drest in a little brief authority
Most ignorant of what he's most assured,
His glassy essence,— like an angry ape,
Plays such fantastic tricks before high heaven,
As make the angels weep."
— MEASURE FOR MEASURE.

WE shall show that the socialist movement rests upon and proceeds more or less logically from a mere materialist basis — that it concerns itself with the questions of wealth production and distribution mainly because in its view the conditions under which economic necessities are produced form the fundamental groundwork from which all social, intellectual, religions and other institutions emanate. Frederick Engels puts it as follows:

"The juridical, philosophical, and religious ideas are the more or less remote offshoots of the economical relations existing in a given society."

"The Appeal To Reason" (June 6, 1903) says:

"The economic conditions of any country, at any period, form the basis of all human effort. All social, political, legal, moral and religious institutions are built upon the economic basis."

George D. Herron, under the Caption, "There cannot be any Reconcilation between Capital and Labor," in "The Metropolitan Magazine" and "The Appeal to Reason" (May 16, 1903) says:

8

"Socialism begins with this—that the history of the world has been economic. The world's sentiments and religions, its laws and morals, its art and literatures, are all rooted in the struggle between classes for the control of the food supply. Moses and Jesus, Wickliffe and Mazzini, Marx and Millet are products of the stress and injustice of intensified economic conditions. War is but a final mode of economic competition. Religions, in their first and purest expressions, are all economic revolts—appeals and protests against the ownership of souls involved in economic ownership."

"Laws, creeds, governments, morals, and arts are chiefly the expression of those who have lived off of other people, and who have made laws and religions, and arts and morals for the purpose of compelling these others to support them while they should fight or preach or make laws or write books."

These three quotations, from Engels, "The Appeal to Reason" and Herron are sufficiently authorative to form a correct starting point from which to view the basis of socialist doctrine and to get a glimpse of socialist logic. Socialism rests upon the assumption that all human institutions of whatever nature "are the more or less remote offshoots of the economic relations." Or as George D. Herron more plainly puts it "The world's sentiments and religions its laws and morals, its arts and literature, are all rooted in the struggle between classes for the control of the food supply."

Let my traducers answer, does or does not socialism deny the validity of revealed religion and does it attack or defend the basis upon which the church rests.

The "materialist conception of history"—the foundation stone of socialist philosophy is clearly laid down in "Socialism Utopian & Scientific" in which Frederick Engels, the author, says,

"The materialistic conception of history proceeds upon the principle that production, and, next to production, the exchange of its products, is the ground-work of every social order; and that in every social system, that has arisen historically, the distribution of the products, together with the social divisions into classes and orders, depends upon that which is produced, and the manner in which it is produced, and also upon the manner in which the articles produced are exchanged. According to this, the prime causes of all social changes and political revolutions are to be traced, not to the heads of men, not to their increasing perception of eternal truth and justice, but to the changes in the manner of production and exchange; they are to be traced, not to the PHILOSOPHY, but to the ECONOMICS of the respective epochs. The awakening perception that existing social institutions are unreasonable and unjust, that sense has become non-sense, and right wrong, is only an evidence that, in the methods of production and forms of exchange, changes have silently taken place with which the social order, fitted to the previous economic conditions, is no longer in keeping. Hereby it is at the same time implied that the means for the removal of the discovered abuses must be latent and more or less developed in the changed conditions of production themselves. But these means are not to be INVENTED by the brains, they are to be DISCOVERED, with the aid of the brains, in the material facts of production that are on hand."

Engels' materialistic basis of history alleges that economic development causes to be built up and to be outgrown all human institutions, religious or otherwise — and this work is accepted as authority by the overwhelming majority of socialists of national and international repute.

Ernest Belfort Bax, who is perhaps no lesser authority than Engels himself, declares that "the result of economical revolution implies a correlative change in the basis of ethics and religion." ("Ethics of Socialism.") Indeed he stands at the head of this department of the school, in the view of the "Social Democrat," the official organ of the Social Dem-

-ocratic Federation of London, England, which says in its issue of January, 1903, "Bax is the philosophic reasoner and exponent of Socialist theory and doctrine," of the world-wide movement.

Certainly this is not a superficial attack upon religion, but it is profoundly hostile to the belief in a Creator — perhaps I may be pardoned for the use of the word profoundly in this connection. What would be the reason for attacking the church when socialists at one fell swoop could take the ground from under it?

But listen to Marx ("Capital," page 32) "Christianity with its *cultus* of abstract man, more especially in its bourgeois development, Protestantism, Deism, etc., is the most fitting form of religion in which the present mode of ex- change of commodities takes place." Let us take further testimony from "the Appeal to Reason" (May 16, 1903).

"Fifty-five years have now passed by since Karl Marx formulated his materialist conception of history, and gave to the world its first science of economics. The Communist Manifesto reads like a document written yesterday. The multiplication table must have been the same six thousand years ago as it is today. A truth is a truth for all time. Therefore, when Marx analyzed society and found that ethics, morals and religions are all the products of economic or material conditions, he was able to predict with certainty the future conduct of society, even as does the astronomer predict the coming of an eclipse."

In order to obtain a comprehensive view of socialism, it must be borne in mind that socialism expresses an economic change in the existing order as a means of revolutionizing the political, ethical and religious forms of society.

One of the "great discoveries" accredited to Marx and Engels is that they were the first to formulate the idea that the economic change is the fundamental cause and the means whereby the forms of all other institutions are changed. Is

it then necessary to "attack" the church when it will fall in
upon itself once the coöperative commonwealth is established?
Certainly not, if there were a sufficient development of self
control amongst the devotees of socialism. But bitter feeling
will have its way despite the better prospects of "ringing in"
the unwary. "Catching flies with molasses" is the better
way to force inroads to the heart of trade unions. In one
word "as a vote catcher" the assertion is commonly made,
especially by new adherents of the socialist parties, that "socialism is an economic and political science, and as such has
no connection with any religious institution or belief."
("American Labor Union Journal," March 12, 1903.) Ignorance of socialist philosophy is in part sponsor for this
opinion. For newcomers are quite innocent of the fact that
the socialist propaganda follows its due course despite the individual attempts to turn it to one side or another. But the
denial of its underlying principles is more often the deliberate
attempt to conceal from the general public the real import of
its aims in the interest of gathering numerical strength.
While such statement is always prompted by the desire to
make the doctrine as little distasteful to the camp followers
and sympathizers as possible.

"Father" Thomas McGrady, a new adherent of socialism, in his "Unaccepted Challenges" [If his knowledge of
socialism were as high as his brazen audacity, he would have
issued fewer of them], writes as follows:

"Socialism does not beget atheism any more than chemistry begets infidelity. Socialism is an economic science, not
a religious creed. We must look elsewhere for the causes of
atheism than in socialism. The so-called father of the Democratic party, Thomas Jefferson, was an infidel; and Robert
Ingersoll, the agnostic, was a leading Republican in his day."

Granted, for the sake of argument, that Jefferson was
an infidel, certainly that does not prove that the democratic
party is committed to a programme of infidelity, for the good

reason that Jefferson's "bible" is not accepted as the bulwark of the democratic programme. Yes, Ingersoll was an agnostic, an intellectual bluffer. But Ingersoll's irrational attacks upon religion and the church are not circulated by the republican party as the basis of its philosophy. Therefore, what rational analogy is there in McGrady's statement? Considering the fact that the irreligious teachings of Marx and Engels are circulated as fundamental prodaganda matter? That the "materialistic concept of history," which is a gross denial of the *rationale* of revealed religion, is generally accepted by socialists, not alone in the United States but throughout the civilized world in past cavil. Let us restate it in Marx' own words. "The life process of society, which is based on the process of material production, does not strip off its mystical veil until it is treated as production by freely associated men, and is consciously regulated by them in accordance with a settled plan. This, however, demands for society a certain material groundwork or set of conditions of existence which in their turn are the spontaneous product of a long and painful process of development." ("Capital," page 33.)

Now listen to this: "The American Labor Union Journal" (March 12, 1903) says "the capitalist hireling editor who tries to make socialism a religious question is either an idiot, or he believes his readers to be idiots." Such denial of socialism by socialists may perhaps mislead numbers of western workmen and cause them to break with the American Federation of Labor, which it is the open purpose of the A. L. U. to destroy. But when the editor's followers come to the understanding of what socialist philosophy truly is they may perhaps realize that he not "the capitalist hireling editor" is the idiot. Knowing socialist propaganda they must conclude that it is of grave importance as a religious question as well as a political and economic problem. However, I shall deal with the religious aspect of the matter in another chapter.

The dispute as to socialism being a purely economic question is not new to the history of the party. Ernest Belfort Bax whose opinions are of international importance—but we will allow socialists to bespeak him fair:—

"Ernest Belfort Bax is one of the best known and most versatile and accomplished socialists of Europe. His published works form a small library in themselves and are everywhere held in highest respect by the recognized leaders of the international socialist movement. Perhaps the best known of his works are *The Religion of Socialism*, *Ethics of Socialism*, *Outspoken Essays*, *Outlooks from the new Standpoint*, *Life of Jean Paul Marat*, *Handbook of the History of Philosophy*, *Story of the French Revolution*, *A Short History of the Paris Commune*, and, in conjunction with William Morris, *Socialism: Its Growth and Outcome*. This quite formidable list represents, I believe, less than half of his original works, in addition to which are numerous translations, including a volume of Schopenhauer's *Essays*, and Kant's *Foundations of Natural Science*.

"Born in Warwickshire, England, in 1854, he studied in Germany—music first, then philosophy. The Paris Commune of 1871 aroused his sympathy and led him to study socialism. He was one of the founders of the Social Democratic Federation in England and during the twenty odd years which have elapsed since then he has ever been an active worker in the cause. It was he who first induced William Morris to join the socialist movement, and perhaps that fact weighed with him when he joined with Morris and others in forming the socialist league. But, like almost every one of the others, he returned to the federation, and ever since has been prominently identified with it. He is a familiar figure at all international congresses of the socialist movement." "The Comrade," New York (December, 1902).

In his review of Kirkups' "An Enquiry into Socialism," Mr. Bax says, editorially in "The Commonweal," Vol. 4, No. 116:

"While fully agreeing with those socialists who would avail themselves of all, even the most apparently trifling efforts tending to raise the present condition of the working classes, . . . yet nevertheless I think too strong a protest cannot be raised against the habit of either blinking or minimising the ideal which all true socialists have in view. It is undeniable that there are certain well-meaning but 'philistinic" persons who are forever going about with tongue and pen trying to convince weak minded and timid hearers or readers that the modern proletarian mountain is, after all, only pregnant with a sort of big mouse. The way they do this is sometimes specious, and hence it is difficult to convict them *in flagrante delicto*. For instance, their first proceeding is to draw a ring-fence round economics and insist that socialism is economical and has nothing to say on any other aspect of human life than that of the production and distribution of wealth. . . . .

"Let us take up Mr. Kirkup's chapter on *Current Views on Socialism*.

(1.) ''Mr. Kirkup starts with the marriage question. The opposition between the 'bourgeois property marriage' and that which will take its place is of course sought to be toned down. While admitting that most leading socialists have attacked the modern or Christian marriage with its indissolubility or quasi-indissolubility, Mr. Kirkup 'cannot see that *as a theory of economic organization* socialism can have any special teaching adverse to marriage and the family.' Now this is because Mr. Kirkup chooses to set up a ring-fence again, ignoring his own definition of socialism given above as 'a theory of social organization, based on a new scheme of economic organization.' The passage quoted above implies that there is only one form of marriage and the family, that of the modern Christian and the bourgeois. Of course as a "*theory* of economic organization,' socialism need not

15

have any special teaching 'adverse' to this; but as a matter of practice the modern marriage and modern family is sustained by the modern system of property, and when the latter gives place to something else, so must the former: . . . It is also not true to say that the views on this question of the 'leading socialist writers' referred to as attacking the present marriage system, have been 'strenuously opposed within the socialist schools.' I challenge Mr. Kirkup to show a single case in point.

(2) "Socialism is 'by many' believed to be hostile to Christianity, etc. Of course here Mr. Kirkup must step in and plead that 'the connection with views of this nature is purely accidental.' It is on a par with the attempt in the 'Britanica' article (vol. xxii, p. 220) to make out that Socialism is not more international than any other movement (artistic or literary, for example). So here, Mr. Kirkup trots out his favorite notion about Socialism not being more hostile to Christianity than Continental Liberalism. It is difficult to think that a man of Mr. Kirkup's reading can fail to see that the internationalism, like the anti-Christianism of Socialism, is a very different thing from the Internationalism of art or commerce, or the anti-clericalism of the Radical. Of course, having drawn this ring-fence round the economical theory of Socialism, it naturally follows that he can exclude everything else but pure economics from the essence of Socialism. But this economic-and-nothing-but-economic Socialism is a 'metaphysical abstraction.' One of the greatest insights of Marx was that of the connection of the economic with the other aspects of human life. And Socialism as a revolutionary theory of society implies an ethical, religious and political revolution as a consequence of the economic one. As such its opposition to the *present* forms of these things, which in their turn are based on the economics of present society, is a matter of Socialistic principle and in nowise 'non-essential' or merely a question of temporary policy as with the Con-

tinental Liberal, who, for the rest, never contemplates anything but the curtailment of clerical influence. I would put
it to Mr. Kirkup and those other professors of the 'science
of Socialism made easy to the middle-class philistine,'
whether they think it would be compatible with Socialism to
have a clerical class setting themselves up as spiritual teachers
and living on the labor of others, or even allow the small
minority who habitually frequent 'places of worship,' to
monopolise lands and buildings for the purpose of their cultus.

"Mr. Kirkup further states that Socialism 'has also been
associated with Christianity, Catholic and Protestant.' Now
in how far is this true ? In the same sense in which it has
been associated with orthodox views as to the family, etc. The
fact of the matter is this: Socialism has by a process of
natural selection become the name of a great movement beginning with the present century, having for its end the re-
organization of human life, moral and material, on a basis of
equality of rights and duties. This movement, on its theoretical no less than on its practical side, is distinguished by
certain well marked stages. The theory of socialism as a
coherent doctrine began with the three great utopist systems
of Robert Owen, Fourier and St. Simon. Not one of these
systems took what I may term the abstract-economic view of
the subject. They all regarded human life as an integral
system, and never dreamt of separating its several aspects.
They were all anti-Christian, all opposed to the modern form
of marriage, and if not explicitly international they were at
least implicitly so. The latter schools of French socialism
have always had something to say in the same sense on the
subjects of religion, marriage, and racial boundaries, that is,
always in a sense hostile to the existing forms of these institutions. Finally, modern 'scientific' socialism, while ac-
centuating the economical revolution implied in the word, has
none the less insisted on the fact that the other aspects of
human life must undergo a corresponding change.

"So much for the growth of Socialist theory. But — and here lies the *équivoque* of Mr. Kirkup's position — concurrently with the later form of this development of true theoretical socialism there has been a series of spurious and bastard systems, clearly distinguishable as such, and which have sprung consciously, or unconsciously for the most part, from a dread of the new economic change. They may be known by this very sign, that they appear to adopt the economic side of socialism while overtly rejecting the notion of the other social changes which that side implies. But when more nearly viewed, it will be found that they do not really accept the economic revolution at all, but merely some scheme which can be made to bear a superficial resemblance to it. Like Pharaoh's soothsayers, the bourgeois also 'did so with their enchantments.' 'Christian socialism' such as that of the Comte de Mun in France on the side of Catholicism, or of Herr Stöcker in Germany on the side of Protestantism, the various co-operative schemes with which the working classes have been from time to time deceived, belong to this spurious socialism. As the devil of mediæval fancy, or Walpurgis night, travestied the proceedings supposed to take place before the judgment seat of God, so the modern bourgeois travesties the aspirations of the real proletarian movement in a series of artificially produced countermovements. In this sense only can it be said that socialism has been 'associated with Christianity, both Catholic and Protestant.' It is not easy to understand that those desirious of maintaining a class society, and recognizing the importance and 'danger' of socialism, think if they but hold the proletariat in leash tied to three venerable institutions, 'the hearth, the throne, and the altar,' or any one of them, that the proletariat is by the very fact rendered harmless. 'Oh, drudge, where is thy sting? Oh, slave, where is thy victory?' Not under the ægis of Christian, philanthropic, or co-operative 'socialism' we must rest assured.

MATERIALISTIC DOCTRINE OF SOCIALISM.

"I have desired under the form of a review of Mr. Kirkup's new book, where the practice appears in its rankest form, to call attention to the illegitimacy of the attempt so often made nowadays to limit the word socialism, in a mechanical manner, to the sphere of economics — while objection is taken to its being applied to what the economical change implies in other departments of human activity. Such a limitation is not logically nor historically valid."

Proof! Did I not tell the Massachusetts Socialists that there is proof — overwhelming proof that "free love" and no God are parts of socialist philosophy? Better politicians than citizens they may bluff their camp followers, but "the damned spot will not out."

If the "Father" McGrady's, the "A. L. U. Journal" and other new upstarts in the socialist movement who are so free with "challenges" want an American authority on the question of socialism as a mere economic movement, here it is: Editorial, "The Comrade" (New York, May, 1903):

"We can no more hope to escape the struggle against the religion of capitalism than we may hope to escape the struggle against its economics. And we have no business attempting to escape it. Yet there has been more than a tendency in that direction in our ranks of late. 'Socialism is simply a question of economics,' says one. 'It has nothing to do with morals,' says another. 'Socialism is nothing more nor less than a matter of economic theory,' and so on. In most instances those who thus narrowly define socialism are the first to complain of what they are pleased to describe as the 'rigid and barren materialism' of the followers of Marx. They do not, apparently, see that their own fear of the issues before them, which these answers are vain attempts to evade, have made of their socialism a cold, barren, harsh materialism, without one solitary spiritual attraction. Only when we are brave enough to be true to the world, and to ourselves, concerning our faith, shall we be able to discern its full spiritual beauty. When that courage is ours, and not till then, the glory and inspiration of socialism will also be ours."

Is "materialism" being outgrown as the acknowledged foundation of socialist belief ? I should say not ! For "The Comrade" is the best of authority. It is an illustrated monthly published in New York city, edited by John Spargo, formerly a leader in the English socialist movement. George D. Herron is the leading member of its advisory board. "The Comrade" ranks first among the illustrated publications of the United States and also within the English-speaking world.

"The struggle," as the editor of "The Comrade" frankly says, against religion cannot be escaped. "Ring fence" definitions, as Bax terms them, which declares socialism to be an economic question merely, dealing only with questions proper to the science of wealth production and distribution, will mislead only the weak minded, the unwary, but never those who are strong and lack not the understanding.

Socialist authorities from Marx and Engels down to the present day teach that all institutions, of whatever nature, religious, moral, intellectual, ethical, civic, political, etc., etc., are but results of the economic structure and therefore all institutions must change with the development of the industrial world. Upon this ground the socialist movement stands, upon this ground the socialist movement must fall.

Origin and Ethics of Socialism Opposed to Christianity.

> "I had rather believe all the fables in the Legend, and the Talmud, and the Alcoran, than that this universal frame is without a mind. It is true that a little philosophy inclineth man's mind to atheism, but depth in philosophy bringeth men's minds about to religion; for while the mind of man looketh upon second causes scattered, it may sometimes rest in them and go no further; but when it beholdeth the chain of them confederate and linked together, it must needs fly to Providence and Deity."
>
> —LORD BACON.

IT has become quite the "rage" with the third rate literati to float their intellectual wares on the radical market by the use of the catch penny term socialism on the title page. That socialism should stand for any fanciful notion of a superior order which may be airily builded up in the noddle of an author is, after all, quite consistent with the quality of disorder which really lies at the bottom of its fatalistic doctrine. Mrs. Freemont Older, in "The Socialist and the Prince," dubs her hero Dennis Kearny, the anti-Chinese agitator, a socialist. Such writing adds greatly to the socialist strength politically; while the general confusion thus created leads not only to innocent misrepresentation but it also encourages duplicity of conduct in the interest of "spreading the cause."

The Owenites of England were the first to use the terms socialist and socialism in the work of organizing their cooperative schemes. Robert Owen, the founder, is accredited by many writers as having coined them about the year 1830.

In the early and middle part of the last century, the followers of Fourier, St. Simon and others who worked for the establishment of their "utopias of freedom" were also known as socialists.

Karl Marx and Frederick Engels in the days of '48, at the behest of the Communist League wrote the "Manifesto" which strictly marks the beginning of the movement which today is known as modern socialism. Speaking of this document the socialist labor party, voicing the sentiment of socialists the world over, says:

"At a congress of the League, held in London in November, 1847, Marx and Engels were commissioned to prepare for publication a complete theoretical and practical program for the party. This program was called the *Manifesto of the Communist Party*. And the *Communist Manifesto*, as it is now more generally known, may be said to be the basis on which modern scientific socialism has built its world-wide structure."

The first word on the title page of this document, Communist (which is still maintained), was used to distinguish the "Internationals" from the movements of Owen, Fourier, St. Simon and others.

With the disintergration of these utopian schemes and the development of the organization headed by Marx and Engels, the word socialism became identified with the latter; as belonging generically and historically to that body of men who are organized nationally and federated internationally. Within the United States socialists are organized under the several names of Socialist Party, Socialist Labor Party and Social Democratic Party.

That socialism bears no kinship with Christianity the merest glance at the "Communist Manifesto" will show, for that which has already "succumbed" to rationalism has but a fancied existence — "the ignorant superstition of religion" lingers only in irrational heads.

"When the ancient world was in its last throes the ancient religions were overcome by Christianity. When Christian ideas succumbed in the eighteenth century to rationalist ideas, feudal society fought its death battle with the then revolutionary bourgeoisie. The ideas of religious liberty and freedom of conscience merely gave expression to the sway of free competition within the domain of knowledge." ("Communist Manifesto.")

In the interest of human progress the ground must be cleared of the underbrush of confusion which hides socialism proper from the view of many who are under its godless influence; honestly hoping to work through its organization — with its literature for a better order of human society. Its irreligious basis must be exposed; its sophistry and duplicity must be uncovered that those who are enthusiastically looking at its glittering pictures may see the hydra headed monster so glowingly clothed — which, given the power, would throw civilization into chaos and ruin.

How often is the statement made, by those new converts whose ardor outstrips their knowledge, that socialism is identical with Christianity. In "green" socialist papers and in "literature for beginners" one may frequently read the statement that "the ethics of Christianity and socialism are identical," when investigation will conclusively prove that the ethics of socialism is as directly opposite to the ethics of Christianity as the positive is from the negative pole of human activity. Investigation will also prove that once one is thoroughly inoculated with the virus of socialist ethics it will be as difficult to get out of the slime of its ethical fluid into the clear blue light of religious ethics as it is for a fly to get out of a pan of milk into the free air.

Ernest Belford Bax, in "The Ethics of Socialism," frankly give the correct socialist position.

"One word on that singular hybrid, the 'Christian Socialist.' . . . The association of Christianism with any form of socialism is a mystery, rivalling the mysterious combination of ethical and other contradictions in the Christian divinity himself.

"It is difficult to devine the motive for thus preserving a

name which, confessedly, in its ordinary meaning, is not only alien but hostile to the doctrine of socialism.

"If by Christianity be meant the body of dogma usually connoted by the word, it will probably be conceded by those to whom we refer that it is in hostility to progress. If on the other hand, this be not meant, but merely the ethical principles Christianity is supposed to embody, then, even if these principles were distinctly and exclusively Christian, which they are not, we challenge them to show this connection or even their compatibility with socialism. If, again, they fail in this, as fail they must, the whole matter is resolved into one of sentiment. And for the sake of retaining a catchword, for such it is, and no more, under these circumstances, they would compromise principles, and throw a sop to the *status quo* in its most hypocritical form.".

We challenge those socialists who are using, ignorantly or willfully, the "Christian catchword" to accept the challenge of Bax (who is undisputed authority within the socialist camp) to the "compatibility" of socialist and Christian ethics. It were just as fitting to speak of Christian atheism as to speak of Christian socialism, in either case the two words swear at one another! Christianity connotes the individual relationship and moral responsibility of man to his Creator ; the recognition of God's revelation to man in the person of Jesus Christ, which finds its material embodiment in the Christian church. Socialism and atheism deny the existence of God and His revelation, and so consequently deny the moral responsibility of man to Him. Socialism declares His church to be the result of economic conditions, and that its present form will be annihilated with the introduction of the co-operative commonwealth. It denies the moral responsibility of the individual, declaring that the "social body" will become morally responsible once it has perfected its form — once the tools of production are collectively owned — when the last class shall have been emancipated.

But we will allow Bax to speak further "on the subject of which he is master."

"According to Christianity and the ethics or religion of introspection generally, regeneration must come from within, must begin in the heart and mind of the individual. The ethic and religion of modern socialism, on the contrary, look for regeneration from without, from material conditions and a higher social life. The ethic and religion of socialism seek not the ideal society through the ideal individual, but conversely the ideal individual through the ideal society." ("Ethics of Socialism, page 19).

This is plain enough! Bread and butter — a plenty of it for society will make the individual man moral!

"The new ethic of socialism has no part nor lot with asceticism. In the first place, it grudges the amount of energy required to be expended by the individual in his effort to acquire the 'self-dicipline,' so called, which is only another name for the moral tight-rope dancing which the Ethic of inwardness postulates as its end." ("Ethics of Socialism,' page 21).

This insulting reflection upon one of the highest religious qualities is quite in conformity with the "economic determinism" of socialist doctrine. "Self-discipline" indeed! — they truly have but little of it in their lawless philosophy.

What, the ethics of socialism and Christianity identical? Kindly read this from Italian socialists.

In the Italian organ of the socialists, the *Avanti*, Christianity was recently called "the dirt-heap of modern thought,' and an article on this subject closes with the words: "The civilization of social democracy will never befoul itself with Christianity." ("Literary Digest," May 23, 1903; and "A. L. U. Journal," July 30, 1903.)

It is difficult to select from such an abundance of matter in proof of my assertions that socialism and atheism are both cut from the same web of anti-religious cloth. But I will next bring forward Dr. Edward B. Averling, who has played an important role in the socialist movement. Edward B. Averling was professor of chemistry and physiology at New College, London, England. He was also professor of comparative anatomy at the London Hospital. A member of the London School Board in 1882, vice-president of the National Secular Society, from which he was forced to resign. His chief literary works are, "Student's Marx," "Student's Darwin," "Heackel's Pedigree of Man," and the translation of Marx' Capital, vol. 1, also the translation of Engels' "Socialism."

Perhaps after all Dr. Averling was best known to the rank and file as the "free husband" of Karl Marx' daughter who met such a tragic death—A fitting consumation of their utter defiance of religious and moral obligation within the family sphere.

Dr. Averling writes, in "To-Day," a socialist magazine;

"Whether anything is done or nothing is done, little that is of any real or lasting value can be done until men and women fairly face the fact that the terrible condition of our poor is due, as are so many other ills, to the two curses of our country and time. These two curses are Capitalism and Christianity.

"Mr. Headlam is sorry I do 'not think it worth while to expose the evils' of capitalism. I do. But I know that others are at this good work, and I know that Christianity and Capitalism support, and are supported by, each other. They are Siamese twins. They live, they die together. A blow at one, is a blow at both. Christianity is a pander to Capitalism, bringing to it for prey the fair virgin called Labor, beguiled by the hope of a beatific hereafter.

"We can scarcely wonder that certain impetuously honest natures among the socialists exclaim against the admission of priests to the party. The priest in this respect is in the same position as the capitalist. He is a monopolist. A capitalist can join the socialist party as an individual, and will be welcomed as a man. But he must denounce even if he cannot renounce, his capitalism. The priest also is admissible to our human, earthly, natural society as an individual, and is welcome as a man, but he must denounce his priesthood and all its pretentions to relation with the supernatural. And whilst we cannot fairly, or for the time wisely ask the capitalist to give up his sources of income, and therefore of work for the good cause, we can ask the priest to do this. There are other means of livelihood more lucrative in some cases, and more honest in all.

"——— In Christianity we see not only a supporter of the greatest of social evils, but a system that by its fundamental principles vitiates human thoughts, and distracts the attention of mankind from the natural and actual. Against these therefore we fight. So indissoluble are these two, so absolutely does the happiness of the future race depend on their downfall, that we re-echo with a modification the cry of Voltaire, " *Ecrasons l'infâme.*"

How well the socialist priests in the United States are obeying this instruction of giving up the priesthood—All the ex-ministers are now quartered upon the socialist movement. Whether it be more lucrative to them or not it certainly is of advantage to the general public that those of sometime sacred calling classify themselves, by renouncing the One True God for that "material force which makes for progress"— for socialism, the fundamental principles of which " vitiates human thought, and distracts the attention of mankind from the natural and actual "— aye and from the possible, thanks be to God !

How illy grounded is the faint iteration of well meaning converts that socialism and christianity are identical ethically in face of so many stout assertions of acknowledged international leaders, James Leatham says, " What we have to do on behalf of the ethics of the Social-Democratic State is to separate them from precepts enjoining duty to God and from any other commands for which there is no social and secular warrant." ("Socialism and character," page 43.)

My readers may think me somewhat too far a-field? I will therefore return home to the United States and take the testimony editorial by "The Comrade." (New York, May, 1903.)

"Let us turn our eyes from what we find satisfaction in seeing, to ourselves. Candor compels the admission that the pallor of fear and the paralysis of its impotency are upon us. We have lost the courage of our faith, if, indeed, we ever had it to lose.

"Take, for example, the question of ethics. How often do we see quoted in our own press, from the *Encyclopaedia Britannica*, that familiar fallacy that 'the ethics of christianity and socialism are identical.' It is not true; we do not ourselves, in most cases, believe it. We repeat it because it appeals to the slave-mind of the world. It is easier so to act, than to affirm, what in our very souls we feel to be true, that socialism as an ethical interpretation of life is far removed from Christianity, and of infinitely greater beauty and worth. The ethics of Christianity, like its practices, are characterized by a monstrous disregard of the common life. Christianity and tyranny are and for ages have been firmly allied. The ethical teaching of Jesus even was not socialism; even his pure, sweet spirit had no clear concept of that great common-life standard which the race was destined to reach through centuries of struggle and pain. But the system which bears his name never knew the ethical teaching of Jesus. There is no wrong, however terrible, which has not been justified by Christianity; no movement for human liberty which has not been opposed by it. Its very basis is a lie and a denial of the basic principle of Socialism. Its own infidelity to the common life of the world sets it at the antithesis of Socialism.

" We must be careful to avoid cramping ourselves and truncating our faith to suit the Christian measure. Christianity is not big enough, nor pure enough, nor noble enough, to measure our great world-faith. To identify Socialism with Christianity we must first ' Christianize ' it; we must abandon its highest and loveliest meanings. Socialism Christianized would be Socialism emasculated and destroyed.

" To appeal to the slave-mind of the world, to play upon its weakness and its bondage, either by the use of such ill-founded judgments as the one quoted to support our case, or of the sacerdotal vestments and titular prestige of ecclesiasticism, is to appeal to, and by the appeal to confirm, the ignorant prejudices with which priestcraft has always held the mass-mind in bondage. It is at once a self-betrayal, and a betrayal to those of whom we appeal. Socialism needs no religion to support it, and if it did it could not receive support from outworn dogmatic Christianity. When we have the courage to take hold of it, Socialism will become for each of us a religion immeasurably grander and truer than what we call religion to-day."

No, Mr. Editor, socialists have not "lost the courage of their faith " when the identicity of Christian and socialist ethics is claimed. In many cases they who use the phrase know it to be false — it is a convenient "catch-word"— an entering wedge to split men from their religious affiliations.

But you should justly turn your tables — I will do so for you. The "slave-mind " of our time turns to the " Communist Manifesto " for its ethical foundation, for its faith, which occupies so little space that it would be difficult to cramp it into smaller compass. But hear the intellectual confusion, the moral degeneracy of this document lauded by the socialist press. Do socialists still have the brazen impudence to tell me there is no proof of my accusation against the socialist party on this score?

" No socialist should neglect to have the Communist Manifesto in his library. Every paragraph, every sentence is replete with suggestive thought and strong philosophy. It is one of the most, if not the most, remarkable pamphlets ever issued. With its publication Marx and Engels made what future historians will consider the beginning of an epoch." ("The Advance," February 9, 1901.)

And this from the "Communist Manifesto" itself:

"Nothing is easier than to give Christian asceticism a socialist tinge. Has not Christianity declaimed against private property, against marriages, against the State? Has it not preached in the place of these charity and poverty, celibacy and mortification of the flesh, monastic life and Mother Church? Christian socialism is but the Holy Water with which the priest consecrates the heart-burnings of the aristocrats."

This is good German beer-saloon philosophy! It requires but a superficial analysis of this quotation to see the negative, the irrational turn given to the three great principles, charity, poverty, celibacy. Principles when viewed from the sublime standard of the world's great religious institutions rest upon the pinnacle of man's attainment.

The attempt to belittle the service of religious teachers, thousands of whom devote their lives, under the vows of poverty, chastity and obedience, to the uplifting of mankind is, to say the least, the rankest ingratitude to the benefactors of the race. To characterize the work of the church as an "effort to consecrate the heart burnings of the aristocrat" is but a fair, or rather foul, sample from the "fathers of the materialistic conception of history" but worthy of the shallow and atheistic reasoning of the socialist world.

Socialism International.

Pull down the mask that hides the haggard face of the pretenders that a full view of chaos may stand revealed before the light of day.

The principles of religion, of marriage and of government extend beyond man's territorial divisions; they are international, they are universal, they concern all men.

IT seems scarcely necessary to bring proof of the international character of socialism beyond the mere citation of the opening statement made in each and every socialist political programme, whatever its specific name may be, which reads substantially as follows: "The Socialist Party reaffirms its adherence to the principles of International Socialism." But it is imperative to enforce the fact of its being an international organization, paying allegiance to the self-same set of principles wherever its standard is set up. And for two general reasons. First, many socialists (?) are themselves illy acquainted with their own philosophy when boiled down to plain every-day terms—they are not "class conscious." Second, because of the petty sharpness of socialist tactics. Honest inquiry is met with duplicity like this, "You don't see anything about free love in our platform, do you?" No, truly, there is nothing about free love in the socialist platform but the principles for which you declare embrace that doctrine.

The party platform of the several countries takes up such specific matters as it deems best as a means to the one aim and end. Thus we find the socialists of Germany increasing their representation with the cry " Bread usury " and " Dear meat." In France, although disharmony and disintegration prevail within its own ranks, the five socialist parties are united in the campaign to deprive the religious teachers of their schools. In the United States the socialist vote is increased by the advocacy of the government ownership of the coal mines. Does it follow that lower tariff duties is socialism in Germany? Does it follow that the disposessing of the Catholic orders is socialism in France? Does it follow that government ownership of the coal mines is socialism in the United States? No! certainly not, these measures are but means to the end. But the means employed to centralize political power into socialist hands, that one day they may overthrow the present order and inaugurate the regime advocated by Marx, Engels, Babel and other leading socialists of the world.

Socialism is not international merely for reasons of sentiment or of theory but for reasons of experience also. The defeat of the Communards of 1848 in their attempt to establish socialism in France, furnished the experience which convinced socialists of the necessity of international organization. Since Austrian bayonets restored to France the political power which had been seized by the Communards it has been a matter of common conviction, with them, that the capitalist governments of Europe and America would not permit the setting up of a socialist society by the working class of any nation so long as the united military power of the remaining capitalist nations retain the power to overthrow it. Hence the necessity of establishing a co-operative commonwealth which shall include the civilized world. Hence, also, the shibboleth "workmen of all countries unite you have nothing to lose but your chains and a whole world to gain."

When confronted with, to them, the objectionable features of modern socialism "sentimental socialists" frequently declare "I am not that kind of a socialist, I am an American socialist." This view is not tolerated by socialism proper.

"The Haverhill Social Democrat," July 20, 1901, writing upon this subject says: —

"There is no such thing as European socialism or American socialism. There is only one kind of socialism the world over — *International Socialism*, which means everywhere the same, among the socialists of Haverhill as well as among the socialists of a city of a similar size in Germany, France, Belgium or England."

We may note in passing that history records the utter failure of the attempts to establish socialism in miniature. For it must be borne in mind that that which socialism is organized to abolish on the one hand and that which it is organized to set up on the other extends in scope far beyond even national boundaries. Therefore, it is that local and national questions must not be mistaken for its objective point — for its ultimatum. It would set up the co-operative ownership of capital. It would abolish all existing institutions.

Socialist Tactics.

How much wood could a wood-chuck chuck
If a wood-chuck could chuck wood?
A wood-chuck would chuck just as much wood
As a wood-chuck would chuck
If a wood-chuck could chuck wood.

SOCIALIST tactics have become well established; not alone with the management but with the rank and file as well. It is their policy to develop what a prominent leader has termed "socialist minds." The socialist begins upon his "subject" with "radical stuff" to "break the ice." He knows very well that the "stuff" which he puts out is not socialist argument, but it serves to wean the man from his beaten path by its attractive style, by its flashing darts, which hit almost anything that the present-order-man may have in mind.

"The Appeal to Reason," which has been dubbed "The Appeal to Imagination," has for years been declared to be "the best socialist paper to make recruits with," simply because it did not put forth "scientific socialism." It commonly confounded socialism with Christianity; the referendum as socialism; it declared the governmental experiments of New Zealand to be socialism; the North Carolina Liquor Dispensary was socialism. In short, any popular measure that would stir up the imagination of men and attract them to the socialist movement was said to be socialism. For the purpose of developing "socialist minds" the "Appeal" was always in demand. It even went so far as to hail the election of some populist and of some radical democratic mayors, governors and congressmen as "socialist victories." However this paper is now reformed. It is considered "scientific." About one year ago the proprietor engaged a new editorial staff of "class conscious" socialists. Men who advocate "the materialist basis of history," "economic determinism," atheism and

34.

all the rest. In nearly every issue of the socialist papers published in the United States one may read articles of a "reform" character, which stray far and away from the measures which socialism properly stands for — that is they are not revolutionary.

This is necessary tactics, otherwise, from the fact that socialists may not properly deal with "reform measures," the socialist party is obliged to refrain from participation in public affairs under the present "capitalist regime." Therefore, logically, until such time as it shall have captured all the offices from the President of the United States down to the selectmen of a country town and at one fell swoop turned the capitalist class, foot, horse and dragoons, out of political doors, it cannot take control of the ship of state and turn it into an "administration of things." This dilemma has brought down upon the most devoted socialist heads the nickname of "impossibilists." The Socialist Labor Party of the United States falls under this classification. It was at their national convention in 1900 that they threw down the "immediate demands" of their political programme. The Socialist Labor Party will not tolerate "reformers" within its ranks, all must be "revolutionists." De Leon says scratch the back of a sentimentalist and you will find a crook. It will not dare to centralize political power by the practical aid of "immediate demands." It is truly the most "uncompromising" division of the world movement. It has the severest logitian at its head. It has the courage of its convictions; that is to say the basic principles of socialism correctly lead to fanaticism. Its membership grows "beautifully less."

The socialist may hang on either one of the horns of his dilemma. He may preach that which he knows is not socialism, to gain converts. Or he may preach that which he knows to be in strict conformity to socialist principles and lose converts. The logical outcome in either case is that

35

the party goes out of existence with its mission unfulfilled. On the other hand, it is whittled to a point and the point cut off, while on the other its bubble is blown so large that it bursts into nothingness.

Socialist tactics would make the establishment of their scheme impossible if their principles did not render it so.

"Gonzalo.

    I' the commonwealth I would by contraries
    Execute all things; for no kind of traffic
    Would I admit; no name of magistrate;
    Letters should not be known: riches, poverty,
    And use of service, none; contract, succession,
    Bourn, bound of land, tilth, vineyard, none:
    No use of metal, corn, or wine, or oil:
    No occupation; all men idle, all;
    And women too; but innocent and pure:
    No sovereignty: —

Sebastian.   Yet he would be king on 't.

Antonio.   The latter end of his commonwealth **forgets** the beginning.

Gonzalo.

    All things in common nature should produce
    Without sweat or endeavor; treason, felony,
    Sword, pike, knife, gun, or need of any engine,
    Would I not have; but nature should bring forth,
    Of its own kind, all foizon, all abundance,
    To feed my innocent people.

Sebastian.   No marrying 'mong his subjects?

Antonio.   None, man; all idle; whores and knaves.

Gonzalo.   I would with such perfection govern, sir, To **excel** the golden age.

Sebastian.   Save his majesty!

Antonio.   Long live Gonzalo!"

                    ("The Tempest," Act 2.)

Lesser tactics, which while they do not prove the impossibility of their scheme, do show that quality of degeneracy into which men fall who defy and deny moral responsibility. One may, for example, see in a copy of "The Worker," the leading socialist weekly of this country, an editorial declaring that its columns are open to free discussion on party affairs, by the party membership, while its editor is at the same time returning articles, of an impersonal character, opening up to view some one of its principles, or some one custom of its propaganda. "Free speech" and "freedom of the press" has been accorded only to those who are on the "inside." But persons of some power who may hold philosophies contrary to the accredited school; to those who will not be partners to the advancement of party leaders who hold and practice pernicious socialist philosophy, — to such the "freedom of the press" is cut off, and, at best, his reputation is damned with faint praise. This Turk will bear no one near his throne. So soon as one with marked ability steps out of the beaten socialist paths the "freedom of the press" is used to attack his character; he is branded as a traitor, coward — in short, the billinsgate vocabulary is hurled against him. Never, save in the notable case of Bernstein in Germany, has the subject-matter of a serious objector been debated. But I must not give over credit — Bernstein's matter was confined strictly to the technical economic field.

It was the lack of "freedom of the press" which in part caused the break in the Socialist Labor Party of 1899. That break, incrimination and recrimination, brought forth the present socialist party from the loins of the "split" and the Social Democratic Party. "The Worker" is as "intolerant", though not as able, as the dam from which it sprung. Look at "The Worker" for proof. There one may see the contradictory tactics of the socialist press — the intolerance of those who with "brave liberty" on their lips, yet, when the power is theirs, out-Russianize Russian tactics.

An underhanded article, which freely displays the meth-

37

ods employed to develop "socialist minds," was published in
"The Worker," March 16, 1902, which was signed by the
New York State Committee of the Social Democratic Party.
We quote: "Archbishop Corrigan and Bishop Quigley
alike charge socialism with hostility to religion . . . these
charges are unqualifiedly false, and we challenge their
authors to quote one phrase from our party platform that
would in any way tend to support their accusations. They
cannot do it, for socialism has no concern with religion."
The members of the New York State Committee know full
well that this is a dodge! I give them the credit of knowing
as well as any set of socialist officials in the United States
that the principles of socialism are not taught in their platform. They know that the platform is merely a "working
programme"; they know that the platform is but condemnatory and declaratory in character; they know the economic
teaching of socialism is not to be found in their platform;
they know that the philosophies of Marx and Engels, which
form the groundwork of socialism, are not to be found in
their platform; they know that the "economic determinism,"
of Ferri and Loria is not in the socialist platform; they know
that the socialist attitude on the State is not to be found in
their platform — save as all these positions are covered by
the fact that the platform is a socialist document, which fact
is proven by *prima facie* evidence. The platform itself an-
nounces the allegiance of the socialist party to the principles
of "International Socialism." Clearly, "the principles of
International Socialism" must be learned in order to know
the meaning of the platform.

Would the New York State Committee refer one to its
platform to learn the socialist attitude on the money question? No, most decidedly no! The Socialist Party, the
Socialist Labor Party, and the Social Democratic Party are
all dumb on the money question — not even a declaration in
favor of nor against money. In fact, if one were to look in

socialist platforms for the development, — the use or the abuse of money, — one would conclude that the United States were lower in the scale of economic development than that which Robinson Crusoe found himself in after his famous sea voyage.

Both the Republican and Democratic Party platforms define their respective attitudes on money legislation. But should one desire to learn the origin of money; what it is; what constitutes its value; how the volume of its value is set up; its functions of measure of value and standard of price determined; etc.; etc., he must have recourse to works not embodied in these platforms. Certainly, the knowledge of money is dependent upon the understanding of economic law. But while this knowledge, or lack of knowledge, is expressed by a statement on money, the argument deduced from the economic phenomena is not traced—the development of value from its intellectual concept, as it presents itself in the stage of barter up to its independent money form is not given. Added knowledge, historical knowledge, not the understanding of primal economic law, is required to trace the use of gold and silver through the higher order of industrial exchange—a knowledge of the history of money legislation. Now let them answer fairly, could one rationally look for all this in a political platform? Could one reasonably look for anything more than a postulate which would necessarily rest back upon republican or democratic principles?

If one desire to learn the socialist attitude on money he must study the question as related to socialist literature, as related to socialist principles, the only authority in the matter. Now, it does not follow because the socialist platforms of our country do not contain one word on the subject of money that they have not a universally recognized attitude in regard to it. Karl Marx in " Capital " ably analyzes the functions of money, and were socialists generally as well versed in the economics of this book as they are in the disruptive philosophy which runs through it, they would not be advocating for the "future society" the inauguration of "time checks," which (did they but know it) precludes the possibility of rendering unto each man his economic value. Marx was exceedingly reticent upon this as upon other details. He would not give "cook-shop receipts for the future society." Socialists of today are not so wary. I said, they have a universally recognized attitude on the money question; they are committed to the destruction of money (along with the state) to the impossible task of giving each man the value which he creates although they will have no means by which to measure its volume.

No! not one word upon money in the socialist platform, but it does not follow, for all that, that socialism does not concern itself with the question of value. "The abolition of the wages-system" — "The working-class are being robbed of their values "—"The full value of his product is demanded by the socialist" and dozens of like phrases assure one most positively that money is of much concern to socialism.

Now let us look a little closer at socialist tactics—tactics intended to blind those adherents and sympathizers, who still cling to religion and the church, to the facts in the case.

What does this mean? one may find it in the socialist platform. I quote: "The possession of the means of livelihood gives to the capitalists the control of the government, the press, the pulpit, and the schools, and enables them to reduce the workingmen to a state of intellectual, physical and social inferiority, political subservience and virtual slavery."

Relate this simply, for the time being, to the pulpit and to the schools, and we shall see whether there is no attack— veiled but none the less an attack—upon religion. What is a pulpit, in common language, but the place where religious instruction is given to church goers? Church goers certainly are not as a rule atheists, they are adherents of the church and believe in religion. What is the necessary inferencehere? Why most assuredly that the pulpit is a means of reducing "the workingmen to a state of intellectual, physical and social inferiority, political subservience and virtual slavery."

What is connoted by "socialists' minds" ("socialist minds" which are already developed) by "the schools" in this connection? Most assuredly this, that "free, secular, and compulsory education" will deprive parents of the time-honored privilege of educating their children in such institutions as they deem advantageous and wise. Either religious or secular.

Now I cannot estimate the New York State committee so low down in the scale of "socialist minds" that it needs further development to be aware of that which is common socialist knowledge. Hence I am assured that it is employing "socialist tactics." Tactics which require duplicity of conduct. Tactics which throw light upon the false argument employed by the Social Democratic party of New York in its challenge to Archbishop Corrigan and Bishop Quigley. What? "Not a phrase in our party platform that would in any way tend to support their accusation" that socialism is hostile to religion? We have seen that the socialist platform is not entirely dumb on this question. Although the case is not yet dismissed. I quote further from the socialist party platform: "The socialist party . . . reaffirms its adherence to the principles of international socialism." Pray what are "the principles of international socialism"? This is the question first to be settled in order to read the correct meaning into the utterances of their platform. The question may be simply stated. Would the principles of international socialism "in any way tend to support their accusations" that socialism is hostile to religion? Yes! yes!! one hundred yeses would not overemphasize the correctness of our answer.

But even more dangerous to the life of society, than is the basic and sustained attack upon religion — which flows from the fundamental principles upon which socialism rests

— is their attack upon the life of the family. Socialist tactics relative to its real position upon marriage is as slippery as an eel. Instead of answering one's straightout question their tactics are to turn the mind away from the core of the matter. They prate about the sex immorality of to-day, for effect, it is good propaganda. For pray mark this, they use not their own standard in condemning vice but the religious standards of the old and the new revelation. Loudly inveighing against the breaking up of the workingmen's homes by the exploitation of the capitalist class, as though sex purity were conditioned upon plenty of bread and butter.

This shifting — sliding — method of meeting inquiry and argument came into socialist vogue with the "Communist manifesto," and it is still followed faithfully throughout the "scientific" school. Let me give an example from that document which socialists allege to be beyond all price valuable to sociological science. This is the voice of the Socialist Labor Party: —

"The principles enunciated in the 'manifesto' are as true to-day as they were fifty years ago, and it is upon these principles that the Class Conscious Proletariat of the United States is hammering its way to the Socialist Republic."

While this is the slippery argument! while it does not deny its own philosophy, it does not openly meet the issue raised.

"Abolition of the family? Even the most radical flare up at this infamous proposal of the Communists.

"On what foundation is the present family, the bourgeois family, based? On capital, on private gain. In its completely developed form this family exists only among the bourgeoisie. But this state of things finds its complement in the practical absence of the family among the proletarians, and in public prostitution.

"The bourgeois family will vanish as a matter of course when its complement vanishes, and both will vanish with the vanishing of capital." 42

Is the "completely developed form" of the bourgeois unlike the working class family? No! certainly not, for according to socialist reasoning the capitalist mode of production fashions all institutions by its own inexorable force.

Then the family will vanish? Certainly, yes; on the introduction of socialism the family will vanish. Will socialism abolish the family? Oh! no! It won't be necessary, it will of itself give place to "sex fondness" which will of itself introduce a herd of human animals upon the introduction of the socialist regime. What is it after all that constitutes a family? Why that primal, that necessary unit in sustaining human society — the father, the mother, the child. Let us rend the veil by putting the matter with brutal frankness. Shall the human race breed like rabbits or shall marriage be maintained as a sacrament? On which side in this discussion is socialist philosophy postulated? Kindly read the chapter on the family and you will conclude that it stands with the rabbits.

The issue of free love has been uncomfortably near the surface since the Massachusetts State convention in 1902, where it was forced into the arena of discussion. The following appeared in the Social Democratic Herald, June 20, 1903 : —

"'Were the Social Democrats of Germany ever in favor of community of wives as Father Sherman and the National Economic League pamphlets claim?' asks an Illinois correspondent.

"Simply, and plainly and emphatically, *no!* The very idea is absurd. Marx, in his Communist Manifesto, written in 1848, touches on this calumny, and even takes the pains to explain how it naturally occurred to the bourgeois mind. Under capitalism everything is property, and wives are looked on by some as a species of possession. So when the capitalist mind conceived the error that socialists wanted to socialize ALL property, the idea readily sprang up that women, being also a sort of property, would have to be socialized! In other words, the believer in capitalism, with his usual stupidity, did not see that socialism seeks to make common property ONLY of that part of wealth that is used to create more wealth, and so supposed that such property as womankind was in danger. And to quote Marx again, the socialists would have no reason to ' introduce community of women ; it has existed almost from time immemorial ! ' See the point? "

Yes, though I see far beyond the point which you intend to make. First, however, I must consider whether this is the brassiest of brazen impudence or whether you have still an "undeveloped socialist mind." I most devoutly hope the latter is the fact. I was long ignorant on the matter myself. But all the same the text is most mischievous, most vicious. It swings in line those who feel like dropping out of the socialist party.

Your denial will not stand in place of proof. And your argument is too specious — too diffuse — too thin, to conceal the devil crouching behind it. You cannot close the discussion here : truth will not admit of your conclusion.

It is not a question of "the stupidity" of the "capitalist mind." But a question of knowledge or lack of knowledge on the socialist position in regard to marriage.

Public. All institutions, marriage included, are developed up in conformity with the prevailing mode of economic production, you say?

Socialist. Yes, under the law of economic determinism.

Public. Then marriage is not a sacred institution ?

Socialist. No, certainly not. It was introduced by the exploiting class for the protection of private property.

Public. What would constitute a socialist marriage?

Socialist. Why, love, of course. Love is the only basis upon which may be built a permanent and enduring marriage relationship.

44

Public. Then if love should cease the marriage would no longer be valid?

Socialist. It would not.

Public. And would the parties be free to find other mates at their own pleasure and convenience?

Socialist. Oh yes! of course! socialism desires freedom in all things. A free family, a free society will only be found on the other side of socialism.

Public. Would not this cause the breaking of the marriage bond?

Socialist. No. For you see there would be no marriage in the present sense, in the bourgeois sense. It would be swept away along with all other capitalist institutions.

Public. Therefore, that immorality, adultery, in polite language, community of wives which has existed almost from time immemorial would be the accepted practice, provided it pleased men and women to fall below all recognition of the moral law.

Socialist. Well yes, you know one's body is his own, he may do with it as he pleases.

Public. Personal happiness is the moral standard; is that correct socialist doctrine?

Socialist. Yes, you are right, there is no other basis for the moral law.

Public. I see! Your materialist conception of history rules out of question the will of Almighty God.

Socialist. Certainly! That belief is but the ignorant superstition of the dark ages brought over into modern times. When the future society shall have perfected itself the *collective will* shall inform the individual what the moral law is. Until then we socialists will do the best we can to propagate the socialist doctrine. Once we get hold of the political power we will abolish both ecclesiastical and civil marriage. Then we could conform to the truth and beauty of socialist ethics such as no man can command in his ordinary life. Do you see the point? 45

Public. Yes; I see the deformity and the blasphemy of it, clearly.

If socialism were bold and candid, openly exposing its philosophy and the consequences of its practice, we would have little reason for showing the duplicity of its tactics.

A. M. Simons in "Boyce's Weekly," May 6, 1903, under the caption of "Capitalism and the Home," very subtilely attacks the sacred character of marriage. After going on with a horribly correct picture of the stress under which thousands of America's poor live, the article concludes by saying:

"These are the 'homes' that it is alleged socialism would destroy. I fear that we must plead guilty to much of the indictment, for to declare for the preservation of such conditions would be to make the idea of socialism a hideous nightmare to all thinking men and women. Socialism will undoubtedly return the father and mother to the family circle, permit the selection and maintenance of a permanent place of residence, shut the woman and child from the factory, and the factory from the home. It will do away with the army of the underpaid, abolish at once the prostitute, the tramp and the parasite, and secure the entire product to those who produce it, and thus make possible all that humanity has learned to love in the word HOME."

No, Mr. Simons, these are not the homes that "it is alleged socialism would destroy." You have but pictured the poverty which woefully abides in American homes, while you have not pictured the plenty, the luxury which abides in the larger number of American homes. Now it is not feared that you will destroy the poverty, the plenty nor the luxury of American homes. The "fear" relates not to the material substance, scant or bountiful, necessary to maintain a home. But, Mr. Simons, the "fear" is, and justly too, that socialism would break the natural tie, the human tie, the sacred tie, the tie which binds the father, the mother, the child, in one family while life lasts. The "fear" is natural, it is wholesome because socialist principles strike at the very root of the home — at the marriage system — And no amount of sophistical writing shall be allowed to pass current as argument in the protection of socialists against their philosophy which, if practiced, would destroy the home for it would break the marriage bond. Lashing the "capitalist system" is not sufficient to betray your fell purpose. Kindly play the part of a brave man and out with your convictions as to the origin, the development, and the future state of the family — then one will be enabled to see that the future home will be, though never so richly furnished, a shed to shelter such human animals as "choose" because of "sex fondness" to herd for the night together.

Having painfully learned socialist principles myself, I give this little book to the public that it may the more readily become acquainted with the tactics of socialists and the principles of international socialism.

From 1848, the time of the Communist Manifesto which locked the form of socialist reasoning and tactics down to the present day, the authoratative writers and managers within the socialist world all use the same negative and sophistical style of reasoning. By which means the thought and the hope of undisciplined minds and hearts are turned from the real issues before the American people into irrational action. By loud mouthed denunciation of the present social order, or by the glamor of brilliantly colored pictures of the material prosperity of the socialist regime, using their unwarrantable tactics the while, many are roped within the socialist camp working for that which they would not have. Perseus wore a magic cap that the monsters he hunted down might not see him, while socialism dons the magic cap over its hydra head that the monster it is may not be seen by those whom it would devour.

Public Ownership.

" It is the philosophy held by those who shall one
day succeed to the helm of state upon the issues
now slowly gathering to a political head that shall
determine whether the earth shall see a display of
blind force that shall out-Herod Herod, or whether
that same force having been educated to self-discipline, shall use the citizenship, so dearly bought
by our fathers, that it shall add security to our
political liberties by the extension and expansion
of the phenomena which demonstrate the principle of democracy as related to the superior and
inferior opportunities of men within the departments of industry, commerce and finance."
—MARTHA MOORE AVERY.

SOCIALISM is often defined by those whose enthusiasm
is higher than their knowledge of the subject as the
"public ownership of public utilities." Socialists will have
none of this — neither will the Judiciary of Massachusetts,
though for other reasons. The judicial opinion is in substance as follows: public utilities are those things which require a governmental function, such as the distribution of
water, gas, electricity — commodities which necessitate a
single enterprise with supplies emanating from a single
source — those things which require the use of the public
highways, etc. We may then have the public ownership of
all possible social utilities without the introduction of socialism, without a change in the "economic system."

Ere socialism had raised its ugly head in the political
world the fathers of this republic had embodied the principle
of public ownership of social utilities in their local, state and
national life. Thus it is that the further ownership of public
utilities may be adopted by municipalities and states without
overstepping the boundaries of our constitution, while the

control of business not public in its nature requires a constitutional amendment.

The demand for the public ownership of social utilities by the "political state" is opposed to the ultimate purpose of socialism, for every additional public service taken from private hands into the control of the civic body adds to the power and functions of the existing government; that is to say, it extends the power of the state which it is the socialists' mission to abolish. Thus it will be seen that socialism works by contraries.

"There is a very general idea that socialism means an extension of the powers and functions of government," says "The People" (New York, Sunday, May 13, 1900). 'This is a very natural misconception, but it is a dangerous misconception and ought to be guarded against.' Socialism does not mean the extension of government; on the contrary it means the end, the elimination of government. 'Government, the authority of a part of the people over the lives of the other for, in theory, of all the people collectively over the lives of all the people individually, is simply a result of the division of society into classes with conflicting interests. With the end of class divisions, the necessity of government disappears. The 'tyranny of socialism' is a bugbear, with no reality behind it. Socialism means individual freedom.

"This is a point which ought to be made as clear as possible on every possible occasion." ("The People," New York, Sunday, May 13, 1900.)

A. M. Simmons, Editor of the "International Socialist Review," in "Boyce's Weekly," Chicago, March 18, 1902, when speaking of the extension of the power of the state into the domain of specific industries, says:

"The present state is simply an instrument for the carrying out of the will of the present capitalist class in the political field.

"Occasionally this class finds it to their interest to use

their government to own and operate some industry, but to call such ownership and operation socialism, is a ridiculous misuse of the word."

It would give us much pleasure if this point were made as clear as possible, as "The People" desires, "on every possible occasion," for the vote recorded for socialist party candidates in the on-coming time would grow like the tail of an ox, downward.

Many enthusiasts read "New York Journal" editorials and, mistaking their demands for extending the power of the state as socialism, are led into voting the socialist party tickets, little knowing that the distance between the two ideals is as great as that between the two poles of human achievement.

The position of the Socialist Labor Party on the question of municipal, state, or national ownership of public utilities, — of public ownership short of the complete ideal of socialism, is from the international socialist standpoint considered the "most scientific." This party at its last national convention (1900) abolished its "Immediate Demands," some of which were measures relative to "extending the power and functions of government." This action was caused by the growing sentiment in favor of public ownership, which is progressively more favorably advocated by voters and legislators, in many states, irrespective of party lines. These men have no sympathy, nor would they give quarter to the negations of socialism, which would abolish the home, the state, and the "soul."

The Socialist Labor Party defines its attitude on the "programme of municipal reform" in part as follows:

"At their last national congress, the socialist municipal councillors (of France and Belgium) appended to their programme a declaration, frankly stating that all such municipal measures as they could now devise for the relief of their constituencies were of necessity palliatives under the capitalistic system, and could not be relied on to curtail to any extent nor for any length of time the capitalistic power; that they should therefore be viewed, not as socialistic institutions, but as mere expedients, through which the working-people might be enabled to more successfully and vigorously carry on the class struggle; and that under no circumstances should the workers rest content with municipal improvements which in the nature of things must be entirely inadequate and temporary; but that they should sternly move onward to the conquest of all the public powers, with a view to the entire uprooting of capitalism and the firm planting of socialism.

"In the same spirit, and with a perfect knowledge of American conditions in all parts of this country, the National Convention of the Socialist Labor Party, held at New York in July, 1896, passed a resolution instructing the National Executive Committee "to elaborate a general programme of municipal reforms for the information of the people and the guidance of socialist officials; it being expressly understood, however, that such programme shall in no sense be considered as a part of the socialist platform, but that it shall be presented as a mere set of demands for the relief of the working-people and the redress of flagrant wrongs under the capitalistic system, and that the term 'Municipal Socialism,' frequently used of late by ignorant persons in reference to such demands, is hereby repudiated."

The Indianapolis Convention, which nationally united the "Debs' division" with the "anti-DeLeon" faction of the socialist movement into the Socialist Party (known as the Social Democratic Party in the states of New York and Wisconsin), adopted a programme of municipal reforms with this caution: "In advocating these measures as steps in the overthrow of capitalism and the establishment of the Coöperative Commonwealth, we warn the working-class against the so-called public-ownership movements as an attempt of the capitalist class to secure governmental control of public utilities for the purpose of obtaining greater security in the exploitation of other industries, and not for the amelioration of the conditions of the working-class."

There was a strong minority against the adoption of the "immediate demands." But in despite of a threatening nearness to another party split, they were adopted by a vote of 5,358; while there were 1,325 votes cast for the complete abolition of these demands, which have no more claim to be termed socialism than had the extension of suffrage to the black man below the Mason and Dixon line.

George D. Herron was the harmonizer at the Indianapolis Convention and the author of the "compromise programme," which was adopted. Of public ownership he says:

"Capitalism will seek to defeat socialism by giving it some of the things for which it seeks. We cannot have the coöperative commonwealth without having the whole of it. Capitalism may give the socialist movement one-half or even nine-tenths of what it demands and still retain the control of power. For instance, the public ownership of so-called public utilities, without the social ownership of all the tools of production, would simply bring forth a new middle class and delay the industrial development that would issue in socialism. Capitalists know this very well, know it much better than the working-class, and are preparing to save themselves by their knowledge." ("The Appeal to Reason," May 16, 1903.)

Another Reverend gentleman who, like Professor Herron, but gives voice to the opinion held by his predecessors and all "class-conscious" socialists on the public ownership of public utilities, Rev. Thomas McGrady, says:

"To speak of socialism in its milder form is like speaking of Trigonometry in its milder form, or of a subdued and meek Table of Logarithms. Socialism does not advocate a governmental control of railroads, telegraphs, etc., but a public, coöperative ownership of all the means of production and distribution. Governmental control and coöperative public ownership are as different from each other as darkness is from light. In Germany, for instance, there is governmental control of railroads and telegraphs, but the common people still pay the same taxes and continue to be ' touched' on behalf of the many public activities." ("Unaccepted Challenges.")

Ernest Unterman, an editor of "The Appeal to Reason," formerly associated with the "International Socialist Review." Mr. Unterman has translated many German socialist works into English, chief among which is "The Origin of the Family," by Frederick Engels. In his pamphlet, "Capitalism to Socialism," Mr. Unterman says:

"The opportunist wish to make socialist experiments, before the people understand the essence of the political socialist movement. The revolutionary socialists insist that the people shall know the foundation of political socialism, before they try any ' practical' experiments."

"The most striking proof of the utter failure of municipal capitalism as an educator of socialist minds is furnished by the English towns, where the majority of the working class, after a generation of municipal ownership, still continue to vote capitalist politicians into office.

"The same is true of Switzerland, where the object lesson of more than twenty years of direct legislation and national ownership of railroads has not succeeded in impressing the workers with the truth that they can only escape capitalist exploitation by organizing as a political party distinct from and opposed to the capitalist parties."

"The transformation of municipal capitalism into municipal socialism is the mission of the socialist party. This transformation is again a political problem. It requires the transformation of capitalist minds into socialist minds, and must be fought out along the line of ' Working class vs. Cap-

53

italist class,' or broadly speaking, 'Socialism vs. Capitalism.'
Municipal Socialism in its complete form cannot come without
the conquest of the state and the nation by the socialists. A
socialist municipality within a capitalist state is impossible."

"Municipal Socialism requires the abolition of capitalism
and of class rule. It is founded on local autonomy. And it
finds its most important function in the administration of those
great industries which could not be brought under collective
control while the capitalists remained the ruling class."

"Finally, it must be emphasized, that neither municipal
capitalism nor state capitalism are a means of educating the
working class to class consciousness and arraigning them
solidly against the capitalist class."

In an article published in "The Worker," March 15,
1903, Mr. Unterman takes to task the "Collectivist Society"
for its attitude upon public ownership. We quote:

"The Collectivist Society, in a recent bulletin makes the
following statement.

"Government-owned railroads and mines would not be,
under the present state, instalments of true socialism. And
yet it must be said that they are probably indispensable steps
toward true socialism. It is almost certain that we must pass
through an era of non-socialist public ownership before we
reach the era of socialism. From this point of view the
socialists ought to co-operate with those who, without the full
socialist mind, are working for public ownership.

"By what methods are we more likely to increase — by
devoting our whole energy to making socialist minds, or by
following the advice of the Collectivist Society and assisting
capitalist and semi-capitalist minds in obtaining something
which is professedly not socialism? Cannot these capitalist
minds, on account of their superior numbers, carry any
measure they desire, without the co-operation of the socialist?

"The Collectivist Society claims that theirs would be the
right course, because 'it appears clear that a system of state

ownership of all principal industries is a much more favorable environment for the creation of the socialist mind than a system of universal private competition, or a system of industrial oligarchy, such as is now supervening.' But this is a most fallacious way of reasoning. State capitalism, which the Collectivist Society itself calls 'a woeful example of public ownership,' does not educate socialists on account of its co-operative management. The socialist mind must be produced by socialist propaganda, and the mere illustration of the practicability of socialism afforded by capitalist public ownership is of little or no value in demonstrating their special class interests to proletarians. Switzerland, Germany, Austria, Russia, and other countries which have for a generation practised state capitalism, are ample proof of this fact. If anything, these state industries make the propagation of socialism still more difficult by tyrannical decrees, martial law during strikes, and a spy system which does not even respect the secrecy of the ballot. In fact, the capitalist environment offers much better chances for socialist propaganda than that of state capitalism.

"This whole argument of the Collectivist Society, then, amounts to nothing else than to an attempt to weaken straight socialist propaganda in the interest of those who wish to see 'a gradual and painless growth of society into socialism.' This is the argument always put forward by those who are comfortably enough situated to await a 'gradual' deliverance from capitalism. But for the great mass of the proletarians this deliverance cannot come any too soon, even if it comes at the expense of a little temporary inconvenience to the 'middle-class socialists.' To follow this advice and help to introduce middle-class socialism, would end, in the language of the Communist Manifesto, in a 'miserable fit of the blues.'"

John C. Chase, socialist ex-mayor of Haverhill, Mass., in "The Coming Nation," June 14, 1903, gives his opinion. "Government ownership of railroads and other institutions of like nature is not a cure, nor is it even a palliative remedy . . . . There is no cure for our ills, short of the absolute abolition of capitalism."

Henry Mayers Hyndman, than whom no international authority on socialism stands higher, states the socialist position as follows:

"There is no possibility of reducing the existing anarchy in production and distribution to order by anything short of this collective ownership of the great means and instruments of production and distribution. This inevitably involves the overthrow of private property or company ownership of those great means and instruments of creating and distributing wealth. And this again carries with it the disappearance of the class state, and the establishment of an organized commission in which private ownership will be confined within the narrowest possible limits."

"Those who talk of 'municipal socialism' as if it were possible to segregate mankind into petty little units with no power to regulate the general production, first nationally and then internationally, overlook the most striking features of the economic development which is going on around them."

.   .   .   .

"Mere palliatives, such as those which have been advocated for years by the Social-Democratic Federation, and are now being adopted in some shape by both the existing capitalist political factions, are, after all, but palliatives; although the men who have been most active in championing them, have carried on this 'practical' propaganda with the direct object of preparing the way to a complete and, if possible, peaceful transformation. But wage-slaves under better conditions remain wage-slaves still; and the causes of the economic and class antagonism remain untouched by any half-measures. No improvements of the capitalist system of production can change or seriously modify the bitter struggle which must go on so long as that system endures in any shape.

"The time is coming when the expropriators will be themselves expropriated, and it is for the rising generation of Englishmen to decide whether in this country the substitution of organized co-operation for anarchical competition shall be brought about consciously and peacefully, or unconsciously and forcibly." ("The Commercial Crisis of the Nineteenth Century," pages 172, 173.)

Many more authorities might easily be quoted, but these will suffice to show that the disciples of modern socialism but follow the teachings of the founders. Frederick Engels in "Socialism from Utopia to Science" lays down the basis and makes the argument from which latter day socialists take their pattern.

"Neither conversion into stock companies nor State ownership removes the quality of capital from the powers of production. With the stock-companies, this fact remains obvious. On the other hand, the modern State is but the organization which capitalist society gives itself in order to maintain the external conditions of capitalist production against the attacks both of the workmen and of individual capitalists. The modern State, whatever its form, is essentially a capitalist machine; it is the State of the capitalist; the ideal total capitalist. The more numerous the productive powers are which it takes in hand, the nearer it is to that ideal total capitalist; all the more citizens does it exploit.

"Since Bismarck took to the plan of State ownership, a certain false socialism has arisen, and even degenerated here and there into a certain degree of sycophancy, which declares off-hand all State ownership, the Bismarckian variety included, to be socialist. Indeed, were State ownership of the tobacco industry socialistic, Napoleon and Metternich would be counted among the founders of socialism. When the Belgian State, from purely common political and financial reasons, built its own main railroads; when Bismarck, without any economic necessity, took possession for the State of the principal railroad lines of Prussia, simply with the view the better to organize and utilize them against a war, to rear the railroad employees into voting cattle for the government, and, above all, to furnish himself with a new source of revenue that should be independent from parliamentary enactments — neither was in any way a socialist measure, directly or indirectly, conscious or unconscious. Else, were the Crown's Royal Maritime Company, the Crown's porcelain factory, and even the regimental tailor likewise socialist institutions."

It is but fair to assume that the inquiring mind will rest content on the testimony given; that government ownership of public utilities is not socialism. Therefore it has no legitimate grounds to be classed as such. The political programme of the American Federation of Labor (which appears in the chapter on trade unions) could as well be called socialism, yet socialism and its programme annually meets its Waterloo at the A. F. of L. convention.

The purpose of this division is clear. It is to separate socialism proper from that indistinct notion of it which causes many a man, aye, and woman too, to aid in the propagation of socialist doctrine, which is as far away from the ideals which they seek to realize as heaven is from hell.

Evolution.

"Eternal, infinite God, I perceive Thy omnipotence in the works of Thy creation, and am like one stricken daft with admiration and wonder. Every part of Thy handiwork, the most infinitesimal as well as the most sublime, is alive with power and wisdom, with unspeakable perfection. The benefits that accrue to us poor mortals from Thy works prove Thy infinite goodness, their beauty and harmony bespeak Thy wisdom, their perpetuosity and fruitfulness Thy eternal power."
—LINNÆUS.

THE world in which one lives is as large as one's attained capacity to conceive of the universe as a whole.

Evolution from the standing ground of socialism, from a belief in "economic determinism," and evolution from the standing ground of revealed religion, that God is the Designer and Creator of the universe, is quite opposite in character.

What Darwin put forth as a theory the socialists proclaim as a science. They have drawn a "ring fence" around their universe and have solved its riddle. "Economic determinism" explains (to their satisfaction) the genesis of all human institutions. "Natural selection" in the struggle for existence creates design. Man has been transmuted from microbe to vegetable — from vegetable to animal — from animal to man. What form he may take will be determined by the pressure of future forces upon him.

The leading socialist authority upon this subject is Enrico Ferri, whose work, "Socialism and Modern Science," has been translated into many languages, appearing in English in 1900, of which "The International Socialist Review," voicing the opinions of socialists generally says,

"Since the translation of Marx's 'Capital' there has been no greater contribution to the socialist movement of the English-speaking world than is afforded by this work. . . .

The chapters on 'Socialism as a Consequence of Darwinism' and 'Evolution and Socialism' constitute the most logical exposition of the fundamentals of socialism to be found in the English language. It is difficult to see how they can be read by any one with reasoning power and not be convinced of the truth of socialism. The book is a perfect arsenal of ideas for socialist writers and speakers, and must form a part of the equipment of every well-armed socialist."

On page 35 of Ferri's book we find this statement: "We ascend in the biological scale from vegetables to animals, and from animals to man." Page 51,

"In the natural, biological domain, the free play of natural (cosmiques) forces and conditions causes a progressive advance or ascent of living forms, from the microbe up to Man."

This doctrine is universally accepted as the science of the socialist school. Born of the conceit of "a little knowledge" any straw is grasped at which will prop up the atheistical beliefs. Socialists proclaim with Proudhon and other anarchists the belief that authority is pernicious, whether it be the authority which comes from the man as master of the family; whether the authority be expressed by the state, or whether it be the authority of God, it must be abolished before mankind will be "free."

The Darwinian doctrine is accepted as proof that through social evolution (through the action of the "class struggle") man will attain unto the ideal socialist society. The "class struggle" in the sociological world is declared to be the complement of the "struggle for existence" in the biological world. An analysis of economic class evolution, as conceived by socialists, would be quite beyond the scope of this book. It is well, however, to note that socialist belief in the complementary relationship of these two schools is so fixed that the fall of one would involve the fall of the other.

One thing is certain, that the Darwinistic and socialistic philosophical deductions expressed in conduct lead to the

degeneracy of men, by robbing them of the religious qualities which elevate them above the purely animal world.

The authority of God is overthrown by this doctrine,
which declares necessity to have shaped forms. Paul La
Fargue (son-in-law to Karl Marx) in his work, "Socialism
and the Intellectuals," says, "When Darwin published his
'Origin of Species' he took away from God his role of
creator in the organic world as Franklin had despoiled him
of his thunderbolt."

This from Enrico Ferri, "Science and religion are in
inverse ratio to each other; the one deminishes and grows
weaker in the same proportion that the other increases and
grows stronger in its struggle against the unknown.

"And if this is one of the consequences of Darwinism,
its influence on the development of socialism is quite obvious."

Leonard D. Abbott, a prominent New York socialist, in
a review of "Darwin and Marx" ("The People," Vol. 9,
No. 33), says,

"The fundamental theories of both Darwin and Marx
are still vehemently combated by the majority of men —
naturally so, for an admission of their truth carries with it
the downfall of popular religion and our existing social system. These brave thinkers directed their shafts against the
most cherished and deeply rooted of human beliefs, and it
would have been impossible to have expected their theories
to win popular credence without violent opposition from the
conservative minds who have made a barrier before every
new idea in the world's history. But truth must inevitably
prevail in the end, and as the years roll on, each adding its
weight of evidence to the Darwinian and Marxian doctrines,
a gradual revolution in the minds of the people takes place.
Speed the day when the mists of superstition and prejudice
shall roll away, and the teachings of Darwin and Marx find
universal acceptance!"

The books of those biologists which can be made to

support the atheistic belief are to be found listed in nearly all socialist catalogues. In many cities classes are established for the study of this disruptive doctrine, which is considered necessary to the understanding of socialism. Edward B. Averling, a "free" son-in-law of Karl Marx, has written a book entitled "Student Darwin," which is the socialist text-book on this subject.

What scientist worthy of the name would to-day risk the statement that science has "taken away from God his role as creator in the organic world"? It was, apparently, with this design that Darwin started his investigations, while, despite his atheistic views, he was forced to the conclusion that God was at least the Creator of a few original forms.

Ferri, in the name of what socialists term "science," throws the oft exploded question, — "And God, who created him?"

It is said that Robert Ingersoll confessed to a friend that "Lambert gave him hell" in his (Lambert's) "Notes on Ingersoll." In a recent socialist attack upon Martha Moore Avery, for declaring that the Socialist Party is under the control of atheists, an ex-priest, who was eulogizing the atheistical biologists, charged her with arrogance and igno-rance" as deep and as dense as that which enshrouds the mind of the Rev. Lambert." In answer to the flippant interroga-tion of Enrico Ferri, and to the socialists who depend upon their five senses alone to inform them as to the meaning of human phenomena, I need not do better than to present the Rev. L. A. Lambert's matter, which, although from an in-tellectual point of view, will give them what Ingersoll said the Rev. Lambert gave him, I hope, from a moral point of view, it will pull them from out of that hot place into a state of mind which will set their faces towards heaven.

"If knowledge comes through the senses alone, how can I know that Mr. Lacy exists? I never saw, heard, touched, tasted or smelled him. Now if there be no other means of acquiring knowledge than through the five senses, how can I know that he exists, since none of my senses testifies to his existence? He has never come within reach of any of them. So far then as my senses are concerned he is to me as that which is not. Ah, but did you not read his 'Reply to Lambert's Notes on Ingersoll?' I have read a book with that title, but which of my five senses tells me that the book ever had an author? My senses tell me that a certain book exists, but none of them tell me that it ever had an author or that an author was necessary. I have the knowledge that a book must have an author. As this knowledge could not come through the senses, which testify only to the book's existence, it must have come to me through some other source, and therefore knowledge does not come to us through the senses alone, whether they be five, six or twenty.

"What then is the mental process by which I came to that intellectual state in which I can affirm Mr. Lacy's existence? My reason, enlightened by the idea of being in general tells me that a book could not come into being without a cause or author. My senses tell me that a book is in being. My reason then says, *therefore* its author also exists, and this affirmation of reason to itself constitutes what we call knowledge. It follows that my knowledge that the 'Reply' had an author comes from reason and not through the senses. It is the result of a judgment of reason.

"True, the senses supply the reason with sensations or the raw materials of thought, but just here their office ceases. And here comes the real difficulty. How can the reason, because conscious of a sensation, affirm anything more than the existence of that sensation. How can it pass from the consciousness of a sensation, to the idea of a real being external to itself? If the reason have nothing in it but the sensations supplied by the senses, how can it form an intellectual judgment and affirm the existence of some thing that is not itself nor a sensation? For instance, I have a sensation of hardness, smoothness, weight and dimensions; how can my mind from these data affirm the existence of something that is neither smoothness, hardness, weight or dimensions — namely substance? The mind on receiving a sensation invariably makes this affirmation. It cannot make it from data given by the senses, for the senses deal only with the qualities of things, as hardness, smoothness, etc., and not with things themselves. The mind then must have data of its own which, joined with the data supplied by the senses, enable it to affirm the existence of beings external to itself; which enable it to say: 'I have a sensation, *therefore* something exists, something besides myself is in being.' But how did the mind acquire in the first place the idea of being? It could not get it from sensation alone, for these are but modes of itself. And if we ask, how can the mind, from its own modes or modifications, infer the existence of things external to itself, we are brought back to the original difficulty. The mind cannot acquire the idea of being from the senses, for they only supply it with sensations of qualities, but do not supply the logical *nexus*, between qualities and real, subsistent beings. How then does the mind originally acquire the idea of being? There appears to be but one answer to this question, namely, it never acquired it, it is innate and coexistent with the mind. This idea of being is the light of reason; it is that which makes the mind an intelligent being, and enables it to interpret sensations and from them to affirm the existence of things; which enables it to say: 'There is a knock at my door, *therefore* there is someone without.' This *nexus* between sensations and realties is the *Pons asinorum* of the philosophers and it has occupied their attention in all times.

"It is admitted by all logicians and philosophers, and indeed by all men who think at all, that it requires at least two ideas to form a judgment. When the mind affirms that something exists, it forms a judgment. In doing this it must have two ideas, the idea of a sensation and the idea of being. The first comes through the senses; but whence comes the second? It must come from within; it must exist originally in the mind, for the theory of sensationalism cannot account for it, but always supposes it.

"Now then as the senses alone cannot account for the first judgment of the mind they cannot account for knowledge, for all knowledge is the result of judgments. I grant that in our present state of existence the mind cannot acquire knowledge without being stimulated into activity by those external stimuli which are supplied by the senses. But this does not prove that knowledge comes through the senses. It proves that the senses are a necessary *condition* of knowledge, but not that they are the *origin*, or *only* condition of it.

"Let us now come back to the point from which we digressed. What is the process of the mind in acquiring knowledge of a thing? The senses supply the mind with certain data called sensations. The mind having intuitively or innately the idea of being, and comparing it to the idea of particular sensations, forms a judgment to the effect that the sensation is caused by a being and that therefore a particular being exists. The particular being in the present case is a book called a 'Reply etc.' The mind still enlightened by the idea of being, also affirms that the book cannot come into being without a cause or author, and that therefore the book has an author. It then says: 'Therefore the author exists —therefore Mr. Lacy exists.' And this is the way I come to know that Mr. Lacy *is*. This knowledge it will be observed comes not from the senses, but from a conjunction of the senses with *reason* or *intellect*.

"This being premised, we can now consider the question: 'How can we *know* that God is?' We have seen how we know that you exist, namely, because you did something — wrote a book. Well, there is another book called the Book of Nature. It is an admirable work, an exhaustless source of instruction, pleasure and amusement. Unlike some books it bears reperusal; unlike others it never requires a second edition. It has a way of reproducing its leaves as Time's skeleton finger stains and mars them, and presents fresh pages to its readers as they hurry past from the cradle to the grave. Humanity, as it rises and sinks wave after wave, gazes on them in admiration as it passes away. But the book remains ever ancient and ever new while intelligences flit past it and are gone. It may appear a want of literary etiquette on my part to make a comparison, and yet I must say that this Book of Nature gives evidence of more creative ability than you have displayed in your 'Reply to Lambert's Notes on Ingersoll.'

"Now if your book proves *your* existence, why should not this magnificent Book of Nature prove the existence of *its* author? If my reasoning be sound in one case why is it not sound in the other? The process is the same in both. I know you *are* by your work; I know God *is* by his work. If you deny the validity of this reasoning you destroy in me the possibility of knowing that you exist; if you admit it, you admit that there is a way of knowing that God exists. I leave you to seek a fence over which to escape from this dilemma.

"To affirm that God could create himself involves the absurdity that he exists and does not exist at the same time. It supposes him first to exist, for unless he exists he cannot act or create; according to the axiom, that which is not can not act. In the second place it supposes him not to exist in order to be created, for that which already exists cannot be again created. The absurdity of a proposition involving the existence and the non-existence of God at the same time is apparent at a glance. But this absurdity is not involved in the affirmation that God can act at any moment of his being, and therefore act or create from eternity. To show this I will use the illustration of Aquinas: An eternal foot eternally pressed in eternal dust makes an eternal footstep. Here we have cause and effect co-eternal. In the same way an eternal creator eternally creating creates a co-eternal creation." ("Tactics of Infidels.")

The fault lies in the assumption that the finite mind may encompass the infinite mind. This absurdity is reduced to its fanatical conclusion by the socialists' assumption that nothing exists beyond that which man, with his physical senses, can analyze; and the further assumption that the only wants — the primary wants of man may be realized by the satisfaction of his sexual and bread-and-butter desires. Literature of this quality is dished out as "Modern Science." In words common to the street, "it is as old as hell."

Mr. Abbot is correct—"The theories of Darwin (as socialists interpret him) and Marx . . . carries with them the downfall of popular religion," and further correct is he, "the downfall of our existing social system." Certainly, for socialism can but destroy — to build is outside the province of its negations.

The fathers of modern socialism are passed and gone, but they leave behind them a band of loyal worshipers at the shrine of materialism.

"Special mention is due to Darwin, who dealt metaphysics its heaviest blow by showing that the whole organic nature now in existence, plants, animals, and consequently, man also, is the product of an evolution that has been in process through millions of years." ("Socialism from Utopia to Science.")

Many books written by socialists and circulated as socialist doctrine would make it appear that they are more concerned with the dethronement of God than they are with the upbuilding of a better social environment. Their ideal of equality, if expressed at the level of their work, would show chaos rather than order. God grant that their intentions, rather than the doctrines which they promulgate, will prevail — though I recall that hell is said to be paved with good intentions. 67

"I add that not only is Darwinism not in contradiction with socialism, but that it constitutes one of its fundamental scientific premises. As Virchow justly remarked, socialism is nothing but a logical and vital corrollary, in part of Darwinism, in part of Spencerian evolution.

"The theory of Darwin, whether we wish it or not, by demonstrating that man is descended from the animals, has dealt a severe blow to the belief in God as the creator of the universe and of man as a special *fiat*." (Enrico Ferri.)

These quotations given will suffice — though the woods are full of them — to show that the evolutionary standing ground of socialism is on the side of "economic determinism." That man has descended from the animal is accepted without a shadow of doubt. A leading socialist speaker, while addressing a Boston audience, said, "whether you like it or not we are all descended from the ape." They are cocksure of what is still without satisfactory proof to any biologist of standing, to declare that your ancestors were not monkeys would be a gross display of ignorance from the socialist standard of intelligence.

The links are still missing!! and they are to be found before the dividing line which separates man from the animal is eliminated from the time-honored standards, as laid down in the first book of Moses. Man is still king of all he surveys, made in the image of his God.

I am certainly aware that Haeckel in his latest book (which by the way is written with an anti-Christian animus quite unbecoming in a man of science) brings forth his fossil man-monkey of Jarva, his Pithecanthropus Erectus as claimant to the place of Sir Linkship. One freak will not prove the link any more than finding one shell will prove a clam bake.

Man has one distinguishing characteristic, supreme, above all lower animals. He has the conscious art principle. The principle by which he can cause his being to positively express itself above the forces to which the animal is negatively subject. He creates his environment in conformity to his self-created design. By the exercise of his will he may create such environment as will best sustain him. By the exercise of his will he may direct the forces and re-form the substances of nature to the satisfaction of his wants. By the exercise of his will he may direct his energies to the salvation of his soul.

By the human art principle man augments his vision by the use of the telescope, the microscope and the X-ray. With the telephone, the telegraph and wireless telegraphy he extends his power of communication — of speech. With the derrick and the steam shovel he adds strength to his arm. With the railroad, steamship and airship he extends his power of locomotion. Whence came this positive art principle by which man may first create his design and then work it out in substance, if not God given? It is not merely more of the same instinct to which the animal negatively responds in carrying out the designs impressed upon them by the Creator of the heaven and the earth. The atheistical biologists have not even a suggestion which covers this great gap in their theory. Evolution from their standpoint is a mock to common sense.

Socially one may clearly see the process of evolution in the growth, the development of our great American Republic. The design of its progress is not created by the successive necessities for larger liberties. But implanted within the Declaration of Independence was the potential design which slowly unrolls to the fuller demonstration of its inherent principles. Its principle of democracy, active in the principle of evolution, extends, expands and elevates its democratic form, successively erecting a purer, more beautiful and more powerful social structure. Great as has been the advance it has not necessitated a change in its fundamental design. In building the Ship of State there have been modifications only in the detail of the work. The principle of democracy is not evolved, it was perfect from the beginning, but the structure within which it finds its human embodiment may by man be unfolded upon the principle of evolution. We give this merely as an illustration of the evolution of human design which it is within the power of man to create with the help of God.

We will allow a churchman to speak of evolution from the standpoint of religion.

"There never was, nor can there ever be, but one Church of Christ, — a Church immutable like her head and founder, who is GOD. But this Church is a living body, and however perfect she is from her origin, she develops and adapts her beneficial influences apace with the progress of centuries. Man does not possess at his birth that fulness of strength, that beauty of symmetry, that expansion of all his faculties, which add so much to the perfection of his nature. At his birth he possesses all this; but he has had no opportunity as yet to work out its development. But still he is always the same individual, whether he is a tender infant, an adolescent, or a full-grown man. Thus the Church, which was born with the Twelve Men in the cenacle, has grown and developed her strength through the growth of succeeding ages. Like a splendid drapery, which slowly deploys and progressively unfolds its beautiful colors, so the Church has successively opened to the world the treasures of her doctrine and the sanctification which emanates from her bosom." (Mgr. Segur.)

I quote from Henry George, who has put this point clearly, in a popular statement which a school-boy may understand.

"However man may have originated, all we know of him is as man — just as he is now to be found. There is no record or trace of him in any lower condition than that in which savages are still to be met . . . Between the lowest savages of whom we know and the highest animals, there is an irreconcilable difference — a difference not merely of degree, but of kind.   Many of the characteristics, actions and emotions of man are exhibited by the lower animals; but man, no matter how low in the scale of humanity, has never yet been found destitute of one thing of which no animal shows the slightest trace, a clearly recognizable but almost undefinable something, which gives him the power of improvement — which makes him the progressive animal.

   "The beaver builds a dam, and the bird a nest, and the bee a cell; but while beavers' dams, and birds' nests, and bees' cells are always constructed on the same model, the house of man passes from the rude hut of leaves and branches to the magnificent mansion replete with modern conveniences.   The dog can to a certain extent connect cause and effect, and may be taught some tricks; but his capacity in these respects has not been a whit increased during all the ages he has been the associate of improving man, and the dog of civilization is not a whit more accomplished or intelligent than the dog of the wandering savage.   We know of no animal that uses clothes, that cooks its food, that makes itself tools or weapons, that breeds other animals that it wishes to eat, or that has an articulate language.   But men who do not do such things have never yet been found, or heard of, except in fable.   That is to say, man, wherever we know him, exhibits this power — of supplementing what nature has done for him by what he does for himself."   ("Progress and Poverty.")

   Now that Ernest Haeckel has thrown up the sponge, I would ask socialists who follow his school why they still claim a Godless nature — why stick to "economic determinism?" Haeckel confesses that the "innermost character of nature" is still a mystery.   I put it this way, why not affirm that the inherent design asserted as the fiat of Almighty God holds as the rational attitude in preference to the guesses of "little gentlemen" until such time as Original Design shall have been overthrown?

After reading through the slime of atheistic dogmatism which mars painstaking description of valuable data, for which one must be grateful, for facts are facts whatever company they are found in, in the conclusion of his book one may find very good proof of that which he rails against — that which he dismisses with contempt — traces of the Infinite Mind which man cannot fully uncover.

"Only one comprehensive riddle of the universe remains — the problem of substance."

———

"We grant at once that the innermost character of nature is just as little understood by us as it was by Anaximander and Empedocles twenty-four hundred years ago, by Spinoza and Newton two hundred years ago, and by Kant and Goethe one hundred years ago. We must even grant that this essence of substance becomes more mysterious and enigmatic the deeper we penetrate into the knowledge of its attributes, matter and energy, and the more thoroughly we study its countless phenomenal forms and their evolution. We do not know the 'thing in itself' that lies behind these knowable phenomena. But why trouble about this enigmatic 'thing in itself' when we have no means of investigating it, when we do not even clearly know whether it exists or not?" ("The Riddle of the Universe," New York, 1900.)

Here we have the most redoubtable gentleman of the atheistic school quarreling with the existence of God — setting up in His place the Darwin — Haeckel school — and at the "wind-up" of his book, with a stroke of his pen throwing the "essence of substance" contemptuously to one side with the flippant remark that after all we do "not even clearly know whether it exists or not."

Notwithstanding this intellectual somersault of Haeckel,

socialists resting on his and like authority have still the audacity to declare that "God as the creator of the universe and of man as a special fiat has been annihilated."

"Natural science has made a myth of creation; astronomy, mathematics and physics have converted heaven into airy space, and the stars on heaven's tent where the angels sat enthroned, into fixed stars and planets, whose nature quite excludes the presence of such beings as angels. The ruling class, which sees its existence threatened, clings to religion as the support of all authority, a dogma which all rulers have upheld up to the present day. The bourgeoisie believes nothing; it has itself destroyed all belief in religion and authority by its own process of development, and by science, to which it has given birth. Its belief is a farce, and the church accepts the help of this false friend because it needs help." (August Babel, "Woman in the Past, Present and Future," page 146.)

"Man is the product of evolution," says Engels and his school, "that has been in process through millions of years."

The world's authority on "time" denies this possibility.

"If Natural Selection be true, the geological time requisite for the evolving of species such as they exist at present, must be vastly greater than can be allowed by astronomers for the whole life of the solar system. 'This power of selection,' says Darwin in a letter to Sir J. Hooker, 'stands in the most direct relation to time, and in the state of nature can only be excessively slow.' Excessively slow indeed, for as Mr. Murphy, quoted by Dr. Mivart, says: 'Suppose it took 500 years to form a greyhound out of his wolf-like ancestor, how long ought it to take to form an elephant from a protozoon, or even from a tadpole-like fish?' And Dr. Mivart himself finds it 'not easy to believe that less than 2,000,000,000 years would be required for the totality of animal development by no other means than minute, fortuitous, occasional, and intermitting variations in all conceivable directions ; ' that is about one hundred times more than Lord Kelvin allows for the age ot sunlight itself.

"That the force of the objection was fully appreciated by Darwin we have ample proofs in his letters. Thus he writes to Wallace (Life and Letters, vol. iii, p. 114) . . . 'Thompson's views of the recent age of the world have been for some time one of my sorest troubles, so I have been glad to hear what you say,' and again in another place : 'I can say nothing more about missing-links than what I have said. I should rely much on pre-silurian times ; but then comes Sir W. Thomson like an odious spectre.' Moreover, it must be borne in mind that these letters were penned some thirty years since, at a time prior to Langley's bolometric observations on the absorption of the solar rays by our atmosphere. The result of these observations has been to reduce the time allowable for the age of the sun very considerably. Thirty years ago, Lord Kelvin arguing from the action of the tides on the rotation of the earth, from the probable length of time that sunlight had illumined our planet, and from the temperature of the interior of the earth, allowed 100,000,000 years as the limit for the existence of living things upon the globe, and it is to this number that Darwin's letter alludes.'" (Rev. Aloysius J. Cortie, "The Age of the Sun.")

Lord Kelvin (Sir William Thompson), who, in many respects, is considered "the greatest living scientist," in answering Professor Henslow (London, May, 1903) said : —

"Professor Henslow had stated that modern science neither affirms nor denies creative power in the origin of life. Lord Kelvin replied that science positively affirms creative power and makes every one feel a miracle in himself. It was not in dead matter, he added, that men lived, moved and had their being, but in a creative and directive power, which science compelled them to accept as an article of belief. Modern biologists were coming once more to a firm acceptance of something, and that was a vital principle.

Agnostics they might be in science, but they only knew the Creator in His works and were absolutely forced by science to admit and to believe with absolute confidence in a directive power. Lord Kelvin made a rigorous application of the logical law of excluded middle, and contended that there must either be scientific belief in creative power or acceptance of the Ciceronian theory of a fortuitous concourse of atoms. Because biologists could not escape from the conclusion that there was original creative power when they studied the physics and dynamics of living and dead matter, science was not antagonistic to religion, but a help to it. 'A million of millions of millions of years would not give them a beautiful world like ours.'

"Lord Kelvin had put this incisive inquiry: 'Is there anything so absurd as to believe that a number of atoms by falling together of their own accord could make a crystal, a sprig of moss, a microbe, or a living animal?' On reflection he perceived that a crystal was an unfortunate illustration, since in structure it differed from the cellular formation of which plants and animals were made. He accordingly hastened to admit that a crystal might result from a fortuitous concourse of atoms, but contended anew that a similar explanation could not be offered for the origin, existence, and growth of plants and living beings, for which scientific thought was compelled to accept the idea of creative power. Lord Kelvin closed his brief but weighty confession of faith with this striking passage: 'Forty years ago I asked Liebig, walking somewhere in the country, if he believed that the grass and flowers which we saw around us grew by mere chemical force. He answered: 'No! no more than I could believe that a book of botany describing them could grow by mere chemical forces.' Every action of a human free will is a miracle to physical and chemical and mathematical science. This is emphatic testimony from the foremost man of science in England respecting the creative mind as the only possible source of life. It differs widely from the scientific atheism of Darwin, Tyndall, Huxley and Spencer, which was accepted a quarter of a century ago as the highest wisdom of the educated world."

The Rev. D. T. O'Sullivan, S. J., of Boston College, an able theologian and scientist, says : —

" Two important deductions may be drawn from reading the opponents of Lord Kelvin; the first is, that while they deny Creative Power, they offer no alternative; and, secondly, their reason for not accepting Creative Power is that they cannot conceive of it. The first shows clearly the limitations of biology as such and its ignorance of the origin of its own subject matter. Ignorance of a thing can never become an argument for its non-existence. Inadequacy of the means offered by a particular science must be supplemented by other legitimate means furnished by some other legitimate branch of science in order to reach the conclusion which the first science unaided could never attain. In the case under consideration the facts furnished by biology must be aided by a process of logical reasoning upon those facts, and the logical conclusions must be admitted by every reasonable mind.

"This brings us to the consideration of the second deduction of the opponents of a Creative Power — namely, that they cannot admit such a power because they cannot conceive of it. This is a most startling statement in the light of scientific methods in every department of science. If there is one thing that any scientist demands as a matter of belief and to which he appeals in all his investigations it is the principle of causation. Remove this principle and what a sorry picture is presented by the investigator in the laboratory !

" Now, those scientists who rigorously demand the application of this principle in every step of scientific investigation should logically demand it to explain the existence of the universe. Hence to say that they cannot conceive of a Creative Power is to abandon at a crucial point the principle of causation, the chief incentive to scientific investigation.

"Probably scientific atheism is based largely on the misunderstanding of the two great generalizations of modern science. These great laws are the conservation of energy and the conservation of matter. But in reality what do they mean? Simply this: in our hands we can neither destroy or create matter or energy, and that we believe on the principle of causation that the same effect always follows everywhere the same cause, and hence we generalize. But whence matter and energy? Are we to deny the principle of causation here?

"It is refreshing to find such princes of science as Kelvin, Newton, Müller, Locke, Schwann, Pasteur, Liebig and others deeply drinking at the fount of science and impregnated with the true philosophy of science defending from scientific grounds the existence of God in opposition to the agnosticism of Huxley, the materialism of Tyndall, the atheism of Clifford, the skepticism of Fitzjames Stephen, the positivism of Frederic Harrison and the pantheism of Haeckel to understand that science must perforce soon cease her dogmatism, confine herself to her own legitimate sphere and become as she must by right the handmaid of religion."

To affirm with socialists that Darwin has proven "that the whole organic nature now in existence — plants, animals, and consequently men also — is the product of evolution," while neither the data nor the reasoning from the demonstrable facts in the case will admit of such conclusion, is false, and leaves the old Mosaic declaration in control of the fortress of human knowledge; nay, not human knowledge, but the revelation of God.

That "Darwin, by demonstrating that man is descended from the animals, has dealt a severe blow to the belief in God," is true only in one sense; and that is, it has built a bump of conceit on the heads of pseudo scientists, who, accepting the socialist interpretation of Darwin, know nothing of science and still less of religion.

The twentieth century is arming itself with instruments of deeper vision, which once more proves Pope's claim that "a little knowledge is a dangerous thing."

Morally Irresponsible.

"IAGO :

'Tis in ourselves tnat we are thus or thus. Our bodies are our gardens, to the which our wills are gardeners; so that if we will plant nettles, or sow lettuce, set hyssop and weed up thyme, supply it with one gender of herbs, or distract it with many, either to have it sterile with idleness, or manured with industry, why, the power and corrigible authority of this lies in our wills."

THE reappearance of an age-worn fallacy, materialism, which now takes political form with the advent of the socialist party must be met upon civic rather than upon religious ground. The natural and logical result of the teachings of the "materialistic conception of history" is the denial of free agency. Thus does "economic determinism" strike a fatal blow at that attribute of human nature which holds man above the animal impressions to which he is cosmically subject. For its root lies deep down in the denial of Ccreative Power — of Original Design — of God. Its primal attack is upon personal responsibility and its second attack is upon the natural rights of man. Socialist philosophy attacks the fundamental principles upon which our great nation is builded.

A leading socialist giving expression to the "class conscious" dissatisfaction, which is prevalent in the east, with Walter Thomas Mills' lessons on "Social Economy," writes:

"I was astonished to find that his very first lesson contained two fallacious teachings on questions of fundamental importance to what we term scientific socialism, viz: first, the teaching of a design in nature (hence a designer); second, the teaching that men have inalienable or natural rights.

"As to the first I will advance no argument beyond the statement that it is totally at variance with the teachings of

79

modern science. The importance of refusing to sanction it in a work on scientific socialism lies in the fact that when we get involved in intricate sociological questions we find that our main or basic arguments, and indeed our general views, depend upon our ultimate philosophic conceptions. For example : Without the materialistic conception of history, socialist political economy would not be scientific since it would have no relation established between cause and effect. But a materialistic conception of history is dependent upon a materialistic philosophy, hence it conflicts with idealistic doctrines.

"The second fallacy : The doctrine of natural rights is one that probably more than any other distinguishes the old academic metaphysical school of political economy from the modern scientific school. It is a fallacy that is refuted by all the teachings of history, and no person with any valid claim to a knowledge of scientific socialism would teach it. It implies that conditions are changed by a recognition of rights, i. e., by ethical teaching, and not by superior force exerted in the interest of classes favored by economic conditions. To permit the teaching of such doctrine is to vitiate the movement by destroying its class conscious and sternly revolutionary character." ("The Chicago Socialist," July 11, 1903.)

This statement is a correct postulation of the position held by socialists the world over. Certainly ! If man have no natural rights, why then, he has no legal rights. For the basis of constitutional rights lies upon his natural rights as formulated in the Mosaic law, which is the natural law revealed to man by the Almighty Designer.

This socialist doctrine is not new, for the denial of natural rights and the denial of the existence of design in nature is as old as time, and a century ago it found violent expression in the French revolution. The denialists of those days " abolished the soul," they set the goddess of reason on the throne of God and " adopted the guillotine as their symbol in place of the cross." The difference in methods, is the only difference between the denialists of to-day and the denialists of the 18th century. Man comes from the troglodyte, therefore he has no moral responsibility — no natural, no God-given rights — His human form is the result of the necessity in the case, therefore he has not free will.

We will take the testimony of a competent socialist authority.

"To the environment, in the last analysis, to the relations necessarily created by the multiple contacts, actions and re-actions of the environment and the environed are due all the transformations of all organisms and, in consequence, all the phenomena that emanate from them." ("Socialism, Revolution and Internationalism," by Gabriel Deville. New York, March, 1901.)

This clear short statement embodies the basis for the ethical standards adopted by socialists in general. The truth of the matter is that it is not valid ground. And in face of the fact that even Haeckel gives up the ghost as to the "essence of matter"; that is to say he don't know whether each particle of cosmic dust is impressed with its own cosmic design or not, is at least the shakiest ground to stand on. Not to mention the attitude of Wallace, Lord Kelvin, Crooks, and others; shallow assertions positively given is, to say the least, impudently flying in the face of the highest authority of the age.

In "The State and Socialism," by Gabriel Deville, published in New York, December, 1900, a work universally accredited by this school of thought, we find that "The inventions and not the intentions of men have been the cause of progress." This sounds well! The music of its rhythm is mistaken for logic. The simple fact is that the inventions of man have always been preceded by the intentions of men, just the same as the design of his book preceded the appearance of his book. Whether it will be "the cause of progress" remains to be seen.   81

In another part of this book, Deville says:

"Obviously there has been progress. But it is not through aspiration toward the realization of righteousness that this progress has been accomplished. Although men had from the beginning a more or less confused sentiment of justice, progress has been brought about neither by this sentiment nor by the idealist manifestations of the human conscience."

Why revere the memory of the great — men of noble purpose — men determined to work righteousness into human relationship? Surely only those whose "aspirations towards the realization of righteousness" have prepared for us this glorious twentieth century. Surely we enjoy the result of the aspiration and self-sacrifice which is now embodied in the laws, the structure and the life of our civilization.

"It is not the conscious mind of man that determines the form of his being, but, vice versa, the social form of his being that determines the conscious action of his mind." ("Critique of Political Economy," Karl Marx.)

This is an excellent specimen of Marxian philosophy in a nutshell. It annihilates free will and personal responsibility. And it predicates society alone as justly punishable for sin and crime. A very convenient doctrine by which to saddle individual immorality upon the social body.

"Socialism is not arbitrary destruction and reconstruction, but a natural process of development . . . neither 'statesmen of genius,' nor 'demagogues who stir up revolt' can guide the course of events according to their will. They believe that they direct the current, but are really borne along with it." (August Babel.)

This is also clearly fatalistic. All self effort is unavailing. According to their jargon the only conscious man is the "class conscious" man.

"Political or scientific theories are natural phenomena and not the capricious and ephemeral products of the free

wills of those who construct and propagate them." (Socialism and Modern Science," Eurico Ferri.)

If man is not endowed with free will — if he be not free
to choose between two courses of action, why hold criminals
responsible for crimes committed? If the power to use one's
faculties as one may determine be not a privilege granted to
man by his Creator, why establish deliberative bodies to en-
act public sentiment, public opinion, public judgment into
law? Why, indeed! Society is the criminal, not the individual — open the doors of the prisons and set the thieves
and the murderers free — set them *free* to roam where they
will.

"The right of freely dissolving the marriage tie, which
was recognized in primitive society, has been gradually re-
placed by the absolute formulæ of theology and mysticism
which fancy that the 'free will' can settle the destiny of a
person by a monosyllable pronounced at a time when the
physical equilibrium is as unstable as it is during courtship
and at marriage. Later on the reversion to the spontaneous
and primitive form of a union based on mutual consent im-
poses itself on men, and the matrimonial union, with the increase in the frequency and facility of divorce, reverts to its
original forms and restores to the family, that is to say, to
the social cell a healthier constitution." ("Socialism and
Modern Science," page 103.)

If one be not *free to will* to follow the lusts of his flesh
— if one be not *free to will* to follow the aspirations of his
soul, why then, to strive to purify the body and elevate the
mind by overcoming temptation is merest moonshine. Why
exercise self-control — why discipline one's sex passions?
Why indeed? Socialists say that "sex fondness" is the
standard of sex purity. Let us put this socialist doctrine into
simple English. One but entertains himself with the idea of
free will, it is not "scientific." With the increase in the frequency and facility of divorce — with religious restraints

broken — the practice of free love will restore to society a healthier set of men, women and children who in nowise are supposed to know who their parents are.

"The new morality must proclaim war to the knife with this abstract morality centering in the individual. The new ideal proclaims that no action is morally wrong that has not directly anti-social consequences." . . . "The perfection of the individual, not through himself but through society, is the motto of modern socialism, and this doctrine involves a complete inversion of the traditional ethical theory." ("The Problems of Realty.")

Certainly it does! Free will denied, personal responsibility and so personal morality is absurd — so also is social morality absurd, but the "socialist mind" is not rational enough to perceive this fact.

"We bring ethics back from the clouds. . . . Morals being purely secular in origin and purpose should be kept free from all contact with religion." ("Where we Stand," Spargo, page 19.)

Considering the fact that moral and religious conduct is based upon free will, and the further fact that socialism rules free will out of court, this instruction is as ambiguous as it is gratutious.

Political Atheism.

"Reason and experience, both forbid us to expect that national morality can previl where religious principles are excluded."

GEORGE WASHINGTON.

THE volume of atheistical literature in circulation within the socialist propaganda is stupendous! Underlying the political attack upon the economic system there lies the determined purpose of uprooting institutions having as their basis revealed religion.

The reader's attention is kindly called to our purpose of giving the authoritative decrees of socialism rather than to give an argument in defense of religion.

The tactics of socialism are elusive, to say the least; one may turn one page finding there a declaration against religion, and another to find the assertion that socialism has nothing to do with religion.

In my years of experience within the socialist party I have known but two or three devout Christians and no orthodox Jews to retain membership in the organization. If men of some little faith came in, it was soon broken down or they left the movement. The old German members, who launched the socialist organization in this country, having imbibed atheism with their beer at home were — and these same members now are rank atheists — cannot hear the name of God without giving expression to contempt. Their hatred of devotion in Christian or Jew knows no bounds; their disgust at church attendance is undisguised.

James Leatham, a prominent English socialist frankly gives voice to the irreligious character of the movement. I quote : —

"At the present moment I cannot remember a single instance of a person who is at one and the same time a really earnest and intelligent socialist and an orthodox Christian. Those who do not openly attack the Church and the fabric of Christianity show but scant respect to either the one or the other in private. . . . And while all of us are thus indifferent to the Church, many of us are frankly hostile to her. Marx, Lassalle and Engels, among earlier socialists; Morris, Bax, Hyndman, Guesde and Babel among present-day socialists — are all more or less avowed Atheists; and what is true of the more notable men of the party is almost equally true of the rank and file the world over." ("Socialism and Character," 1897.)

Edward B. Averling, a sometime leader of the atheistic movement of Great Britain, is good authority — the best of authority; he says: —

"Marx was an avowed Atheist. And those who desire to know the scientific reasons for the materialism of Marx, Engels, Babel, Leibknecht, Guesde, Lafargue, Adler, Plechauff — in a word, of all the founders and teachers of scientific socialism — should read the whole of the introduction written by Frederick Engels in 1892 to my translation of his 'Socialism, Scientific and Utopian.'" ("Charles Darwin and Karl Marx: a Comparison.")

In this work the "Materialist Basis of History" is promulgated, which has for its complementary principle the denial of Creative Power.

"It is our duty as socialists to root out the faith in God with all our zeal, nor is any one worthy the name who does not consecrate himself to the spread of Atheism." (Wilhelm Leibknecht.) John Graham Brooks gives it as his opinion, in his book entitled "Social Unrest," that this statement of Leibknecht's may be duplicated, substantially, from twenty authoritative socialist sources.

Leibknecht was a little later taught, by experience, that direct attacks upon religion was not good politics. At the Halle Congress he said: —

"Instead of squandering our strength in a struggle with the Church and sacerdotalism, let us go to the root of the matter. We desire to overthrow the State of the classes. When we have done that the Church and sacerdotalism will fall with it, and in this respect we are much more radical and much more definite in purpose than our opponents, for we like neither the priests nor the anti-priests."

August Babel, although an avowed atheist, recognized the necessity for different tactics than those employed by the French revolutionists, declared that while he favored the "dethronement of religion," he found that progress towards this ideal lay in the capture of the public powers. (Hence the political atheism masqurading as the socialist party.) In "Woman: Past, Present and Future," page 146, Babel says:—

"Religion will share the fate of the state. It will not be 'abolished,' God will not be dethroned, religion will not be 'torn out of the peoples' hearts,' nor will any other of the phrases be put into effect, of which the atheistic Social-Democrats are accused. Social-Democracy leaves all such foolish attempts to the bourgeois ideologists who tried to realize them in the French Revolution, and naturally came to grief. Religion will disappear by itself, without any violent attack.

"Religion is the transcendental image of the condition of society at any given period. The religion of society changes in the same measure as society changes and as its development progresse. The ruling classes seek to preserve it as a means of upholding their supremacy. This business becomes an important official function, exercised by a caste formed for the purpose of supporting and enlarging the edifice with all the subtility at its command, and thereby assuring its own power and prestige."

Not until after an experience of over forty years did the choler of the atheist-socialist German movement become sufficiently cool for them to recognize the fact that direct attack upon the religious belief of citizens retarded their political growth, and that a masked attack was therefore the best policy. It was at the Erfurt Congress (1891) that they passed a resolution declaring "religion to be a private matter." The American socialists, taking pattern after the tactics of their foreign comrades, from whom their denialist doctrine emanated, have passed similar resolutions in this country, to which they refer with persistent iteration when the subject of religion is up.

When the author presented to the Massachusetts socialist convention (1902) a resolution, the substance of which was that such speakers as attacked theological doctrines or dogmas should be deemed disqualified for the socialist platform, the convention passed a counter resolution declaring religion to be a matter of private opinion.

How strange that a political party is forced to make this declaration! But is this "the modern scientific revolutionary" method of disposing of this question? Agreed, religion is a private matter, looked at from a personal point of view, and it needs no declaration of political parties to establish its standing as such, — but when an organized attempt is made to capture the Ship of State to the end that its religious institutions and its doctrines may be sunk hell deep, then religion is not only a private matter but it becomes a matter of great national import. And such is the danger which confronts the American people — aye, the danger which confronts civilization.

We challenge socialists on this ground: Prove the honesty of your resolution which carries with it the inference that you do not intend to interfere with the convictions, the doctrines of the religious; act up to your declarations by putting a stop to the circulation of the books written by the founders and promoters of the socialist movement; after which adopt additional resolutions denouncing the materialist philosophy of Marx, Engels, Babel, Loria, Bax, Ferri and all other socialist authorities. Or, as Savonarola made a flaming pile of the vanities of his time, so socialists might spread a purifying influence over their followers by making a flaming pile of those abominations which drug the human mind. No, this cannot be done; it would be equal to the complete overthrow of the socialist movement! Then act like men; have the courage openly to defend your convictions, though you fight to maintain the gates of hell.

Enrico Ferri declares that under the influence of "scientific culture" religious convictions will "perish by atrophy."

"It is true that Marxian socialism, since the congress held in Erfurt (1891), has rightly declared that religious beliefs are private affairs.

"Socialism knows and foresees that religious beliefs, whether one regards them with Sergi, as pathological phenomena of human psychology, or as useless phenomena of moral incrustation, are destined to perish by atrophy with the extension of even elementary scientific culture. This is why socialism does not feel the necessity of waging a special warfare against these religious beliefs which are destined to disappear. It has assumed this attitude, although it knows that the absence or the impairment of the belief in God is one of the most powerful factors for its extension, because the priests of all religions have been, throughout all the phases of history, the most potent allies of the ruling classes in keeping the masses pliant and submissive under the yoke by means of the enchantment of religion, just as the tamer keeps wild beasts submissive by the terrors of the cracks of his whip.

"And this is so true that the most clear-sighted conservatives, even though they are atheists, regret that the religious sentiment — that precious narcotic — is diminishing among the masses, because they see in it, though their pharisaism does not permit them to say it openly, an instrument of political domination." (Socialism and Modern Science, pages 62–63.)

It is false reasoning to assume, as socialists do, that "the enchantment of religion keeps the masses pliant and submissive" to the control of base men, and it would advance progress apace if materialists were to become "pliant and submissive" to the will of God. Pages of the world's history are filled with the names of men and women to whom we are indebted for the progress in science and art, who owe their culture and education to the "enchantment of religion."— Nay more, the names that, like mountain peaks, lift up their heads above the oozy horizon of human commonplace are those whose wills are set towards God by the effort to keep His commandments. It is a natural consequence that materialism should hang the head toward the ground. Ferri does not know that the fear of God maketh the heart sweet — that religious fear is quite different in quality from that fear which "the tamer keeps wild beasts submissive by the terror of the cracks of his whip." Were he to raise his eyes heavenward and receive an influx of that light which lighteth the world, it would show him that the passions of men are subdued to calm only by the purifying influence of religion, not by physical fear, nor even by physical indulgence.

"Religion is a private matter" . . . . . "have we not declared it to be such by resolutions; why charge us with attacking the church and its teachings?" Say the socialists: "It is a capitalist trick to throw discredit upon the working class movement." "Well, slander is expected from the Benedict Arnold's once in the party, they are necessary to the success of the movement."

What you could honestly say is that personal opposition as well as opposition to that abstraction the capital system is necessary to the life of the socialist movement. To make progress it is necessary to vilify those who having once accepted socialism as the means of emancipating the wage workers from the degradation of their economic relationship, and now if after close and exhaustive study of it find it to be the political sink pot of atheistical philosophy, one would rid our national life of this pest, he necessarily comes in conflict with those of us who promote those vile doctrines as the messenger of liberty, equality and fraternity.

But let us hear "The Worker;" it sets the pace as the bully-bluffer in dishonest tactics. Here one may see pretended friendship with the church, of the same base metal as its friendship with trade unions which it seeks to use and to destroy. "The Worker" answers its own challenge, in the self same issue in which it is made. Not one word against religion? Indeed, thou art the prince of bluffers!

"Shall the church rule the labor movement?"

"First, he, 'the Bishop of Buffalo,' has declared that the Social Democratic Party (or Socialist Party) 'is everywhere characterized by unbelief, hostility to religion, and, above all, uncompromising and bitter hatred of the Catholic Church,' and that its 'official programs, the platforms of its party conventions, the public utterances of its advocates, its newspaper organs and periodicals breathe hatred and threats against revealed religion, its doctrines and institutions.'

"The Bishop's charge is a sweeping one. We now challenge him, as Bishop or as honest man, to prove, not the whole, but one hundredth part of what he has alleged. He cannot do it, for it is not true.

"Bishop Quigley, let us advise you to reconsider your action. Your attack is an unprovoked one, for the Socialist Party makes no attack upon you or your Church or your beliefs. But if you persist in the attack, let us tell you that there is no organization on earth that can fight as we can. Bismarck has measured strength with us, and failed. Russian czars and French dictators have tried to crush our movement, and they have failed. You will not succeed." ("The Worker," New York, March 9, 1903.)

"The Worker," March 9, 1902, has a translation

from 'Sempre Avantis' (Forward Forever), published in Turin, Italy, the editor, Hon Oddino Morgari, socialist member of Parliament from Piedmont, in reply to the question, "Can we keep a picture of Christ in our socialist headquarters?" says: It can stay, but the picture should be without a halo, and should have the words beneath it: to Christ who was a man and a martyr to the principle of brotherhood among men.' Thus it is that the religious convictions of millions of our citizens are outraged, their belief in the divinity of Christ blasphemed.

Passing from the challenge to Bishop Quigley, on March the 9th, to the issue of March 30, 1902, we find that the editor of "The Worker," who has the brazen face to ask for proof, "not of the whole but one hundredth part of what he (the Bishop) has alleged," culled the following from "The Advance," a California socialist party paper, and hashes it out as fit food with which to develop "socialist minds." These are the points: Does the editor declare the bishop to be dishonest? Does he affirm it to be impossible to prove "but one hundredth part of what he has alleged?" Let us understand this matter! Does this leader of falsifying socialist editors mean to imply that the socialist party stands favorable to or even neutral to "revealed religion, its doctrines and institutions?" Which the bishop says socialism "breathes hatred and threats against?" We are ready to prove that the statement of the bishop is correct. That from the very nature of socialist philosophy it must stand in direct opposition to the philosophy of revealed knowledge — and that socialism "breathes hatred" double dyed against religious law.

"In a letter to 'Advance,' called forth by an article in which the writer intimated that he 'would saddle a Christ upon the movement,' George D. Herron writes as follows:

"I have always been thoroughly opposed to the using of the socialist platform for the propagation of anything known as 'Social Christianity.' I have never, when speaking from a socialist platform, made use of it for religious propaganda. I believe every such use of socialism will result in confusion, disaster and betrayal. Every appeal to men to become Socialists in the name of Christianity will result in the corruption and betrayal of Socialism in the end, and in the use of the movement for private ends. People cannot separate Christ from Christianity. And Christianity to-day stands for what is lowest and basest in life. The church of to-day sounds the lowest note in human life. It is the most degrading of all our institutions, and the most brutalizing in its effects on the common life. The church is simply organized Christianity. For Socialism to use it, to make terms with it, or to let it make approaches to the Socialist movement is for Socialism to take Judas to its bosom. There is not an instance, in sixteen centuries, in which the church has not betrayed every movement for human emancipation it has touched. Official religion and militarism are the two guardians of capitalism, and the subtle methods of the church, in destroying the manhood of the soul and keeping it servile, are infinitely more to be dreaded by the Socialist movement than the world's standing armies.

"Let us keep clean from confusion and self-deceit in this critical hour, and not use the Socialist movement for special propagandas of our own. If we belong to Socialism, if our lives are dedicated to the revolution — and its emancipation of mind and body, then let us give ourselves to it without trying to use it, or without putting conditions in our service." ("The Worker," March 30, 1902, republished from "The Advance.") Could a more open attack be published against the church of which Bishop Quigley is a distinguished member? Especially does it count as coming from the highest official in the socialist party of America — This some-time "professor of applied Christianity" is now the American Secretary of the International Socialist Party. He is correct; he does not, "when speaking from a socialist platform, make use of it for religious propaganda." Just the opposite, Professor! What you say is true. Your platform utterances and printed matter will plainly show that you use your opportunities in the socialist party for anti-religious propaganda. Do I pick up one of your articles, it is a rarity if I do not find in it a direct attack upon religion and upon the marriage system made sacred by it. Notwithstanding the "pure whiteness" of your socialist conscience.

"Christianity to-day stands for what is lowest and basest in life"? "To take on Christianity would be for socialism to take Judas to its bosom"? "Christianity will result in the corruption and betrayal of socialism"? No! Professor, yours is not an attempt to "saddle a Christ upon the movement." You do but tighten the "saddle" of the anti-christ upon the movement — which was ever bone of its bone and flesh of its flesh ere you joined the movement to speed the pace of the devil.

Whether you know it or not Christianity stands to-day for what it ever stood, however far away atheists are from emanating Christian character. You are wrong? Socialism cannot change its lurid color — Judas was dyed in its warp and woof and spun in its specious web long before you gave the pieces of silver to the Secretary of the Massachusetts State Committee, who now guards your party interests as national Secretary. Instead of Christianity betraying socialism, Christianity is being betrayed by socialism.

The Professor says that there is "not an instance in 16 centuries in which the church has not betrayed every movement for human emancipation." Men who read history free from the prejudices of passion know how much of civilization is due to the work of the self-sacrificing religious — know how much the state, the family and the individual owe to religious institutions — know that all the blessings of our time, and they are many, despite the many yet to come, flow from obedience to religious principles. Were Prof. Herron's but a personal opinion one would pass it by lightly — But because it is a sample of the type of "international scientific revolutionary socialism," and because the Professor is one of the two representatives of the socialist parties of the United States to the international committee's headquarters in Belgium, it deserves mention. It is a *rara avis* to find in a socialist publication a statement favorable to religious institutions, but in opposition to the Professor's statement that we have had 16 centuries of church betrayal of every movement for human emancipation, we are happy to present the view of an acknowledged leader of the Social Democratic Federation of Great Britain.

"The relations of the church, the monasteries, and the clergy to the people were also most important from every point of view. There is nothing more noteworthy in the history of the human mind than the manner in which the essential portion of English society in the middle-ages has been handled by our ordinary economists, chroniclers, and religionists. Even sober, and in the main tolerably conscientious writers seem to lose their heads or become afraid to tell the truth on this matter. Just as the modern capitalist can see nothing but anarchy and oppression in the connection between the people and the feudal noble, so the authors who represent the middle-class economy of our time, the Protestant divines whose creed is the devil take the hindmost here and hereafter, fail to discover anything but luxury, debauchery and hypocrisy in the Catholic church of the fifteenth century.

"It is high time that, without any prejudice in favour of that church, the nonsense which has been foisted on to the public by men interested in suppressing the facts should be exposed. It is not true that the church of our ancestors was the organized fraud which it suits fanatics to represent it; it is not true that the monasteries, priories, and nunneries were mere receptacles for all uncleanness and lewdness; it is not true that the great revenues of the celibate clergy and the celibate recluses were squandered, as a rule, in riotous living. As a mere question of religion, Catholicism was as good as any creed which has ever found acceptance amongst men. Abuses doubtless there were, and most of them were bitterly attacked by members of the Church themselves; tyranny and persecution there were, too, in many forms; but the church, as all know, was the one body in which equality of conditions was the rule from the start. There, at least, the man of ability, who outside her pale was forced to bow down before some Norman baron, whose ruffianly ancestor has formed part of William's gang of marauders, could rise to a position in which this rough, unlettered swashbuckler grovelled before him. Sixtus V. was picked out of the gutter; our Englishman, Nicholas Breakspear, Adrian IV., was a poor labourer's son; and these are but two instances, out of thousands, of distinguished ecclesiastics of humble birth.

"However dangerous, also, the spiritual authority of the church may appear to us, it was used for the most part, notwithstanding all the hideous corruptions of the papal court in the days of the Borgias and others, for the people and against the dominant class; and its influence, as history shows, was almost unbounded. Kings and barons alike bowed and trembled before it. The great art of the time, too, was, like all other great art, for public uses, and devoted to religion. But all this was trifling compared with the work done in the way of general education. The conventual establishments and the parish priests did far more than is commonly supposed in the direction of elementary teaching. But the higher education, the universities? Where would Oxford be to-day but for the splendid munificence of bishops, monks and nuns? Fourteen of her finest colleges were founded by the celibate ecclesiastics and recluses for the benefit, above all, of the children of the people.

"Our noble Church of England has turned these magnificent establishments into mere preserves for the upper and middle classes.   So I might go on in refutation of the foolish idea that the greatest institution of the middle ages, the most complete ar.d widespread religious organization ever known on the planet, was a mere collection of idol-worshippers and incense-burners, and its ecclesiastical establishments nothing but dens of iniquity.   My purpose, however, is not to champion the Catholic Church against the attacks of ignorant historians, but to show briefly the useful functions it fulfilled in the social economy of the time."   ("The Historical Basis of Socialism," pages 14, 15, 16, 17, Henry Mayers Hyndman.) As authoritative history Mr. Hyndman recommends " A History of the Protestant Reformation," by Corbett.   Mr. Hyndman then proceeds to show that church property was held in the interest of the people : — that the parish priest was permitted to spend but the smaller part of his income upon himself, two-thirds of it going to the poor and to the service of the church ; — that existing account-books of the monasteries show that a large part of the revenues was spent on travelers, the poor, the sick and in other good works.   In conclusion upon this topic he says: "Granting that large sums were wasted on the useless ceremonies of Masses and candles, that some of the monasteries had a well-managed refectory and an admirable cellar of wine and beer, it is certain, nevertheless, that the abbots and priors were the best landlords in England, and that, so long as the church held its lands and its power, permanent pauperism was unknown."   As this is the testimony of an avowed atheist it should bear some weight with men who call upon facts to substantiate their claims—but not so with socialists generally, all-inclusive condemnation of religious institutions is the fashion which these defamers of religion indulge in excessively.

This is from the editor of "The Worker," he declares that "Religion has all through the ages been a disruptive force." . . . "The Socialist Party," . . . "has no more right to condemn those who believe that men and women can be clean and true husbands and wives without a clergyman's benediction than it has to impose upon its members any one of the many forms of marriage ceremony, each of which has been declared to be the only holy or legitimate one." (New York, April 26, 1903.)

No ! certainly not, the Socialist Party has no " right to condemn " its own teaching. It openly declares its adherance to the principles of free love, which our next chapter will prove. But a self-respecting, law abiding, God fearing body of men organized into a political party have the right and would exercise the right of protecting the integrity of the family by upholding civil and ecclesiastical marriage.

Further on this same editorial, evidently in the interest of mixing the oil and water within its ranks, says : —

" The Socialist Party has no more right to condemn the atheists, be there few or many in its ranks, than it has to condemn the Presbyterians or the Quakers or the Jews or the Catholics. It has no more right to endorse the belief in God than to denounce such a belief."

No, surely, the socialist party has " no right to condemn the atheists " within its ranks, for atheism lies at the base of its propaganda. To condemn atheists, it would be necessary to overthow its " economic determinism," its "materialist conception of history," along with the rest of its " class-conscious " jargon. If it were to condemn atheists the major portion of its membership would be " disciplined " out of the party. If it were to condemn atheists nearly every socialist paper would be searching for a new editor, including " The Worker." No indeed ! It would not do to condemn atheists, for there would not be a grease spot of the socialist party left to tell the tale of its dissolution. But this is after all only a little pleasantry on the editor's part. Just a little sophistry, a little Punch and Judy justice — just a little touch of socialist tactics.

"To say that there is no connection between socialist principles and religious or ethical principles would, of course, not be correct. All things in this world are inter-related, and the fundamental character of socialist philosophy brings it into especially close connections with every other department or system of thought. But it by no means follows that‘ because certain men agree in accepting the idea of socialism and working for the propagation of those ideas and their realization in socialist institutions, those men must agree upon questions of religion or of ethics. Just because socialist philosophy treats the evolving economic system as the basis of all religious and moral conceptions, it follows that, as militant socialists, we must concentrate our efforts upon so changing the economic system as to give us the greatest freedom and harmony in these and other expressions of our life."

Here is more of the same "well written" editorial. It will suffice to convince the "socialist minds," of such as have not the intellectual tenacity to hold the meaning of one paragraph in view while the next is read, of what the editor desires that they should "think." Please note: "Socialist philosophy brings it (the socialist party) into especially close connection" with religion! Granted. So "especially" close is its closeness that it is gnawing at the vitals of what little religious faith there is in the movement. "Socialist philosophy treats the evolving economic system as the basis of all religious and moral conception." This is the point! the vital point, which puts socialism in exact opposition to religious faith and to religious institutions. "Socialist religion" comes up through a well-fed and highly evolved stomach — while religion is revealed to man by God. What does this mean? "We must concentrate our efforts upon so changing the economic system as to give us the greatest freedom and harmony in these and other expressions of our life." What are "these" expressions of our life? Why, to be sure, we socialists must be given the greatest freedom and har-

mony in socialist "religious and moral expression"—that is
to say, we socialists must be given the greatest freedom in
non-religious and non-moral expression; for socialism is an
anti-religious cult. This "greatest freedom," which is to be
given mankind under the socialist regime, will be amidst the
ruins of the church, the state and the family. It will be the
"freedom and harmony" of no restraint, of no condemnation
of sex relations outside the marriage bond, dilated upon in
this editorial. Wild liberty, this!—"Freedom and harmony"
gone mad. One may as well picture an ideal freedom with
ferocious beasts roaming the city streets as to picture ideal
human freedom with religious faith and moral standards
broken. But to this end, affirms this editorial, is political
power sought by the socialist party. "Under the conditions
now existing in this country, political action presents itself as
the method by which this change should be effected."

After this modern blasphemy, these "heretics," as John
Mitchell styled them, these misleaders of civic virtue, have
recourse to their wonted duplicity. Here is a fine specimen
of socialist party tactics. We quote further from the editorial:—

"Whoever seeks to commit the organized socialist movement to any declaration upon other than economic and political principles seeks, wilfully or not, but none the less injuri-
ously if without evil intent, to divide and to weaken the
movement."

We repeat, political action on the part of socialists is
merely the means of changing the whole fabric of society—
economic, political, judicial, moral and religious.—Socialists,
come out in the light! Stand where you belong, as the promoters of political atheism, and we will meet you face to
face.—The defenders of religious philosophy against the
defenders of atheistic philosophy—stand by the words of
your masters, Marx and Engels, in "the most international
production of all socialist literature," the Communist Manifesto.

"The Communists disdain to conceal their views and aims. They openly declare that their ends can be attained only by the forcible overthrow of all existing social conditions. Let the ruling classes tremble at a Communistic revolution."

Come, open to public view the vital difference between the socialist conception of the origin of religious faith and the teachings of the Mosaic and Christian law!

Revelation forms the basis of religious faith and institutions. Socialism makes a mock at revelation and faith; hence the very nature of the beast compels socialists to stand, having the courage of their convictions, diametrically opposed to existing religious institutions.

Religions are built upon the authority of Almighty God. Whether such authority is recognized as coming to the Hebrew nation, whether the authority is recognized in the apostolic successors of Jesus Christ, or whether the Bible is accepted as the authority, all are agreed that Divine Revelation is the source, the one only source, of religious faith and institutions. Socialists affirm that religious, philosophical, artistic, literary and other institutions are the result of economic environment, and change with the changing economic order.

"In the third month of the departure of Israel out of the land of Egypt, on this day they came into the wilderness of Sinai:

"And Moses went up to God: and the Lord called unto him from the mountain, and said: Thus shalt thou say to the house of Jacob, and tell the children of Israel:

"You have seen what I have done to the Egyptians, how I have carried you upon the wings of eagles, and have taken you to myself.

"If therefore you will hear my voice, and keep my covenant, you shall be my peculiar possession above all people: for all the earth is mine."

"And you shall be to me a priestly kingdom and a holy

nation. These are the words thou shalt speak to the children
of Israel.

"And Moses came down from the mount to the people,
and sanctified them.

"And the Lord spoke the words of the Commandments
to Moses.

"And all the people saw the voices and the flames, and
the sound of the trumpet, and the mount smoking: and being
terrified and struck with fear, they stood afar off.

"And Moses said to the people: Fear not: for God is
come to prove you, and that the dread of him might be in
you, and you should not sin.

"And the Lord said to Moses: Thus shalt thou say to
the children of Israel: You have seen that I have spoken to
you from heaven.

"Do not think that I am come to destroy the law, or the
prophets. I am not come to destroy, but to fulfil.

"For the law was given by Moses; grace and truth came
by Jesus Christ.

"And as Moses lifted up the serpent in the desert, so
must the Son of man be lifted up:

"For God so loved the world, as to give his only begotten
Son; that whosoever believeth in him, may not perish, but
may have life everlasting.

"For God sent not his Son into the world, to judge the
world, but that the world may be saved by him.

"He that believeth in him is not judged. But he that
doth not believe, is already judged: because he believeth not
in the name of the only begotten Son of God.

"Jesus saith to them: But whom do you say that I am?

Simon Peter answered and said: Thou art Christ, the
Son of the living God.

"And Jesus answering, said to him: Blessed art thou,
Simon Bar-Jona: because flesh and blood hath not revealed
it to thee, but my father, who is in heaven.

"And I say to thee: That thou art Peter; and upon this rock I will build my church, and the gates of hell shall not prevail against it."

The Ten Commandments stand as the natural law under the old Mosaic dispensation while the Beatitudes make up the law of human conduct as revealed by Jesus Christ under the new dispensation.

Achille Loria, the Italian socialist, is recognized as the "greatest living exponent of economic determinism." We will quote him at length:

"If we examine the psychological influences surrounding isolated or co-actively associated labor, we find they reduce themselves to the following: First, labor, whose productivity is limited, either on account of its lack of association, or by reason of the checks imposed by compulsory association, is unable to dominate matter completely, and finds itself accordingly unable to effectually control the forces of nature. Second, this fact, taken together with the unconscious character of the social relations surrounding the individual, determines a sort of obsession of the mental faculties, and engenders a feeling of degradation and impotence, because he, as an individual, feels himself the victim of social forces, of whose ulterior tendencies he is ignorant, and whose processes he is unable to control. Third, the necessity of reconciling the social conscience to the existence of economic forms which are essentially corrupt, leads, by a systematic falsification of logic, to the institution of a settled sophism.

"These three influences combined — and more particularly the first — result in a psychological phenomenon of extraordinary compass, namely, the idea of the supernatural.

. . . .

It is, therefore, in no wise strange that the religious sentiment is thus developed as the psychological product of isolated or co-actively associated labour.

"Religious ideas, however elaborate and complex, are

all derived from the original feeling of impotence that the human being experiences before the forces of nature; and this sentiment, in turn, is the historical product of either the non-association or the compulsory association of labour. Such is the psychological basis upon which capitalistic society has been able to elaborate its methods of coercive morality. Now, given such psychological conditions, with their resulting mental phenomena, the means of moral suasion which society has at its disposal, evidently reduce themselves to the following: *fear, religion and public opinion.*

"Religion in the sense of an invocation of Divine aid through prayers and offerings, does not of itself imply morality. Morality is a relation between man and man; religion is a relation between man and God; and these two relations may very well be disconnected and exist independently of each other. This is so true that in many religions the moral element is absolutely lacking. . . . . Though religion is thus not necessarily accompanied with moral sanctions, it may, nevertheless, be made to serve as an excellent instrument of moral coercion. . . . In this way God becomes, as it were, the capitalist of heaven, crediting men with the good actions performed during their lifetime, and paying them a proportional salary either in this life or in the life to come. Thus the fear of Divine punishment succeeds in doing violence to the egoism of the individual, deterring him from acting in conformity with his own interests, and impelling him to acts which are opposed to his own, but in conformity with the real egoism of his oppressors.

"After we have once thoroughly grasped the truth that capitalistic property is not a natural phenomenon but a violation of law, both human and divine—the impossible erected into a system—we shall be able to understand how in order to guarantee the persistence of so absurd and contradictory a system it is necessary to draw upon all the passions and sentiments of human nature, corrupt them at their purest sources and divert them into the service of this monstrous engine of iniquity."

If it be true, as Loria affirms, that "The religious senti- ment is developed as the psychological product of co-actively associated labor," then is revealed religion a "monstrous en- gine of iniquity!" Religious precepts and religious teaching a vain delusion and a snare, for "Religious ideas are derived from the feeling of impotence." "God is the capitalist of heaven," leading men "by a systematic falsification of logic" and with "fear of Divine punishment," to perform acts "in conformity with the interest of their oppressors." If this be true, then is the world's history false. The path cut through the wilderness of the ages by the vanguard of the religions is a curse, not a blessing—the democracy of religion which teaches that God is no respecter of persons—that all men are equal before Him is said to corrupt men "at their purest source." This is the false doctrine which socialists put forth as "science."

In his "Notes on Ingersoll," The Rev. L. A. Lambert replying to his (Ingersoll's) falsification of religious effort in behalf of human freedom—which, by the way, exhibits the erratic quality which characterizes socialist writings—brings forth data to prove that the foremost teachers of the past 18 centuries, while standing by the doctrine of Divine punish- ment, act not "in conformity" with the material interests of oppressors, but rather, they have promoted the freedom of the oppressed.

"When I say Christianity antagonized slavery I do not mean that it was by a general, indefinite sentiment, but by actual legislation. I will, in proof of this, give some of the councils which legislated to protect the slave. The council of Elvira, held in the year 305; the council of Epaon, year 517; the council of Toledo, year 694; the fifth council of Arles, year 549; Emerita, 666; the eleventh of Toledo, year 675; Worms, 868; second of Macon, 585; the fifth of

Paris, 614; the third of Toledo, 589; fourth of Toledo, 633; of Agde, 506; Rheims, 625; the third of Lyons, 583; the council of St. Patrick, celebrated in Ireland in 450, required church property to be used in redeeming captives; the second council of Vernenil, 844, did the same. The second council of Lyons excommunicated those who enslaved others. A council held in 922, declared that he who sold another into slavery was guilty of homicide. A council held in London in the year 1102 forbade the selling of men in that city, and called it an infamous traffic. Pope Gregory XVI, in 1839, published Apostolic letters against the slave trade. I might mention many other councils, but I have given enough to show the spirit and tendency of Christianity on the subject of slavery, and that anti-slavery is a Christian thought."

"Capitalistic property" (whatever that may mean) "is not a natural phenomena but a violation of law both human and Divine." Divine law? How may he who denies the existence of God talk of "Divine" law? In short, how may one rationally talk of "human law"? For without God law has no existence. Statute law rests on human law, which in its turn is based on natural rights (which socialists deny the existence of), natural law has as its base Divine law, which is the gift of God.

If "the religious sentiment is developed as the psychological product of co-actively associated labor," the belief in God falls! Divine law and all law fall! Neither "capitalistic property" nor any property remains, for chaos instead of order reigns.

"Capitalistic property is not a natural phenomenon"? What nonsense is this? Is it from off the same piece with "The impossible erected into a system"? Is this "socialist science"? A system — a chain of mutual dependences — an organic whole erected out of the impossible? Not even the stuff of which dreams are made is put into this too, too solid property of the capitalist regime. "Socialist science" might be passed by in silence were it not for the development of "socialist minds" which corrupt the body politic with irreligious clamor.

The Rev. L. A. Lambert, the author of the two books ("Notes on Ingersoll" and "The Tactics of Infidels") the earnest perusal of which would arrest the development of "socialist minds," defines religion as follows,

"By the word religion, when used without adjective or qualification, is meant that primitive and universal intuition or idea which is common to all men, and is one and the same in all, however various their *forms* or *systems* of religion may be. This primitive idea is that of a power superior to that of man; of a Supreme Being who governs all things. From this primitive idea springs the idea of relations between this Supreme Being and man, and from these are derived obligations, duties and the impulse to worship and to manifest that worship by external acts. All the various *forms* or *systems* of religion, true or false, that are known to the world have their origin in this primitive intuition or idea called religion; without it they would be alike impossible. This primitive idea is a fundamental fact of our nature, it is the common property of all men, Christian, Jew or Gentile. The errors of false systems of religion are not in the primitive idea but in the false *development* of it."

Now that we have shown revelation to be the basis of religious beliefs and institutions — now that we have an understanding of what is meant by religion as an unqualified term, this question is pertinent. Is the socialist doctrine compatible with religion?

Suppose we allow Loria to answer? "Religious ideas, however elaborate and complex," are the "historical product of either the non-association or compulsory association of labor." The organizer of the modern socialist movement of France, Paul Lafargue himself a son-in-law of Karl Marx, gives his answer in "The Evolution of Property," page 58.

"Religious rites and ceremonies were instituted to impress upon the superstitious minds of primitive peoples the respect due to private property of the family collectively." Could a statement be more in opposition to the position held by theologians generally? Or take the following answer; it is the latest English utterance from the father of "The materialist basis of history." (Translated and published for the first time by the Chicago socialists this year [1903].)

"Religion once arisen contains material of tradition, hence in all ideological matters, religion is a great conservative force. But the changes which take place in this material spring from class conditions, that is from the economic circumstances of the men who take these changes in hand." ("The Roots of Socialist Philosophy," Frederick Engels, 1903.)

Certainly, "religion is a great conservative force." Religious influences have promoted and sustained the progress of civilization, as against the lewdness of the influence of materialism. For the simple reason that religion set up the standards of morality and commands obedience thereto, which conserves the life of man.

August Babel, who is good authority, has this to say:

"Morality and ethics have nothing to with religion; those who assert the contrary are either fools or hypocrites. Morality and ethics are the expression of conceptions which regulate the actions of men and their relations towards each other; religion regulates the actions of men towards supernatural beings. But ideas of morality are the fruit of the social conditions of mankind at a given period, just as religion is the fruit of those conditions." ("Woman Past Present and Future," page 147.)

It is certain that the animus of the Austrian socialists is directed against religion for this phrase is to be found in their platform. "No religious bodies to have privileges."

Karl Kautsky, than whom no man stands higher in the international socialist movement, has this to say:

"In France, where the traditions of the French Revolution continue to exercise so powerful an action, where the religious orders have become fighting organizations on the side of reaction . . . . we must demand the dissolution of the orders, and the confiscation of their property." ("Social Democrat," London, England, May 15, 1903.)

Or, if you like here is an American authority; two American authorities, in fact; Charles H. Kerr and "The People." Mr. Kerr, in speaking of the churches and their moral teachings, says:

"Their whole influence is on the side of whatever will best serve to strengthen the rule of the capitalist class," and that "In any state of society, the commonly accepted idea of moral or right conduct is such conduct as tends to increase the happiness and well being of the ruling class."

"The People" (New York, February 18, 1900), in commenting upon the booklet, "Morals and Socialism," says:

"How has the ruling class established this control over its members and its slaves? In three ways — through religion; through public opinion; and through the law, with its judges and soldiers.

"Religion is perhaps the most powerful of these means of maintaining class society by inducing the members of the subject class to act contrary to their own interests and in accordance with that of their masters. And Christianity, the religion of the most progressive part of the human family, is the most effective of all. It has operated primarily by the offer of rewards in heaven and the threat of punishment in hell. The lesson has been so well taught that, even where the belief in heaven and hell is gone, the old moral feelings connected with it survive for a long time."

Is all this for or against religion? — Nothing to do with religion? You socialists do all you dare to do, all you can do against it. — For upon your principles this is properly your work. If you are true to the principles of international socialism you can not but be opposed to moral and religious principles — for morals and religion can have no meaning with you save with which to drug the embryonic socialist mind.

We shall now give an authority on the side of revealed religion, and we beg the reader to note its light in contrast to the darkness of atheistic opinion.

"The doctrine that without revelation there would be no moral law is verified by common sense and sound philosophy as well as by the Scripture. The moral law as contradistinguished from physical law is, according to Webster who agrees with the theologians, 'the will of God, as the Supreme moral ruler, concerning the character and conduct of all responsible beings.' Now as the moral law is the will of God it is very evident that that will cannot be known to man unless it is revealed — hence the necessity of a revelation to a knowledge of the moral law. Hence, again if we have no revelation we can have no knowledge of the moral law. The moral law may and does exist in the mind of God, but it is no law for us until it is promulgated, and its promulgation is a revelation.

"The doctrine that there is no moral law without revelation accords equally with Scripture. To show this I need go no further than the text quoted by you from St. Paul. 'These (the Gentiles) having not the law, are a law unto themselves; which show the work of the law, *written in their hearts*, their conscience also bearing witness.' (Romans II, 14, 15.) If the law was written in their hearts it was certainly revealed to them by Him who wrote it in their hearts. This writing of the law in their hearts was a revelation. This is why I have said that without revelation of some kind the moral law cannot be known to man. Had you been familiar with the well known distinction between the divine natural law which was revealed to all men and the divine positive law which was revealed on Mount Sinai you would have understood St. Paul better." ("Tactics of Infidels," Rev. L. A. Lambert.)

We turn again to the darkness of socialist degeneracy:

"It is sometimes said that socialism is neither religious nor irreligious. This does not or should not mean that socialism fails to come into contact with the views of the world and of life which the current religions furnish, or that at a particular stage in its progress it may not take up a position even of active hostility to those religions. What it means is that socialism implies a state of society out and away beyond the barren speculative polemics of the hour.

"In what sense socialism is not religious will be now clear. It utterly despises the 'other world' with all its stage properties — that is, the present objects of religion. . . The socialist whose social creed is his only religion requires no travesty of Christian rites to aid him in keeping his ideal before him." ("Socialism and Religion," Ernest Balfort Bax.)

Does the reader agree with the author that socialists themselves prove that their "social creed" dismisses moral responsibility, the tie which harmoniously unites man to man, for the simple reason that it denies individual responsibility to Almighty God? If not, we will produce further testimony from them.

"All religions the world has ever seen have been imposed for the purpose of preventing the operation of the collective will. They have been mere philosophies of submission, aiming at the subjection of the people. The world has therefore only advanced as the collective will has found halting expression in successive revolutions made against these imposed dogmas, both the church and the state. Thus humanity can hope to advance only as it forsakes all reliance upon any resources outside of the common life. The common life and its common aims, aspirations and efforts must be its own saviour. It makes even now its own heaven and its own hell." (Lecture by G. D. Herron, "The Coöperative Life," Chicago Temple. Printed in "The Socialist Spirit," issue January, 1903.)

Representative James F. Carey of Haverhill, in a speech before the Channing Club of Boston, said:

"Not all the hypocrisy of the pulpit . . . can possibly destroy the rock upon which we of the despised working class build up our philosophy. It (Socialism) is our only hope, and without that hope no promise of heaven, no fear of hell, can cause us to have any interest in life."

And what is that rock? "Economic determinism"— that force called progress, which begins with the troglodyte. And ends — with the devil. This book will smite that rock and call the devils forth into the light of day.

But Mr. Carey is a "class conscious" socialist. His atheism is in harmony with the international leaders of the party.

Karl Marx: "Religion is a fantastic degradation of human nature."

Liebknecht: "Socialism must conquer the stupidity of the masses in so far as this stupidity reveals itself in religious forms and dogmas."

Babel: "We wish in politics the republic, in economy socialism, and in religion atheism."

In a debate between Jean Jaures and Jules Guesde — socialist members of the French Chamber of Deputies—on the question of whether the Social Deputy Millerand had violated the principles of socialism by accepting a seat in the French cabinet, (which position Millerand still occupies; which fact is rending the French socialist parties further asunder), Jean Jaures — after reading from a pamphlet written by Wilhelm Liebknecht in 1869, wherein he (Liebknecht) opposes parliamentary activity on the part of socialists — as reported in "The People," official organ of the Socialist Labor Party. New York, January 12th, 1901, there occurs this scene:

"A few years later, nevertheless, drawn by the irresistible course of events, not only did Liebknecht remain a militant in the Imperial Assembly, but he entered the Landtag of Saxony, where no entrance can be made without a vow of loyalty to the royal and bourgeois constitution:

"'I swear before God' (ironical exclamations from several parts of the hall).

"CHAIRMAN DELORY — Citizens, the itch to interrupt places the interrupters in a bad light. Jaures was only quoting.

"JAURES — Just see, citizens, to what extraordinary misunderstandings can the prejudice lead to that we entertain against one another. I had just told you that no one could enter the Landtag without taking an oath of loyalty to the king of Saxony; I relate to you, I describe to you the formula of the oath taken by Liebknecht in order to enter the Landtag of Saxony; and, behold comrades, somewhat heated, who do not hesitate to tax me with clericalism. (Laughter.)

"Keep in mind that it is Liebknecht who speaks:

"'I swear before God, of being unfalteringly loyal to the constitution; to serve, according to my conscience, by my propositions and my votes, the inseparable interests of the King and the Fatherland. So help me God.'

"There were, comrades, at that time, 'purists,' 'uncompromising' men, who accused Liebknecht of having failed towards the social democracy by taking an oath for the purpose of filling a seat in the Landtag. Whereupon Liebknecht, the admirable revolutionist, answered well: 'What of it? We would be eternally the dupes of the ruling class, if all they had to do was to throw across our path the paper obstacle of the formula of an oath.'

"And I, in turn, ask: When a crime is made out of a socialist cabinet minister's having accepted what I shall call the ministerial formality of seeming solidarity with his colleagues in the cabinet, is that formality more humiliating than was, for the revolutionary socialists of Germany, the oath taken 'before God' to remain loyal to the king?

"I ask you whether we also should allow ourselves to be arrested in our course by those obstacles of paper, before those bureau formalities, and whether we shall hesitate, when our Cause needs it, to throw one of our own into the fortress of a hostile Government? ('No! No!')"

Socialism is the cause and hissing the name of God is the effect! Is it desirable that the teachings of socialism should become the one source of cultivation that materialism be substituted for faith in God? Socialist philosophy it is which "socialist minds" in France have embodied in the Associations Bill and are putting into effect by the confiscation of church property.

So well thought of is this display of ignorance and blasphemy that after it appeared in the Socialist Labor Party's official organ "The People," New York, Jan. 12, 1901, the Social Democratic Party reproduced it in their official organ, "The Social Democratic Herald," Chicago, June 15, 1901. And, too, it was taken from "The People" without being credited — for you must know that these two parties are at swords' points over the best method of turning the trade unions into one gigantic "socialist mind."

One may often hear this remark within socialist circles: "It's no use talking to him, he's stuck on the church." One must be pulled away from his religious affiliations before he is a subject for inoculation with socialist belief. The father of modern socialism averred that religion made men "weak and resigned to their fate." He rejoiced at their lack of faith. No! Socialism does not attack religion? Kindly read this statement from Frederick Engels. —

"English socialism affords the most pronounced expression of the prevailing absence of religion among the working-men, an expression so pronounced indeed that the mass of working-men, being unconsciously and merely practically irreligious, often draw back before it, but here, too, necessity will force the working-men to abandon the remnants of a belief which, as they will more and more clearly perceive—serves only to make them weak and resigned to their fate." ("Condition of the Working Class in England in 1844," page 237.)

Possibly this from James Leatham will convince some one of the fact that "there is no room for God in the socialist movement."

"No exercise of faith is required for belief in the event of socialism ; for socialism is admitted to be inevitable, even by those who abhor it and dread its coming.

"But faith, properly so called, is dead. The belief in God, with all it implies, is now without a *raison d'être.* The original conception of God has everywhere been that of a Creator, a great Master Workman, of the Universe, who made it and who sustains it. But the idea of creation is now given up. The conception of a universe beginning to be out of nothing is found, even by Roman Catholic theologians, to be unthinkable, and they now speak of God and the Universe as 'co-existent eternities.' This is certainly giving away the idea of God as the Creator.

"Nor is the conception of God the Sustainer any longer an intellectual necessity, as it was when men could not account for the phenomena of Nature in terms of the Natural. . . . . There is nothing left for Deity to do." ("Socialism and Character," "A contribution towards a system of applied ethics." 1899. Preface.)

"Nothing left for Deity to do?" But man has much to do, to practice His precepts and obey His commands that poverty, disease and crime may pass off the face of the earth. The stupendous assumption of knowledge of God's work which says there is no "*raison d'être*" for faith is the common attitude of the socialist school, though it is commonly less elegantly expressed.

The following from the "Sozial Demokrat," the Organ of the German socialists, is brutally frank enough to show what the socialist intent is.

"The socialistic state will never be realized except by a violent revolution, and it is our duty to spread this conviction through all classes. . . . . Christianity is the greatest enemy of socialism. When God is expelled from human brains, what is called the Divine Grace will at the same time be banished; and when the heaven above appears nothing more than an immense falsehood, men will seek to create for themselves a heaven below." ("Sozial Demokrat," vol. i, page 310. Encyclopedia of Social Reforms, William D. P. Bliss, page 896–897.)

The socialist movement has nothing to do with religion? So? It seems greatly to concern itself with banishing it from the face of the earth. But there is strength in the reflection, that were the desire of the "Sozial Demokrat" realized — were God and Divine Grace to be banished, we may rest assured that man will be sunk so deep in iniquity and slime that the very word heaven will be unknown to him.

Do new comers talk big of what they know little? or is this to be set down to "socialist tactics?"

"Socialism is not opposed to religion. Neither is Socialism an ally of religion. The Socialist party bears the same relation to religion as it does to medicine, surgery, art and historical and scientific research. It has nothing, whatever, to do with any of these, for the simple reason that Socialism is purely an economical and political question. Will anyone say that the republican party is atheistic because Ingersoll was a republican, or that the democratic party is a Catholic institution because Bishop O'Sullivan was elected a democratic member of the Vermont legislature? Certainly not. Religious belief or unbelief is not a test for membership in the Socialist party. The supreme test is whether a person believes in the complete overthrow of the present wage system and the substitution therefor of the co-operative common-wealth. You may be a Protestant, a Catholic, or of no religion at all, but if you believe in this you are a Socialist." ("American Labor Union Journal," Butte, Montana. Feb. 19, 1903. Editorial.)

I would like to ask the editor of this anti-American Federation of Labor paper whether, in view of this deluge of authoritative socialist quotations, he will still have the audacity to declare "that Socialism is not opposed to religion?" I should like to ask him whether the mere statement that a belief in "the complete overthrow of the present wage system and the substitution therefore of the co-operative common-wealth" will suffice as a test of a man's belief in socialism? Is it not true that this statement of yours is, by socialists, well understood to carry with it the complete overthrow of the present social order? That is to say, the overthrow of the present forms of the family, the religious and the civic life of to-day.

"You may be a Protestant, a Catholic or of no religion at all, but if you believe in this you are a Socialist." You may have been a Protestant or a Catholic, but if you are now a "good" socialist you will be an atheist! If you are not acquainted with the fact that atheism and socialism are one and the same philosophy, even though Montana be on the map, if you still fondly cling to the delusion which I once held, this book will add to your socialist knowledge.

You may speak authoritatively in opposition to the legitimate trade unions of this country; but it is not for you *ex-cathedra* to pronounce upon what constitutes a Catholic's standing on questions which effect his faith and morals; even though ex-priests stand back of your opinions and of your organization.

Leo XIII has declared that a man cannot be a Catholic and a socialist. Neither can a Protestant or a Jew remain true to his belief in God and God's revelation and remain a socialist. You are correct in this, "You may be . . . . of no religion at all" and be a socialist, for the very foundation stone of socialist doctrine is anti-religion.

"Organized society is a huge conspiracy against manhood," and "Truth needs no institutions" says Franklin H. Wentworth, ex-minister and sometime editor of "The Socialist Spirit," in a lecture given throughout the country under socialist auspices. These statements "brought down the house" at his meeting at Paine Hall in Boston. Such catchy phrases win the applause of the unthinking, but when analyzed there is no substance within them. For they merely express negation. This is the ground upon which the Herron school of ex-ministers, who adorn the socialist rostrum, concludes that although religious sentiment is not to be eradicated from the human heart, it, religion, needs no institutions—no material body through which to work its will.

Democracy is a truth. —It is a principle which is embodied within the breasts of men; does it follow that democracy "needs no institutions" within which men are democratically related to one another? Certainly not! Democracy finds an embodiment in the civil structure of the American people. How highly perfected within the nation will be the principle of democracy? Just as high as the flame of democracy burns in the breast of the American people, just so highly will the government of the United States demonstrate democracy. Fancy democracy without an institution through which its quality could be seen, could become real. To do so, one must fancy that which does not exist. —Just fancy one's fancying that which he cannot fancy. Good nonsense this, but not good sense which these ministerial socialists talk, who would retain religion but demolish the institutions of religion. To attempt to separate religion from the Church is mere intellectual tomfoolery.

"You are gentlemen of brave mettle; you
Would lift the moon out of her sphere, if she

Would continue in it five weeks without
Changing." (The Tempest.)

But let us return to the pagan-professor, who is "thoroughly opposed to using the socialist platform for religious propaganda."

"The worship and joy of life, which is our inheritance from the Pagans, is still with us in spite of the Puritan and the monk.

"With Christianity we have, as socialists, a different problem to face. It is the system of Christianity that we have with us, and the spirit of Jesus that is hid and bound; and the spirit of Jesus cannot escape until Christianity is destroyed. There could be no greater antithesis, no deeper gulf, than that between Jesus and the Christian system. And nothing so surely as Christianity stands for all that is worse in capitalism; for all that is weak and mean in the human spirit; for all that represents the basest and most puerile modes of gaining power. There is no such force making for the destruction of spiritual integrity and courage, and for the unmanning and deceiving of the race, as the system of religion which so monstrously bears Christ's name, and so characteristically misrepresents him. Among no class of men is there so beggarly a conception of what it means to tell or be the truth, as among the official classes of religion; and among no other class is there so parasitical a servility. This has always been so, and it will continue to be so as long as there is an official religious class. It is in the nature of things that it should be so; for organized religion is always the economic dependent of the ruling class.

"Christianity is a huge and ghastly parasite, consuming billions of treasure out of the labor and the patience of the people, and is supremely interested in keeping the people in economic and spiritual subjection to capitalism. The spiritual deliverance of the race depends on its escape from this parasite. The world must be saved from its salvations.

"But soon the church will have no sources of power within itself. It will discover that capitalism cannot save it, since capitalism cannot save itself, and will then seek to fasten itself upon the socialist movement — not for the sake of socialism, but for the sake of ecclesiasticism, or the religious system. With these approaches of Christianity the Socialist revolution should have nothing to do. To Christianize socialism would be to destroy it, and to perpetuate a capitalized and decadent Christianity. Every attempt of the church to serve Socialism will be for the sake of self-preservation, and not for the sake of the Socialist cause, just as churches are established in working-class quarters of the city to "reach the masses," not for the sake of helping them to freedom and justice, but for the sake of exploiting them as spiritual property for the church." (George D. Herron.) Socialists do not make an attack upon the church? So highly do Socialists prize this, Herronic effusion that from "Wilshire," the millionaire socialists' magazine, it was reprinted in the "Advance," official organ of the California socialists, November 9th, 1901; and also in the New York "Worker," Nov. 10th, 1901.

Socialists do not make an attack upon the church? Have then words lost their wonted meaning? "There is no such force making for the destruction of the spiritual integrity and courage and for the unmanning and deceiving of the race." Dr. Herron proceeds to charge religious teachers with being liars. Of course this is done in academic language, there is no class of men who have "so beggarly a conception of what it means to tell or be the truth." He also charges them with being servile parasites, and without qualification declares that they have "always been so."

Ministerial socialists failing to revamp their churches into socialist organizations, with the materialist conception of history as the basis of faith (if faith it may be called) immediately mount a high horse and assume the position of infallible interpreters of religious law. It was one time the hope of the writer that religious men would enter the socialist movement and thus add to it the quality it so greatly stood in need of — but I confess my error. In the first place religious qualities cannot be grafted upon this atheistic trunk. In the second place the use of religious phraseology, indulged in freely by the ex-ministers, but pushes true religious emotions further into the slush and slime of materialism. One has but to read Dr. Herron's publications while he was yet a minister of the Congregational Church, and compare them with his recent works, from which the effusions quoted in this book are taken, to behold a rapid degeneracy in the quality of his work. This intellectual decay is common to men of religious training — once departed from their religious moorings they drift into the irrational method of argument native to the atheist. Ambition is not a virtue in religious circles but ambition puts men of little might in the full view of the socialist party.

Should any minister be misled into the socialist movement, thinking it to be an avenue through which to better the economic condition of the working class, he will sooner or later bring down upon himself the wrath of the "class-conscious" socialists. They will not tolerate true religious philosophy within their ranks. Without exception everyone of the ministers who have entered the socialist party have adopted their philosophy of "economic determinism" and have enforced its materialistic teachings with the prestige of their former religious standing; or they have left the party wiser if not better men.

Socialists have no use for religious teachers they have times without number declared them to be "hypocrites" and "humbugs."

J. Bruce Glasier, a prominent socialist of Great Britain, says:

". . . In fact, frankly speaking, I don't want clergymen to become socialists — at least to any great extent. They serve the cause admirably as enemies — they would spoil it as friends. Wherever two or three clergymen are gathered together, there, surely, are hypocrisy and humbug in the midst of them! The blacker the hosts of the enemy become with clerical coats, the nearer and the easier will our victory be." ("Men who are Socialists," "The Commonweal," Vol. 4, No. 139.)

We next present to the attention of the reader a disciple of George D. Herron, Rev. William Thurston Brown, for merly pastor of the Plymouth Church, Rochester, New York. He is a favorite socialist sermonizer. Rev. Mr. Brown was the candidate of the Social Democratic party for Lieutenant Governor of his state at the last election. I quote from a "sermon" published in the "Socialist Spirit," June, 1902.

"The truth is, as all thinking men are aware, we have no such thing as intellectual honesty in the sphere of religion. We have made religion a department of human thought and action in which moral principles do not figure. We have not even succeeded in getting a conception of God that has any moral quality. The deity men pray to and exhibit in theological systems is not a moral being. He does not act in accord with immutable principles, but at his own caprice or to meet unforseen emergencies.

"Ethics has nothing to do with the Christianity of today.

"It is intellectual dishonesty which seems to me altogether the most dangerous and menacing form of dishonesty prevalent in the world. And if any other country can excel our own in this respect, I could not on short notice name the country. I may be wrong, but after considerable observation it seems to me we hardly know the meaning of intellectual honesty in this country. At least, I doubt very much if the Christian Church has any knowledge of it. And I know no reason why it should have. Unless I am seriously mistaken, we have branded as infidels and atheists about the only persons who have begun to cultivate the virtue of intellectual honesty."

Here is more testimony from Rev. Brown, who is a leader in the socialist party. We think that when a prominent socialist puts on paper the statement that the "putrid and decaying carcass" of religious institutions are a menace to the life of man, and furthermore when that scandal is printed and reprinted in leading socialist publications, that there is color for saying that socialism is a menace to the church. Don't you?

"If ever in the history of the world any human institution was completely and finally discredited, it is the religious institution, whose putrid and decaying carcass here at the beginning of the twentieth century menaces the life of men.

"Never in all the past did the religious institution seem more impotent or despicable than now. Scientific research dissipated — as the meridian sun dissipates vapor — the whole philosophy upon which accepted religion is made to rest. And he who would enter its ministry must first of all envisage in his imagination a non-existant and impossible world, in order to become the mouthpiece of its message of fear to minds still steeped in ignorance and superstition. It stands before the world as a foe to research, an enemy of freedom of thinking, a purveyor of baseless superstitions, a morally impotent and an ethically monstrous factor in human society. The fearful hypocrisy to which we have come has been recently disclosed, not only in the moral obliquity of missionaries abroad and ministers at home, but far more in the spirit of unconcern with which the majority of our religionists treat the exposure made by our greatest satirist, Mark Twain.

"What does the church offer? With what would it satisfy this new soul-hunger, too deep for words? With a baseless superstition about heaven and hell. With a lot of dry-as-dust dogmas. With creeds and rites, with manufactured sins and fictitious virtues. With a dualism that is destructive of all truth and sincerity. With a separation of life into 'sacred' and 'secular'—as if life could be divided! As if it were not the supreme sacrilege thus to cleave asunder the divine unity of life!" ("The Social Crusader" and "The Advance," July 20, 1901.)

Rev. Mr. Brown declares religion "calls for the abandonment of reason." Verily the socialist party is a fit subject for inoculation with reason. The fact of the matter is that socialists are intoxicated with visions of liberty. This drunkenness has led to the loss of the reasoning faculty, everything is seen not in rational relation, but in monstrous proportion, Rev. Mr. Brown, whose motives I believe to be above question, must have forgotten that the art and science of the centuries has been safeguarded by the church. If religion "calls for the abandonment of reason," how is it that Bacon, Magnus, Gerbert, Copernicus, Cusa, Becquerel, Kepler, Linne, Fontenelle, Galileo, Faraday, Descartes, Galvani, Newton, Ampère, Boscovich, Volta, were men of science? they were religious men? Oxford and Cambridge, Aberdeen and St. Andrews, Upsala and Copenhagen, Paris, Toulouse and Montpelier, Freiberg, Leipsic, Heidelberg, Tübingen, Wurzburg, Cracow, Prague, Vienna, Bologna, Naples, Pisa, Turin, Rome, Salamanca, Seville, Valladolid, Coimbra, Lorvain are celebrated seats of learning, established during the middle ages by the Church and its religious upholders. Were these places established "for the abandonment of reason"?

"Moral principles do not figure" in the sphere of religion. Is this your judgement? Surely the light of your candle must be hid under a bushel. For you see by the darkness of "infidels and atheists" and so mistake intellectual drivel for the "virtue of intellectual honesty." At least the light of your candle flickers low in the blaze of socialist passion. That socialism is a false light which lures men to their destruction, this book is meant to show.

" I imagine, indeed, that in anything worthy to be called a co-operative commonwealth there will be no use for the profession which has consumed some of the best years of my life. For teachers there will always be a demand in any desirable social order. For men and women who can produce something useful or beautiful there will be need. But I cannot conceive a place in any sane social system for a profession whose dogmas and doctrines call for abandonment of reason and the suppression of science. The clerical profession lives to-day only because ignorance and superstition remain.

" The religion of the Church had no scruple whatever against any sort of mastership or any sort of slavery *that was profitable.*

" For a time I thought the fault lay in the individuals composing the Church. What was needed was a conversion of the Church to Christianity. It was Ruskin, an avowed agnostic, who declared that no one ' could sit at his table, unless he sat blindfold ' in the midst of the misery created by our commercial cannibalism. But I have yet to find one man or woman, in good standing as a member of the Christian Church, who gives any evidence of possessing even the conscience of this agnostic. It is left for the awful Anarchists and the dangerous Socialists to show any marked disturbance over the world's social misery. So, a considerable part of my preaching was devoted to the attempt to acquaint the Church with the character of the man it professed to revere. But, so far as practical results are concerned, it was a waste of time and strength.

" Finally, contemplation of the problem of social justice led to a new reading of history, a new look at life. And the conviction steadily took shape in my mind that my whole philosophy as to the paramount influence of the individual in determining human institutions and social conditions, was wrong. Reading, experience and reflection forced me to the philosophy of economic determinism, and I could not name a document of equal length which seems to me to contain so much truth as the 'Communist Manifesto' of Marx and Engels.

"Of course, the acceptance of the idea of an animal origin of the human race and the main conclusions of materialistic evolution involved a complete reconstruction of my thought world. I thus saw history to be an upward struggle out of animalism toward a goal which no man is capable of naming." ("How I became a Socialist," William Thurston Brown, in "the Comrade." New York, May, 1903.)

Oh! the pity of it. The blind are unable to lead the blind save on the path of darkness to death. This sad confession by Rev. William Thurston Brown of his unconscious down-fall to the groveling level of "economic determinism" is very good evidence that atheism is organizing politically to destroy religious institutions and the civilization which is sustained by them.

In support of the fact that the socialist leaders, from Karl Marx and Engels down to the clerical collar socialists of to-day, have all attacked religion, look at this from "The Daily People," Friday, June 5, 1903 (official organ of the Socialist Labor Party).

"It is high time that we Socialists dropped our timidity about attacking those priests and ministers who, under the guise of religion, and wrapped in its sacred folds, so underhandedly attack and falsely represent Socialism.

"The working people are rapidly becoming aware of the fact that the Church of to-day is the same as it has always been — a stumbling block and bar to progress and civilization. It makes no difference what its creed may be, whether it be Roman Catholic, Presbyterian, Methodist, Lutheran, Episcopalian or any other kind of creed, they all stand united as defenders of capitalism."

Their timidity must be dropped? "The People" most

assuredly confounds timidity with diplomacy, with duplicity.
— Socialism in its very nature is the exact opposite to religion. Socialist tactics are not so much an evidence of
timidity as of double dealing by which the unwary man of
faith is engulfed in the psychology of socialist atmosphere to
his undoing. But it is not our purpose to show so much your
"timidity" as it is to show your anti-religious principles.

Here is something from J. Sketchley in "Our Task
To-day."

"In every age and in every country the Church and the
State have been the great centres of despotism. The Church
and the State, the throne and the altar, the priest and the soldier, have ever made war on the people. It is the same to-day.
In almost every age efforts have been made to reform the
Church, to diminish its power, to free it from corruption.
Rivers of blood have been shed, and thousands of martyrs
have given up their lives for the purification of the Church.
But the Church is still the great engine for enslaving the
minds of men, for binding mankind in ignorance and superstition. And the same with the State. For how many generations have not the best of nature's nobles laboured and
suffered and died in their endeavours to reform the State.
But the State is still supreme. It is still the great centre of
despotism, still the seat of centralized tyranny. It still claims
unquestioned obedience to its decrees. The State, like the
Church, is a relic of barbarism. If we would raise man to
dignity, in place of the Church we must have a free and
rational system of education. If we would raise man to liberty, in place of the State we must have the free organization
of society." ("The Commonweal," vol. 4, No. 137.)

Destroy "the Church, and the State, the throne and the
altar" and substitute "a free and rational system of education
and a free organization of Society." That is to say reduce
civilization to chaos and eradicate from man the consciousness of his Divine origin.

Let us introduce another follower of the Herron school, Franklin H. Wentworth:

"Social democracy has unquestionably given the death blow to the church in Germany, and the pope has but to glance at the city of Berlin to find a justification of all his fears regarding socialism. German philosophy, born out of the Lutheran reformation, began the work which the social democracy has well nigh completed. Compared to the capital cities of other nations the percentage of church attendance in Berlin is amazingly low. With a population of nearly 2,000,000 Berlin to-day has less than sixty churches.

"Although the German 'war lord' is zealously devout, as is usual with gentlemen of his distinguished characteristics, the German people persistently stay away from the churches. There is more fun in philosophical discussions in the beer gardens and in drowsing through the afternoons at the Philharmonic concerts.

"It is not the Catholic Church alone which recognizes in social democracy a foe. The Protestant Church of Germany has been allied to the state since the disfranchisement of the Jesuit societies, hence the socialist leaders make no secret of opposition to the church. To every church in Berlin, in fact throughout Germany, there are half a dozen halls devoted to socialist propaganda. Social democracy finds headway easy against a church long since riddled into shreds by Nietzsche, Schopenhauer, Kant and Hegel." (Editorial, Socialism and the German church, "The Socialist Spirit," May, 1902.)

Did we not say that the "Communist Manifesto" was beer garden philosophy? And is not this editorial proof that socialism is now bearing its vile fruit?

The "Communist Manifesto" is the fountain source of enthusiasm from which these ex-ministers drink to the dregs the cup which pollutes the human heart and stultifies the human mind. It is so big with self-pride that it will not stoop to answer, "The charges against communism made from a religious, a philosophical; and, generally, from a ideological standpoint are not deserving of serious examination." (Communist Manifesto.)

We shall next present the testimony of five socialist papers: And we kindly ask public consideration as to whether or not there is truth in the assertion that "Socialism has no concern with religion."

The People's Press, Chicago, January 10, 1903:

"Now that the Holy (?) Church has come out and declared OPENLY AGAINST SOCIALISM, the socialists MUST, either come out the same way, and declare against and FIGHT *the hoary Beast, 'Mother of harlots'* — ROME! or, SHUT UP SHOP!!!" Editorial.

"For us we fear the enmity of the (Catholic) church less than its friendship — and this we should say equally of any other church or any other organization accepting the capitalist ideal." ("The Worker," May 1, 1902.)

"The waves of Socialism are washing against the walls of the Vatican, and it is doubtful whether the next Pope will remain in the classic land of Papal tradition or move to some more comfortable place. Unless it retires to one of the poles of the earth, ecclesiastical hierarchy, like all other despotism, will soon be crowded off the earth." (International Socialist Review, Chicago, Ill., Aug. 1902.)

"The anti-Socialist agitation of the churches thus proves once more that the continued disuse, or misuse, of any faculty finally results in its degeneration. Having taught and believed, or professed to believe, for centuries, certain ideas which are opposed to the plain evidence of our sane senses, the clericals have become victims of their own methods. Having stifled the demands of reason in every possible way, they have finally lost all powers of reasoning themselves. As a class, they have dulled the minds of vast masses by their collective efforts. But now, they are falling into the very pit which they have so long dug for others. Instead of advancing with the times, we see them engaged in the mad attempt to fall into the spokes of the whirling wheels of progress, and of grafting, mediæval superstitions into the mental life of a society living under fundamentally revolutionized economic conditions." ("Appeal to Reason," April 11, 1903.)

"So it is with the churches. Far better is it to have the open hatred and opposition of the Catholic Church, from the Pope down to Father Heiter, than the maudlin sympathy and friendship of some of our would-be friends, who, in the name of friendship, would make the Socialist movement an appendage to the church, and socialism a prop for an infidel Christianity. Let us have the fight; in this case it is a good deal better than the friendship. There has been too much of a tendency in the movement of late to measure Socialism by the measure of Christianity; too much attempting to link the two. Let us beware of these attempts! Socialism has nothing to gain from any such alliances; the church must gain at the expense of the Socialist movement. The very word Socialism embodies an ethical concept infinitely higher than anything that organized religion has ever known. Nothing could well be more dangerous than the no doubt well-meant attempts to prove Socialism true by an appeal to religion. Favorable enough to the latter, these attempts are disastrous to the former. It is no business of ours to prove anything of the kind. It is for us to proclaim and defend our own social faith. If that is not in accord with the teaching of the church — well, so much the worse for the church!" ("The Comrade," New York, April, 1902.)

These five quotations from five socialist papers speak for themselves on the question at issue for the United States. We shall conclude this division of our work with the presentation of data from seven international socialist authorities. Quoting from world-renowned authors. And, too, we present the question, whether or not there is truth in the allegation that "Socialism has no concern with religion." Should the answer be, as we think it must, that socialism greatly concerns itself with religion with the purpose of destroying it from off the face of the earth, we desire to ask the American public one further question — Shall socialists be given the political power with which to work damnation?

First and foremost stands the German movement, from a political and from a literary point of view. Karl Kautsky, Editor of "*Die Neue Zeitung*," Stuttgart, Germany, author of many socialist books, several of which have been translated into English. Writing on the subject of "Anti-Clericalism and Socialism" in the "Appeal to Reason," Girard, Kansas, February 21, 1903, says:

"The capitalist class cannot carry on a serious and destructive fight against the church, It is now conservative in its nature, and incapable of any great revolutionary act.

"The capitalist class and the working class cannot fight together against the church. The class interests of the working class demand a plan of action totally different from that of the capitalist class, also in religious matters. The working class occupies a peculiar position among the present social classes. It is a subject class. It rules no other class and cannot elevate itself over any other class in the economic order. When the working class will conquer the political power, it can only abolish all classes and also suppress its own character as a class. It cannot use its political power to put a new ruling class into the place of the present one.

"The working class, therefore, aims at the conquest of the political powers for the purpose of eliminating all instruments of class rule from social life, not with the intention of making them its own. For this reason it is opposed to the church, which constitutes one of these instruments of class rule. 131

"But the church does not limit itself to this function. The religion which it professes and teaches still meets the pressing wants of great masses. Being a subject class, whose mental and spiritual liberty is restricted by all other classes, the working class must declare for religious freedom. Without this it would prevent the mass of believers from satisfying their religious cravings, and thus come into contradiction with its own historical mission."

Second, Enrico Ferri, Socialist Deputy of the Italian Parliament, Editor of ."The Avanti," a socialist daily, Rome, Italy, whom the " International Socialist Review " of Chicago (April, 1903), declares to be the foremost exponent of socialism now living, has this to say in the "Social Democrat" of London, England, on October 15, 1902:

"When one undertakes socialistic propaganda and organization then it follows that human conscience must be opposed to every form of intellectual dictation, and still more to the clerical spirit. But socialists need not engage in a direct anti-clerical propaganda. They are free thinkers, and must, therefor, respect the faith of sincere believers, especially if they are peasants, among whom it is impossible to engage in an anti-clerical propaganda.

"If some of the middle classes carry on an anti-clerical agitation the socialistic party should not stop them. They should rather help them against an assault of reactionary forces."

Third, Henry Quelch, Editor of "London Justice," official weekly newspaper of the Social Democratic Federation of England since 1892, is considered the leading editor in the socialist movement of Great Britain. He gives his position in an article entitled "Clericalism and the Socialist Attitude Thereto."

"The Social Democrat," March 15, 1903:

"In answer to your letter asking me for my opinion as to the attitude of the Socialist Party towards the Church, I think that the only line to be taken is that of uncompromising hostility.

"The Church is a powerful, crafty, and resourceful enemy. It is, perhaps, a mistake to provoke her, but she can never be the friend of democratic progress, or of the intellectual development of the people, and will always be their irreconcilable foe. The more friendly she is the more dangerous she will be.

"As an institution, the Church stands for obscurantism and for reaction. There is no iniquity so vile, no crime, however monstrous, that the Church has not blessed and sanctified if perpetrated in the interests of the rich and powerful.

"The Church is one of the pillars of capitalism, and the true function of the clergy is to chloroform the workers, to make docile wage-slaves of them, patient and contented with their lot in this world while expecting a glorious reward in the next.

"As long as the Church holds the minds of the workers in its grip, there will be little hope of freeing their bodies from capitalist supremacy."

Fourth, we present the testimony of Emile Vandervelde, member of the Chamber of Deputies of Belgium; the acknowledged leader of the socialist movement there. He is the author of books having an international circulation. Writing for the "Le Mouvement Socialiste" and "The Social Democrat" (January, 1903), he says:

"Beaten in Holland, crushed in Belgium, reduced to a minimum in Germany and in Austria (we do not speak of England where the question is a different one), the Liberal Party can only continue to exist in Europe either, as in Spain, by granting the demands of the Church, or, as in France and Italy, by obtaining the support of socialists.

"In France, for instance, we see most of the socialist forces taking part in the struggle, enthusiastically helping the Radical tactics, advocating against the Church the use of violent and vigorous laws, and also attacking virulently all religious ideas. And . . . the anti-Ministerialist Socialist deputies are not the least to urge the Government by vote and by speech when it is violently struggling against the Clerical and Nationalist forces.

"In the end the question to be solved is What is the essential aim of socialism? There is not a socialist who would hesitate to say that it is the emancipation of the workers, the freedom of the proletariat — and by this freedom we mean its complete freedom, the abolition of all slavery in the spiritual sphere as well as in the material sphere.

"Is it not a fact . . . . that some of our comrades advocate the union of all workers, and on the other hand act so as to make that union morally impossible? Is it not sad, for example, after a lecture in which we have stated that the socialist party respects all beliefs, to hear comrades . . . begin singing that odious verse of the 'Carmagnole' which I have for my part, never heard but with feelings of disgust:

'Throw Christ in the gutter,
The Virgin in the stable,
And the Pope to the devil.'

"I leave them the Pope — for painters of the Middle Age put in hell the monks and popes, but why should socialists be so inconsistent or so ridiculous as to insult the Crucified One — the victim of Pharisees and priests, or to vilify the Virgin — the sublime image of maternal grief? Do they think that these attacks will bring to socialism the workers who are still faithful sons of the Church? And as a general rule do they think that by forbidding processions, by ordering priests not to wear their cassocks, by organizing public dinners on Good Friday, by proposing oppressive laws against Catholics, that they will advance the cause of the Revolution? . . . .

"Can a sincere believer follow the Church's teachings and yet be a socialist? . . . . We are bound to admit that both in philosophy and politics there must be war between socialism and the Church."

Fifth. Ernest Belfort Bax, who is introduced elsewhere, in "The Religion of Socialism" ("The Modérn Revolution," page 77), records his opinion.

"The religious aspect of our capitalistic civilization is dogmatic Protestantism. . . . . . The predominantly commercial states of Christendom are the predominantly Protestant ones, ... The religious creed of the capitalist *bourgeoisie* is dogma, *minus* sacerdotalism. The religious creed of the land-owning aristocracy is sacerdotalism, with a nominal adhesion to dogma. The watchword of one is, an infallible Church; the standard of the other, an infallible Bible. The Romish or High-Anglican squire represents incarnate land, on its religious side; the Babtists haberdasher, incarnate capital.

"And now we come to the question, What is to be the end of these things?

(Page 81.) "Socialism has been well described as a new conception of the world presenting itself in industry as co-operative Communism, in politics as international Republicism, in religion as atheistic Humanism, ... The establishment of society on a socialistic basis would imply the definitive abandonment of all theological cults, since the notion of a transcendent god or semi-divine prophet is but the counterpart and analogue of the transcendent governing class. So soon as we are rid of the desire of one section of society to enslave another the dogmas of an effete creed will lose their interest. As the religion of slave industry was Paganism; as the religion serfage was Catholic Christianity, or Sacerdotalism; as the religion of Capitalism is Protestant Christianity or Biblical Dogma; so the religion of collective and co-operative industry is Humanism, which is only another name for socialism.

"There is a party who think to overthrow the current theology by disputation and ridicule. They fail to see that the theology they detest is so closely entwined with the current mode of production that the two things must stand or fall together. . . . But ere we reach our reconstruction we have the last agonized throes of Revolution to pass through. The privileged classes, it is too much to hope, will surrender without a struggle. But we are nearing the catastrophe. Our churches and chapels, our prisons, our reformatories, our workhouses, may be filled to overflowing, but the end is approaching. Already the discerning may see the open tomb in the distance, already hear the chant of the goblins of destiny indicating the determination of the mad chase and the dissolution, it may be by a quiet enthanasia, it may be in blood and fire, of the ghastly mockery of human aspiration we call 'the civilization of the nineteenth century.'"

Sixth, Leon Furnemont, member of the Belgian Chamber of Deputies ("Social Democrat," August 15, 1903), says:

"Cesar de Paepe (a prominent socialist leader) wrote in 1863:—'Whatever Socialists and Christians may say there is no connection between the Christian idea and the Socialist idea, between evangelical brotherhood and equal justice, between charity and reciprocity of services, between the religious community and industrial association, between prayer and work, between theology and the science of social economy, between the Church and the Revolution.'

"And Babel, in an essay republished by Vorwaerts in 1901, said:—'Christianity is the enemy of liberty and of civilization. It has kept mankind in slavery and oppression. The Church and State have always fraternally united to exploit the people. Christianity and Socialism are like fire and water.'

"This enables us to say that the *free thought movement*, that is to say, the struggle against religious prejudices, favors the progress of the Socialist idea.

"Theoretically, no one denies that Socialism is an *integral* doctrine, a true *system of the cosmos* having for its aim the *complete* enfranchisement of all human beings. And, moreover, how can we conceive a fraternal and free society with morals of submission and slavery?

"The present day Socialism, which is called scientific in order to distinguish it from the abstract theories of the first reformers, is based on the *materialist* conception of history. Could one imagine a more complete elimination of the absolute, without which no religion is possible?

"If the direction of civilization is exclusively determined by the forms of economic production, religions themselves only appear as excrescences of a capitalist society, which are destined to disappear with it.

"It is feared that the affirmation of a rationalistic and scientific philosophy would keep away from our organization a certain number of working men who still believe in the faith of their fathers. That is a vain fear; for revolutions, even of a social kind, are always the work of a minority, and the mass only understands afterwards.

"Should we make war on the Church? But against whom should we fight? Should it be against the windmills of the doctrinaires?

"We must wage an unrelenting war against the Church because she foments civil war among the workers. We must take away from her her control over public education which she uses to corrupt children who would otherwise become socialists.

"We must fight her without weakness, for she is the only power which has dogmas, hierarchies, riches and agents who systematically attack us. We must attack her because her economics, her politics, her ethics are contrary to our ideal.

"We must attack her because she is the only reactionary force which has any strength and which keeps us in voluntary slavery, and that is worst of all, as these Christian working-men have really lost all idea of trying to become free.

"And finally as Babel says, 'Human progress demands that war should be waged against all privileges and all arbitrary power; the Church like the State, rules the individual. We must fight against everything that is based on authority and blind belief, and which tries to destroy science and civilization that Socialism is endeavoring to maintain. Socialism, that is to say humanity, will realize the moral laws which the Church has pretended to use for the oppression and the exploitation of the masses."

Is it true that socialism is opposed to religion? We submit, to the candid mind, that our claim that it is is substantiated by the evidence which we have produced. The inauguration of socialist principles (if that were possible) would sound the death knell of religious principles.

Karl Kautsky testifies that socialists intend to use political power to oppose the church, because the church is an "instrument of class rule." Because the church forces the submission of the working class to the employing class, and this false sentiment is reechoed through the socialist world.

Enrico Ferri advocates a double policy, the breaking down of faith, but with such caution (that political progress may not be retarded) that the peasants may not be led to "think that this was an anti-religious propaganda."

Henry Quelch, with his English frankness, makes an unqualified attack upon religious institutions.

Emil Vandervelde's statement that "there is not a socialist who would hesitate to say that it is the emancipation of the workers, the freedom of the proletariat — and by this freedom we mean its complete freedom, the abolition of all slavery in the spiritual sphere as well as in the material sphere," goes unchallenged throughout the socialist world. While he has the good taste to bewail the blasphemous conduct of his "comrades," he is free to say that there is open "war between socialism and the Church." And Bax, "one of the best known and most versatile and accomplished socialists," with commendable frankness declares that "the establishment of society upon a socialistic basis would imply a definitive abandonment of all theological cults."

The sixth author we have quoted counts for more than one for he himself quotes from two men of the highest standing in the international movement. Leon Furnémont is perfectly well aware of the fact that the socialist philosophy forbids the possibility of belief in God, and he is clear in his expression of his own doctrine, "could one imagine a more complete elimination of the absolute, without which no religion is possible?" Certainly not, the socialist denial of the existence of God is complete, and its logic is relentlessly materialistic. Its courage is as good as its logic but its good courage and its good logic because founded upon bad principles would, if it could work utter destruction to those institutions which are founded upon good principles, which are sustained by good logic and which are defended with good courage. Mr. Furnémont cuts the issue free from intellectual rubbish, he says, "We must wage an unrelenting war against the church." . . . . And this is the "freedom" promised !

Seventh, and weightiest — for all socialist law and prophecy hang for authority upon the words of Marx, we give from "Secret Society in Switzerland" the following quotation which speaks for atheism in such clear tones that comment is entirely unnecessary. "We shall do well if we stir hatred and contempt against all existing institutions; we make war against all prevailing ideas of religion, of the state, of country, of patriotism. The idea of God is the keystone of perverted civilization; the true root of civilization; the true root of liberty, of equality, of culture, is atheism."

Does socialism concern itself with religion? We freely leave the question to the judgement of those of our fellow citizens who shall have read this mass of data, which is but a small part of the anti-religious writings in use by the propaganda of the modern socialist movement.

The "Paine Halls" of the country are empty and barren. They can scarcely raise the funds to keep their members from freezing! With the death of Ingersoll, their power as a distinctive organization was ended. Atheism has now found its new body, its political body in the socialist movement. As political atheism it (socialism) asks for the suffrages of the working class, for the strongest weapon of the state, with which "to overthrow the whole existing social order." One may well say with Ferdinand, "Hell is empty, and all the devils are here."

"Woe to you scribes and Pharisees, hypocrites; because you go round about the sea and the land to make one proselyte; and when he is made, you make him the child of hell twofold more than yourselves."

With my collaborator Martha Moore Avery I may truly say:

"From all the facts historical and present I must perforce conclude that the Socialist movement is a world-wide attempt at the disruption of the civilization made by the race. That it stands for devolution and not for evolution toward the perfection of human affairs. In short, that Socialism and anarchism are after all cut from one and the same web of cloth. Socialism is the right wing and the more powerful for destruction, in that it seeks the political power as its weapon of disaster rather than the stupid, the more impatient method of personal assault. It is the more dangerous in the same degree that political power is advanced over the strength of individual power.

POLITICAL ATHEISM.

THE RANK AND FILE WHOLLY MISLED AS TO THE REAL IMPORT OF SOCIALISM.

"That the rank and file of the organization as well as the voters generally are wholly misled as to the real import of Socialism I well know. And that hundreds of idealists are engaged in centralizing power in the hands of men who would use it without scruple for a purpose as far as hell is from the heaven of their enthusiasm I am free to presume. That the Socialist party is swinging into line the numerous negative hobby horses driven by sir knights of the quill I know by the flocks of erratic newspapers declaring for Socialism which find a nest in my waste basket.

SODOM AND GOMORRAH PREPARING THE WAY OF DESTRUCTION.

"I take upon myself the task of making amends as far as I may to my country and to Almighty God for the offences I have unwittingly committed in working to give power to that philosophy which I now see clearly to be an abomination — to be the blare of false gods which leadeth to destruction, rather than to that benign light which leadeth into wisdom. It has pleased me to give over all that I have thought necessary to the service of this movement — this seducer of civic virtue — this defamer of God and man — this movement whose light is darkness and whose intellectual and moral darkness grows blacker, and by swift marches. It shall now be my pleasure to give over all that I deem necessary to the promotion of industrial equities as against this devil with its specious cry of liberty while it develops its mailed fist of social might to crush liberty — this devil who cries for bread and feeds out poison — this devil who denies God and strides toward the temporal throne — this devil who talks of love and breathes the foul taint of lust — this devil who stretches out his arm to grasp the mighty sword of political power in a free land. It shall not be given him ! Though it may seem that

Sodom and Gomorrah are preparing anew the way to destructio..! First and most easily the rich are corrupting the State for private gain, for pride, for power. Next, the poor are belied into the confidence of ignorance over knowledge; vice over virtue; sophistry over philosophy — in short that the Ruler of the Universe has abandoned His seat of wisdom, of love and of justice and that the working class may set up a new order — with Babel in command.

"There need be no wild alarm, but there is need that the grave issue which confronts this nation be probed to its centre and that the service of righteousness be called in to aid in making the adjustments necessary to the growing demands of industrial democracy."

To this end I submit the data herein contained that false lights may not lure honest men to false faiths.

Free Love.

"Bless ever bless, thy servants, Lord,
Whom thou dost join in sweet accord,
The Bridegroom and the Bride;
In sorrow, sickness, and in health,
In tribulation and in wealth,
Be Thou their Help and Guide."

COULD men but realize what civilization owes to the religious teachings of the past and present and how much the future happiness of life is dependent upon the maintenance of the God given standards of morality, one would encounter less indifference to religious teachings, than one meets with in his daily walks of life. Were the practice common, of denying all things which one cannot mentally encompass, as it is with those who throw aside the belief in God, the world's advance would be cut off. Whether one have the light with which to realize the blessings of God's law or not; it is still a demonstrable fact — demonstrable to those who have the power to penetrate into the Great Sea of Light that God has designed man to lead a life of purity if he would win happiness. If man so wills he may so shape his destiny as to live harmoniously with his Creator here and enjoying the blessings of life everlasting. God's law requires of man that he shall so elevate his animal passions that he may become ennobled and reign in peace over his dominions. He has provided man, by His revelations, with the knowledge whereby to guide his course through this life. Whether one wish it or not man must obey God's commands, or into a sink of iniquity he must fall?

What doth it avail if one get bread and butter with which to fill his belly, if he maintain moral standards that consign him to the pig pens of life?

What happiness for man, even in this short material existence, if the institution of the family be destroyed and the land filled with men and women broken in virtue and in health — crazed with the passions of sex? The standards of morality were set centuries gone past. — We shall either obey them or suffer the tortures of the damned.

"Adam said: This now is bone of my bones, and flesh of my flesh; she shall be called woman, because she was taken out of man.

"Wherefore a man shall leave father and mother, and shall cleave to his wife: and they shall be two in one flesh.

"But to them that are married, not I but the Lord commandeth, that the wife depart not from her husband.

"And if she depart, that she remain unmarried, or be reconciled to her husband. And let not the husband put away his wife.

"The Pharisees tempting him (Jesus), said: Is it lawful for a man to put away his wife for every cause?

"Who answering, said to them: Have ye not read, that he who made man from the beginning, *made them male and female?* And he said:

"*For this cause shall a man leave father and mother, and shall cleave to his wife, and they two shall be one flesh.*

"Therefore now they are not two, but one flesh. What therefore God hath joined together, let no man put asunder.

"They say to him: Why then did Moses command to give a bill of divorce, and to put away?

"He saith to them: Because Moses by reason of the hardness of your heart permitted you to put away your wives; but from the beginning it was not so.

"And I say to you, that whosoever shall put away his wife, except it be for fornication, and shall marry another, committeth adultery; and he that shall marry her that is put away, committeth adultery."

Here we have the simple yet most vital and holy ideal of the relationship of husband and wife. It is God's law that monogomy shall be maintained. One man one wife—one and inseparable.

Socialists, as we have without a shadow of doubt proven, deny the existence of God. Socialists, whom we have without question proven, deny revelation. Socialism stands for the political power to the end of abolishing religion. And what is connoted thereby? Why, that all institutions that in turn are supported by the influence and teachings of religion —they must fall. Did I not say socialists were opposed to the family? That they were free lovers?

Denying, as they do, the existence of God, they logically deny the revelative standards of the old and new testaments: They are left without a standard upon which to hold to marriage. One is not bold to say that the present elevation of the family life is wholly due to the sacred environment in which it has been sustained. Many are the crimes and sins committed within and without the bonds of matrimony. But is that the fault of the God given standards? Or the discipline of religious institutions which have struggled to maintain them? No! It is the fault (and suffer they do for their own folly) of those who have departed from the standards of religion — of those who have not lived in accord with the ideals which they know to be good in the sight of God.

The work of religion has not yet been accomplished — not yet perfected. The periodical attacks of atheism, it has withstood, has been a stumbling block to its work of upbuilding the race. Religion has survived materialistic attacks in the past — and fear not — this latest political attack, which seeks to break the bonds of matrimony by control of the civic power, will also fall by its might.

In opening our case [which is to prove that socialism would destroy the sacred institution of the family] let us present the evidence of Professor Herron, who is an able exponent of the philosophy of socialism; and who has somewhat experienced the practice of it — with the full approval of the socialist party. He says:

"Without regard to our liking, Socialism is coming; it is manifestly the near stage of historic development. The socialistic road is the opening highway which humanity will next travel, whether we want to or not; and if we have anything to say to the world, or anything to give which we think it ought to have, we shall have to go along and stay with the people to the end of the journey. If it is free land we are after, or a free religion, or a free family, or a wholly free society, we shall only find it at the other side of Socialism, or along the socialistic way." (George D. Herron in "The Coming Nation," March 28, 1903.)

We have seen their position on "free religion"—that is, their advocacy of no religion — in the last chapter. We may now see that the "free family" merely means no family at all. This abuse of the term "free" has been the catch ball of the atheists in all the long gone ages. It is logical that the political atheists of to-day — inheritors of the heresies of the past — juggle with it to attract unwary lovers of human progress.

"The free family" (one of which the Professor has partially established), the completion of which "we shall find on the other side of Socialism," will not be bound by the education of the Church, nor will the protecting arm of the state be thrown around it.

Frederick Engels declared that "Three great obstacles block the path of social reform — private property, religion and the present form of marriage."

Consequently socialists stand for the abolition of private property; for the abolition of religion; and the abolition of the family.

Oscar Wilde, who became famous, as well as infamous, by putting his creed into practice, said:

"As for the virtuous poor, one can pity them, of course,

but one cannot possibly admire them. They have made private terms with the enemy, and sold their birthright for very bad pottage.

"Socialism annihilates family life . . . With the abolition of private property, marriage in its present form must disappear. This is part of the programme. . . . It converts the abolition of legal restraint into a form of freedom that will help the full development of personality, and make the love of man and woman more wonderful, more beautiful, and more ennobling." ("The Soul of Man Under Socialism," by Oscar Wilde, run in "The Challenge," a California socialist paper, and in "Millionaire," socialist "Wilshire's Magazine," June, 1902.)

In "The Historical Basis of Socialism," H. M. Hyndman says (page 452):

"Thus breaking down and building up go on slowly together, and new forms arise to displace the old. It is the same with the family. That, in the German-Christian sense of marriage for life and responsibility of the parents for the children born in wedlock, is almost at an end even now, . . . and must result in a widely extended Communism."

This gentleman, in common with all "class conscious" socialists, would destroy the individuality which is developed within the family circle; he would replace the "responsibility of the parents for the children born in wedlock" with communal responsibility. (Of course this relates to the stage of transition from the family to the no-family of the fully evolved socialist society — of the "free society.") — Certainly, for as Mr. H. Ellis, an English socialist and author of "Woman and Marriage" says: "The reproduction of the race is a social function."

But let us turn to the highest possible authorities in the modern socialist movement — to Marx and Engels, in the "Communist Manifesto." — And that this "great document" may gain its proper weight by great adherents to its doctrine, we will present an opinion of it by the late Wilhelm Leib-knecht. Who as member of the German Reichstag, until the time of his death, was the recognized leader of the socialist party of Germany.

"The Manifesto is the work of Marx and Engels. What was supplied by the one, what by the other? An idle question! It is of one mould, and Marx and Engels are one soul —as inseparable in the Communist Manifesto as they remained in their death in all their working and planning, and as they will be to humanity in their works and creations while human beings are living on earth.

"And the credit to have originated this Manifesto, to have provided through it a guide of thought and action, the fundamental principles of doctrine and tactics, for the proletariat — this credit is so colossal that even by dividing it in halves both of them still receive a giant's share.

"If Marx and Engels had never created anything else, if they had been devoured by the revolution, on the eve of which they thundered forth into the world with prophetic vision the Manifesto — they had gained immortality." ("Biographical Memoirs of Karl Marx," Chicago, 1901.)

Now "The Communist Manifesto" may speak for itself on the subject in question.

"Abolition of the family! Even the most radical flare up at this infamous proposal of the Communists.

"On what foundation is the present family, the bourgeois family, based? On capital, on private gain. In its completely developed form this family exists only among the bourgeoisie. But this state of things finds its complement in the practical absence of the family among the proletarians and in public prostitution.

"The bourgeois family will vanish as a matter of course, when its complement (prostitution) vanishes, and both will vanish with the vanishing of capital.

"The bourgeoisie has torn away from the family its sentimental veil, and has reduced the family relation to a mere money relation.

"Nothing is more ridiculous than the virtuous indignation of our bourgeois at the community of women which, they pretend, is to be openly and officially established by the Communists. The Communists have no need to introduce community of women; it has existed almost from time immemorial.

"Bourgeois marriage is in reality a system of wives in common, and thus, at the most, what the Communists might possibly be reproached with, is that they desire to introduce, in substitution for a hypocritically concealed, an openly legalized community of women. For the rest it is self-evident that the abolition of the present system of production must bring with it the abolition of the community of women springing from that system, *i. e.*, of prostitution both public and private."

This reasoning is the legerdemain of now you see it and now you don't. But careful reading of this quotation will show it to be a somewhat veiled but ferocious attack upon the sacred institution of the family. Were this subject matter to come forth dressed in honest garb, the spots of the leper would be clearly seen. It attacks by innuendo the natural order of human life — the Divine ideal of the family. While it openly declares that the family is founded on property. This statement lays the lines for the further hypocritical argument that the scmetimes property in women prevents the untrained mind from readily seeing the material source of the institution of marriage. It falsely alleges the practical absence of the family amongst the working class. Next we have a desperate sample of the underhanded method of innoculating men with the "socialist mind." Words which carry the quality of disintegration with them — words of immoral import to the emotions of the reader, veiled in analytical phrases, rather than a clear intellectual statement which says what is meant and which the mind can grasp. "The bourgeosie has torn away from the family its sentimental veil, and has reduced the family relation to a mere money relation." What may this mean? except that the sentiment of family purity once sustained by religious faith is once for all, by "economic determinism," torn asunder. That under capitalism the buying and selling of sex sentiment goes on apace? After insisting that community of wives is the mode of today—although there is a pretended "virtuous indignation" at the purpose of socialists to establish a system of wives in common. — Then the real cat comes cautiously out of the bag, "in this greatest document on earth." "For the rest it is self-evident that the abolition of the present system of production must bring with it the abolition of the community of women springing from that system, *i. e.* of prostitution both public and private." That is to say, the selling of one's body is private prostitution, likewise marriage is public prostitution. What then? Why, verily — under socialism, neither pretense nor family ties whatsoever.

"Socialism What it is and what it seeks to accomplish." Wilhelm Liebknecht (Chicago, August 15, 1901):

"Thanks to the wrong conditions of society and the state, woman is to-day without rights and in countless cases is condemned to wedded or unwedded prostitution. The intercourse of the sexes is unnatural and immoral — socialism will bring the emancipation of woman as well as of man. It insists on her complete political and social equality and equal position with man. It will destroy prostitution, whether it walk ashamed under the mantle of marriage for wealth or convenience, or whether it run shameless painted and naked upon the street."

But what about that "mantle of marriage" which covers the chaste relationship of father, mother and child? — will socialists kindly meet the issue frankly and answer?

"Woman is today without rights"? How false! Facts

prove from an economic and political point of view (the point of view which socialists are ever prating about) that woman stands to-day greatly in advance of the past, and for that advance she is indebted to religious instruction. Women have the right to the control of her children — the right to own property — the right of suffrage. If she have no rights how can her rights be more safely guarded now than in times past?

"She is condemned to wedded or unwedded prostitution"? This is a regular stock insult, which socialists use freely throughout the world, in their press and on their platform.

"I resent, past speech, the imputation that low wages and hard conditions compel working girls to sell their bodies to be burned by lust. The saving truth is that inclination to feed the flesh and to serve the devil make of poor women and of rich women alike the loathsome opposite of the wives, mothers and sisters whom men and children love and to whom the world pays honor.

"It is the fashion in Socialist speeches and frequently met with in Socialist literature to assume that bread and butter and good clothes are to many, to hosts of women, more coveted than that priceless treasure of the woman's heart, chastity.

"I am free to say that such vicious sentiment becoming generally accepted, would be a most potent factor in inducing women to break from the paths of virtue under the pressure of hard economic conditions.

"Persons holding sentiments of 'easy virtue' either ignore or are incapable of reaching the conviction which lies at the very center of the design of perfect motherhood that chastity is far more to be prized than gold or lands or rank or even life itself. For what is the life of a woman to herself if stripped of the citadel of her self-sanctity? Therefore do you say that she cannot live without vice — then many a woman under stress answers you back again, so be it, dust and ashes is by far the more preferable!

"Do you say that a woman who is pushed beyond the brink of virtue is as good as any man's mother who is virtuous having been protected in the struggle for life? Then I say out upon such slippery reasoning! For I ask about that other man's mother who for long and stormy days, weeks, months and years brought girls and boys to sweet and sound womanhood and manhood upon a wretched pittance? Can a man with such a mother (and alas there are so many) consent to such slimy sophistry? No matter how vociferously it clamors for a hearing. Certainly not! He knows in his innermost heart that the thought, aye the merest motion towards the corrupt suggestion, is abhorrent.

"No, women are not chaste because they are poor and defenseless nor because they are rich and protected. Women are virtuous because they cherish beyond all else the inherent claims of pure womanhood, of pure wifehood, and of pure motherhood upon them. Because there is no happiness outside of sex purity.

"Shall the Socialist movement become a corrupter of women? I trust not! But it is true that intellectual arguments may for a time confuse her inner sense of purity — may for a little drown her sensibilities to vice, may condone her sex sin by the argument of her frightful poverty. Although direst poverty as a constant condition is as a pleasant May morning to the torments of the damned compared to the awful enslavement caused by sex degradation, it falls below all else. To this conscious mental state men are not admitted, for it is to the women of the race that chastity is given for safe keeping. Woman's day of self-reckoning is ever at hand. The bewitching Du Barry was at no time in her career of vice so struck home to the quick as by her own overwhelming self-accusation — 'I am a courtezan.'

"A great responsibility is upon us! Let us not aid in

destroying that peace of heart native to all women, by asserting that the misery of poverty is greater than the tragedy of vice. But rather let us appeal to that love of virtue which sits deep in every woman's heart, even though her hunger for food or her wanton flesh may make strong argument to her in favor of a sex servility which is as black as hell. Do not let us add to her temptations by setting up false standards which declare that virtue and vice alike are conditional upon outward material conditions and interests. Virtue and vice are promoted by man's own will. He alone may say I will or I will not perform this act or that act and thus add strength to his virtue or add strength to his vice. He may by his own volition go up into the purer air of his new and more beautiful earthly estate or go down into the ruins of corrupted temples. Both the nation and the men have their own in their own keeping.

"That the nation may renew its life upon the foundations of sounder economic knowledge and refresh its spirit with purer ideals is the work we have in hand. Let us not then play the opposite, the damnable opposite part, by surrounding the working women of our time with the intellectual snares as to what is and what is not the true course for women to pursue. To break in upon the tower of womanly virtue by undermining its foundation by specious intellectual arguments and mawkish pity which muddles the waters of her moral mirror and so doing perforce despoils her physical body and her mental hope is a campaign in which not one of us can engage when once the realization of such deadly work comes home to us. Shall we not then rather set before the hard pressed working girls of our day examples of womanly courage such as is exhibited by Scott's Rebecca? who held at bay her seducer by the determined purpose of dashing herself upon the rocks far below beneath the window of the tower — that so she mightest keep her freedom — the freedom of her chastity, knowing it to be the blessed opposite of the enslavement purchased by vice.

"To bring this matter to close range, let me put it to you in this brutally frank way: I hear upon Boston Common or in our brave cradle of liberty, Faneuil Hall, Socialist speakers dilate upon the low wages, which, it is true, are insufficient to live upon save eked out by the almost incredible genius of thrift, straightway declare it to be impossible for a woman to live upon so low a sum and by direct imputation cover every girl in our great department stores with the shame of prostitution. There runs through the audience a visible effect! High or higher mounts the sympathy for the women who stagger and fall under industrial oppression — low and lower are the sensations thrown off by the crowd when the flesh is stirred with thoughts of immoral conquest.

"The false standards that are thus set up bear heavily down upon these women from two opposite directions. On the one hand if it be the accepted philosophy that economic hardships are sufficient reason for vicious living then surely these girls are not to be held responsible to standards of virtue! Therefore the intellectual arguments are such as to weaken self-effort to live a life of chastity in the teeth of fierce economic temptation. While on the other hand, if it be accepted as correct doctrine that economic pressure is over much for virtue to withstand, what is to prevent men who come under such teaching from assuming the attitude that lust is not so bad a thing after all and consequently these women are, all said and done, their legitimate prey.

"On the next morning after having heard these speeches I, together with crowds of other shoppers, face these girls behind the counters, what then! Up comes the suggestion, can it be true? Oh! pity, can it be true! How shocking even mentally to debate the question, even for one moment — I feel guilty. Such a thought is a poisoned dagger! To thrust these women before me with suspicious thoughts immediately brings a consequence from which I shrink, both at them and to myself, for if many of them, may be this one of them is that which Desdemona would not speak — still I look along the row at each of them? Oh! horror, I, Othello like, self-convicted, have quickly turned away, ashamed to face even the recollection of these speeches in my heart, much more the girls — knowing full that I was committing a personal offense for which I might justly be struck a blow in the face.

"Let me ask, is not the acknowledged fact of houses of disorder shame enough to openly put upon modern women? Shall we seek to fasten evil suspicion upon whole classes of our hardworking women and thus lay heavier burdens across their shoulders and shame upon mankind?

"Let socialists use such monstrous instruments in propagating a doctrine for the destruction of the family, under the guise of advancing the economic interests of the race. But that we should follow their base standard is too much to believe when once its foul face is seen.

"I know too well the estimate which women put upon their supreme claim to love and to honor, to accept such conclusions or such methods. I protest with all my soul against such treatment of defenseless women!"

Edward Carpenter, a socialist of renown, whose works are circulated by anarchists, too; the founder of "London Justice," a leading weekly, in his latest book ("Love's Coming of Age," 1903, Chicago,) advocates a "free society" in which "free love" will be the rule without "the artificial thunder of the church and the state."

In writing of this book Leonard D. Abbott, a leading socialist of New York, in "The Comrade" says, "During recent years Carpenter had devoted a great deal of attention to sexual problems, and his book, 'Love's Coming of Age,' is as suggestive and notable a treatment of this subject, from the socialist point of view, as has yet appeared in the English language."—Yes, it is indeed suggestive, despite its roseate hue, of the period of Sodom and Gomorrah, in the days before Moses was commanded to wipe these vile spots from off the face of the earth.

Marion Craig Wentworth, reviewing "Love's Coming of Age" for "The Socialist Spirit" (Chicago, November, 1902), says: "This is a comprehensive and philosophical treatise on sexual science and marriage. Like all of Edward Carpenter's productions, it is written from high ground. There is no doubt that as soon as woman is free politically and economically the marriage relation will undergo a radical change. For a comprehension of the possible lines upon which such changes may be worked out one may well turn to this little book of Mr. Carpenter's. It is a real contribution, and the emancipated should not fail to have it upon their book shelves."

But Mr. Carpenter will speak plainly for himself:

"Here there is no solution except the freedom of woman —which means of course also the freedom of the masses of the people, men and women, and the ceasing altogether of economic slavery. There is no solution which will not include the redemption of the terms 'free woman' and 'free love' to their true and rightful significance. Let every woman whose heart bleeds for the sufferings of her sex, hasten to declare herself and to constitute herself, as far as she possibly can, a free woman. Let her accept the term with all the odium that belongs to it; let her insist on her right to speak, dress, think, act, and above all to use her sex, as she deems best; let her face the scorn and the ridicule; let her 'lose her own life' if she likes; assured that only so can come deliverance, and that only when the free woman is honored will the prostitute cease to exist." ("Love's Coming of Age," Chicago, Ill., 1903, page 62.)

That sex immorality has caused many to suffer the tortures of hell, here and now, is known to the sorrow of sinful men and women, whose faces betray more than one's heart can bear to witness. That the cause is economic; and that the remedy is to be had by breaking the religious, the civic and the conventional sex standards is the common opinion of the authorities on socialism. They have nothing to offer but this — to break the bonds that hold sex emotions from falling to the low tone of lust. Without a belief in God there is nothing left upon which to erect a standard which would sustain sex purity up to the ideal standards laid down in the Bible — For if there is no God there is no moral responsibility — no inner consciousness by which one measures his own conduct by the Divine rule. Without God, ideals are left entirely at the mercy of human emotion — of "sex fondness." Lacking the purifying environment of religion, what is there left to the heart's desire but to satisfy the sex passion. Take away the recognition of God from the human mind and mankind is left without the contrast of light and darkness — without the distance between heaven and hell. If there be no God the socialist denial of free will is logical, and human passion may control the human mind.—But women, make no mistake! This is what socialists offer you as a means of solving the sex question. Do you believe in socialism? Then you are a "free woman," you can "insist on your right (without the fear of God or the love of God) to use your sex as you deem best." Is it surprising that this doctrine causes "free love" manifestations to be common to the socialist movement?

That "woman may use her sex as she deems best" is well known to every woman. But the principle of purity implanted in the breast of each and every woman, cultivated by the teachings of religion, tells her that the "freedom" which socialists seek to foist upon her will be at the cost of that most priceless treasure of her heart, her honor.

What is there that "class conscious" socialists may call honor? On the sex question. Do you feel sex passion arise within you? Is that woman attached to you by "sex fondness"? "That is your private business." The state, the church and "the big policeman above" have no moral right to interfere. — Herd together until a new sex attraction sets your passions aflame.

Let me put the power of virginity as the immortal Shakespeare conceived it in contrast to the conquest of lust.

"Prospero:
  If thou dost break her virgin knot before
  All sanctimonious ceremonies may
  With full and holy rite be minister'd,
  No sweet aspersion shall the heavens let fall
  To make this contract grow: but barren hate,
  Sour-ey'd disdain, and discord, shall bestrew
  The union of your bed with weeds so loathly
  That you shall hate it both: therefore take heed,
  As Hymen's lamps shall light you.

"Ferdinand:
                As I hope
  For quiet days, fair issue, and long life,
  With such love as 't is now, the murkiest den,
  The most opportune place, the strong'st suggestion
  Our worser genius can, shall never melt
  Mine honour into lust; to take away
  The edge of that day's celebration,
  When I shall think, or Phœbus' steeds are founder'd,
  Or night kept chain'd below."

But we have more proof, much more. "The People's Press," a socialist paper published in Chicago, January 31, 1903.

"SOCIALISM IS HELL!"

"'REV.' THOMAS J. SHERMAN of St. Ignatius (Jesuit) College — according to the Romanized Capitalistic city press — in his lecture Tuesday night (Jan. 27), in Jones' Hall, Windsor Park, expressed the same opinion of Socialism that his illustrious father did of War. 'SOCIALISM IS HELL!!!'

"The *Chicago Record-Herald* of the next morning, contains the following extract from this Jesuit priest's abuse of Socialism:

"'Socialism in its view of matrimony, reduces the state to the level of a breeding farm. Socialism asks us to vote for the dishonor of our mothers, for the shame of every drop of blood in our bodies. Are we men to permit such a party to rear its political standard in our midst? WHERE IS AMERICAN MANHOOD AND COURAGE, that they do not RISE and DRIVE the advocates of SUCH principles out of the political field? The AMERICAN man who declares himself in favor of *such* Socialism, IS HELL'S LOWEST VOMIT. I have been asked often, 'Can a Catholic be a Socialist?' I reply emphatically he CAN NOT. Socialism is more than a heresy. It is a nest of heresies. Not only can no Catholic be a Socialist, but no truly patriotic American can be one, and no man with sound common sense would be one.'

"Can any Socialist be a Catholic after reading the above lying tirade? 'Where is the American manhood and courage' of the Socialists? Tying their hopes to the tail of the priest-dominated Labor Union kite?" (Referring to the American Federation of Labor.)

With the Rev. Father I too, would ask can any patriotic American — Catholic, Protestant, Jew or Gentile, stand by such doctrine?

"The People's Press" alleges that the Father's statement is a "lying tirade."— I endorse every word uttered by the Rev. Thomas J. Sherman — and most freely affirm that the authorities quoted in this book will abundantly substantiate his claim. Not only does "socialism ask us to vote for the dishonor of our mothers" but it asks us to set up rules for conduct (if the police are not in sight) which would break down the knowledge of morality — ye gods! — this slime is what we are asked to vote for.

William Morris, "poet, artist and socialist," gives in "News From Nowhere" a pictorial presentation of the love relationship under the "free" conditions to come in with the socialist society. ("News From Nowhere" was published serially in "The Comrade," Nov. 1901 — May, 1903.) We quote from this much prized picture of the great socialist poet.

Said I: "That beautiful girl, is he going to be married to her?"

"Well," said he, "yes, he is. He has been married to her once already, and now I should say it is pretty clear that he will be married to her again."

"Indeed," quoth I, wondering what that meant.

"Here is the whole tale," said old Hammond; "a short one enough; and now I hope a happy one: they lived together two years the first time; were both very young; and then she got it into her head that she was in love with somebody else. So she left poor Dick; I say *poor* Dick, because he had not found any one else. But it did not last long, only about a year. Then she came to me, as she was in the habit of bringing her troubles to the old carle, and asked me how Dick was, and whether he was happy, and all the rest of it. So I saw how the land lay, and said that he was very unhappy, and not at all well; which last at any rate was a lie. There, you can guess the rest. Clara came to have a long talk with me to-day, but Dick will serve her turn much better. Indeed, if he hadn't chanced in upon me to-day I should have had to have sent for him to-morrow."

"Dear me," said I. "Have they any children?"

"Yes," said he, "two; they are staying with one of my daughters at present where, indeed, Clara has mostly been. I wouldn't lose sight of her, as I felt sure they would come together again: and Dick, who is the best of good fellows, really took the matter to heart. You see, he had no other love

160

to run to, as she had. So I imagined it all; as I have done with such-like matters before."

"Ah," said I, "no doubt you wanted to keep them out of the Divorce Court: but I suppose it often has to settle such matters."

"Then you suppose nonsense," said he. "I know that there used to be such lunatic affairs as divorce-courts: but just consider; all the cases that came into them were matters of property quarrels: and I think, dear guest," said he, smiling, "that though you do come from another planet, you can see from the mere outside look of our world that quarrels about private property could not go on amongst us in our days."

Indeed my drive from Hammersmith to Bloomsbury, and all the quiet happy life I had seen so many hints of, even apart from my shopping, would have been enough to tell me that "the sacred rights of property," as we used to think of them, were now no more. So I sat silent while the old man took up the thread of the discourse again, and said:

"Well, then, property quarrels being no longer possible, what remains in these matters that a court of law could deal with? Fancy a court for enforcing a contract of passion or sentiment! If such a thing were needed as a *reductio ad absurdum* of the enforcement of contract, such a folly would do that for us."

He was silent again a little, and then said: "You must understand once for all that we have changed these matters; or rather, that our way of looking at them has changed, as we have changed within the last two hundred years. We do not deceive ourselves, indeed, or believe that we can get rid of all the trouble that besets the dealings between the sexes. We know that we must face the unhappiness that comes of man and woman confusing the relations between natural passion, and sentiment, and the friendship which, when things go well, softens the awakening from passing illusions: but we are not so mad as to pile up degradation on that un-happiness by engaging in sordid squabbles about livelihood and position, and the power of tyrannizing over the children who have been the results of love or lust."

Here is a "free" picture of an ideal "socialist marriage." No church, no state! For is it not asserted that "There will be, instead of persons to be constrained, only things to be administered." ("The State and Socialism," Gabriel Deville, New York, December, 1900.)

"Dick and Clara" lived together for two years — two children are born to them — when this ideal socialist woman "got it into her head that she was in love with somebody else." She leaves Dick for this "somebody else." A year passes by, when Clara returns to take up her forsaken bed with her first love.

To be brutally frank, what can prompt a woman, with two children, to leave her home and live with "somebody else" but mere sex passion?

What would become of the race — of women in particular, in a society where, regardless of ecclesiastical and civil law; and without the restraints and the elevation of sex passion by religious and moral training, men and women were utterly "free" to accept the matrimonial relationship? — Not to speak of moral degredation — how long would the physical structure stand the strain that would thus be put upon it?

Reader, kindly compare this low browed atheistic philosophy, though it wear a rose on its bosom, by the "artist socialist" with the great bard's picture of good Queen Katherine, who regarded marriage as a sacrament — then tell the American public for which you vote.

"Queen Katherine:
Have I liv'd thus long — let me speak myself,
Since virtue finds no friends — a wife, a true one?
A woman — I dare say without vain-glory —
Never yet branded with suspicion?

Have I with all my full affections
Still met the king? lov'd him next heaven? obey'd him?
Been, out of fondness, superstitious to him?
Almost forgot my prayers to content him?
And am I thus rewarded? 'Tis not well, lords,
Bring me a constant woman to her husband,
One that ne'er dream'd a joy beyond his pleasure,
And to that woman, when she has done most,
Yet will I add an honour, — a great patience.

Wolsey:
Madam, you wander from the good we aim at.

Queen Katherine:
My lord, I dare not make myself so guilty,
To give up willingly that noble title
Your master wed me to; nothing but death
Shall e'er divorce my dignities."

No "such lunatic affairs as divorce courts" under the socialist regime. No! a "free family" will be the order of that day. — "Dick and Clara" found their children upon her return, thanks to their lying friend Hammond. But what after all does the care of the children signify so long as the Claras and Dicks gratify their sex passion? No? No property quarrels — what a charming picture? But it is questionable whether such a stable thing as "property" could exist under a regime of mere "sex fondness."

The love of mothers for their children is by the muddy mode of socialist reasoning turned into "the power of tyrannizing over the children who have been the results of love or lust." With the Rev. Thomas J. Sherman, we can truthfully say "socialism is hell's lowest vomit."

In "Socialism Its Growth and Outcome," the joint production of Morris and Bax (chapter xxi,, page 298) under the heading "Socialism Triumphant," they say:

"It will be noticed that we have above been speaking of

religion and morality as distinct from one another. But the religion of Socialism will be but the ordinary ethics carried into a higher atmosphere and will only differ from them in *degree* of conscious responsibility to one's fellows. Socialistic Ethics would be the guide of our daily habit of life; socialistic religion would be that higher form of conscience that would impel us to actions on behalf of a future of the race, such as no man could command in his ordinary moods.

"As to the particulars of life under the Socialist order, we may, to begin with, say concerning marriage and the family that it would be affected by the great change, firstly in economics, and secondly in ethics. The present marriage system is based on the general supposition of economic dependence of the woman on the man, and the consequent necessity for his making provision for her, which she can legally enforce. This basis would disappear with the advent of social economic freedom, and no binding contract would be necessary between the parties as regards livelihood; while property in children would cease to exist, and every infant that came into the world would be born into full citizenship, and would enjoy all its advantages, whatever the conduct of its parents might be. Thus a new development of the family would take place, on the basis, not of a predetermined lifelong business arrangement, to be formally and nominally held to, irrespective of circumstances, but on mutual inclination and affection, an association terminable at the will of either party. It is easy to see how great the gain would be to morality and sentiment in this change. At present, in this country at least, a legal and quasi moral offence has to be committed before the obviously unworkable contract can be set aside. On the continent, it is true, even at the present day the marriage can de dissolved by mutual consent; but either party can, if so inclined, force the other into subjection, and prevent the exercise of his or her freedom. It is perhaps necessary to state that this change would not be made merely formally and mechanically. There would be no vestige of reprobation weighing on the dissolution of one tie and the forming of another. For the abhorrence of the oppression of the man by the woman, or the woman by the man (both of which continually happen to-day under the *ægis* of our would-be moral institutions) will certainly be an essential outcome of the ethics of the New Society."

Under socialism 1st —" No binding contract would be necessary " between men and women entering into the sacred relation of marriage, nor no civil bond either. 2nd, Instead of marriage until death do us part, "mutual inclination" will make the "association terminable at the will of either party." 3rd. "Property in children will cease to exist" for "every infant will be born in full citizenship." No father's voice to speak the protecting word — no mother's love to make a heaven of home — Under socialism the infant citizen will we assume live in barracks — Is not this " hell's lowest vomit? "

In answer to an article which appeared in " The Catholic Light," " The Worker " says editorially (Sunday, July 20th, 1902) :

" The writer — who seems never to have read a Socialist book or paper or heard a Socialist speaker — tells the miners . . . that Socialism is an attack on the home, the family, and the church. That the Socialists foment riot and disorder, that they propose to overthrow law and order, religion and morality, that they are 'laying the foundation for a system of confusion, vice, and infidelity.'

" We challenge this writer to cite one speech or written article, in support of his sweeping charges. He cannot do it. The Socialist party does not attack religion nor the church. It officially declares that religious opinion is a private matter, which should be kept separate from politics.

" The Socialist party does not attack the institution of the family nor seek to undermine the home.

" Gentlemen of the 'Catholic Light' it is a dangerous

game you are playing. Honesty is the best policy. In this
age of newspapers and public meetings it does not pay to
falsify facts too recklessly. The miners are learning what
Socialism is by meeting and listening to Socialists and reading their writings. If you keep on misrepresenting Socialism you will succeed only in destroying the miners' confidence in you. We give you this warning in all kindness
and good faith, for we do not wish to quarrel with you."

You "do not wish to quarrel" with them? Neither do
you wish to meet the issue which they raise openly. But
you do mean to employ socialist tactics — to be bold when it
is politically prudent and to be innocent when you dare not
be bold. Do you think the public is daft? You say that
you do not attack the home, when in your published list of
books on sale, in almost every issue of your paper, are to be
found socialist books advocating the destruction of the family.
In the face of the fact of socialist advocacy of free love
it is brazen assumption for you to call the "Catholic Light"
to task by telling them that "honesty is the best policy." But
honesty is not your best policy for if you were honestly to
put your doctrine before the American people they would
have none of it. We say to you "it is a dangerous game"
you are playing and this book will unmask the socialist face.

You are right "the miners are learning what socialism
is." And, too, they are learning that your friendship for
them is as false as your challenge to the "Catholic Light" is
brazen. Under the wise directorship of John Mitchell, whose
life of devotion is given to the defense and elevation of the
miners' homes, the miners will stand in solid phalanx against
the encroachments of the socialist parties upon their trade
union, despite the bewildering picture of material success
with which you would seduce them to your political demands.

"Economic determinism" keeps one's gaze upon the
ground. The low regard in which women are held and the
degrading conclusions as to the "ideal" sex relation, come

alike from this false theory. Karl Marx says, "The first division of labor is that of man and wife in breeding children." — Think to what straits one is put in defence of one's theory when human procreation is classed under the science of political economy. — Here is another sample of a father of the "materialist concept of history." "In the family the man is the bourgeois, the woman represents the proletariat." (Frederick Engels.)

And this from Ernest Belfort Bax is viler still: "The husband is compelled, by custom and by law, to do *corvée*, or to yield up such portion of his earnings as may enable his wife to live in comfort — just as the villein was compelled to do *corvée*, or to pay his lord a proportion of the produce of the fields worked by his labour. The lord had the practical monopoly of the villein's means of existence — the land. Under the most favourable circumstances, he exacted from him a toll, in the shape of a rent, in kind or money, and other dues, for the privilege of working the land. The woman possesses the monopoly of what is, if not a primary, at least a secondary necessary of life to the great majority of men — the means of sexual satisfaction, her body; and for allowing him access to which the law entitles her to demand a rent and dues in the shape of food, clothes, shelter — in short, provision in accordance with the station in life occupied by her "villein," the husband, without any exertion on her part." ("Social Democrat.)

This is a natural consequence of the atheistic philosophy. — With nothing to distinguish the human creation of wealth from the Divine creation of man socialism wallows in the intellectual mire. They cannot see the Divine Law — the positive side of the civic law with its basis in equity, which holds men to paths of duty and honor. No, they see only the negative side — "the policeman's club" — the law which protects woman in the collection of her fee for the rent of her body from her "villein" the husband, as the lord is allowed to collect the fee for the rent of his land.

One may as consistently use licentious French literature in the education of his children as to give them the socialist literature on this subject, — with this disadvantage, however, the socialist literature is seriously put forth as science.

Belfort Bax in "The Religion of Socialism" ("Essays in Modern Socialist Criticism" page 136 — "The Capitalistic Hearth") is altogether too plain of speech to admit of any misunderstanding.

"The throne, the altar and the hearth — the political emblem, the religious emblem, and the social emblem — have long constituted the mystic trinity . . . . In the *bourgeois* world of today the first two terms may be sometimes modified. The middle-class . . . . may even prefer to substitute for it the presidential chair, but in either case it is the "law" — the legal system of a class society . . . . to the altar he might possibly prefer the "Bible," by which he would wish to be understood Protestant dogmas without the inconveniences of direct sacerdotal domination. . . . Beneath throne, altar, and hearth, in their present form, all Socialists know that there lies the market. They know that the market is the bed-rock on which the throne, the altar, and the hearth of the nineteenth century rests, and that this bed-rock shattered, the said throne, altar, and hearth will be doomed."

In his "Outlooks From a New Standpoint" Ernest Belfort Bax has this further to say :

"In the present day there are but two alternatives — the *mystical* sanction of monogamy, and what we may term the *vestryman* sanction. The only rational position for those who take up the strict lines of legalised monogamic chastity and sniff disapprovingly at the fact, or the notion, of sexual intercourse outside this relation, is the mystical — Christian sanction. Such a one must regard marriage and the sex relation generally, as a sacred symbol of a solemn, mystical truth, otherwise he is a blatant fraud. For though he may 'most powerfully and potently' believe in the economic or vestryman sanction, yet this alone, while it might lead to reasoned remonstrance, could not possibly evoke any genuine unction of the kind one is accustomed to associate with conventional laudations of chastity, and condemnations of its breach, or with finger-pointings at the non-respectable woman. For this sanction has a quite peculiar flavour, which could in reality only be caused by an outrage on our deepest feelings, such as would rend our hearts, and not merely our trousers' pocket. The unctious saint, if we are persuaded of his sincerity, one may respect and even love, but the unctious vestryman no man can love. Besides, the 'vestryman' sanction — that is the one consisting of mere economical expediency — loses its direct force in at least two cases within the limits of our present society. It loses where the question of offspring is eliminated by 'practical malthusianism,' or other causes. It loses it where the offspring are as well provided for as they would be in marriage. It loses it, as a matter of course, where the economic basis of society, from being individualistic, has become Socialistic. The vestryman or trousers-pocket sanction of marriage is, therefore, obviously not of a nature to give the institution a fundamental ethical basis, and hence, we are justified in saying that monogamy as an ethical principle collapses with the collapse of theological mysticism. For this reason, the various Christian sects are trying to constitute themselves the custodians of monogamy and the conventual sexual morality, as the only remunerative occupation left them, except 'charity,' after the loss of public interest in God, Christ, etc. In addition to the Christians there are the Positivists and miscellaneous rhetoricians who seek to prop up monogamy by phrases. They are, however, a very feeble folk, so far as this question is concerned, we have already pointed out the only two solid arguments for the monogamic principle and the sexual abstinence it involves. Now, these good people can't exactly accept either the 'mystical' or the 'vestryman' position. Hence, they take refuge in deliciously vague declamation on the nobility, on the loftiness, of the ideal which handcuffs one man and one woman together for life. We are never allowed to see precisely where the nobility and the loftiness come in, but we are assured that they are there. The mere commonplace man, if left to himself, would probably think that it rested entirely upon circumstances, upon character, temperament, etc., whether the perpetual union of two persons was desirable. There are excellent men and women [possibly the majority] born with dispositions for whom a single permanent union is doubtless just the right thing; there are other excellent men and women who are born with lively imaginations and bohemian temperaments for whom it is not always precisely the right thing. Now, the plain man of ordinary reflection would imagine that all these phases of human nature have their justification and their corresponding ideals. No, says the Positivist, or other rhetorical upholder of strict monogamy, there is only one absolute ideal, and on the procrustean bed of this ideal all men and women must be stretched.

". . . . . It is clearly the duty of every individual to protest against it openly by word and deed, rather than for the sake of gaining the applause of mawkish sentimentalists to sanction it either tacitly or avowedly.

"Herein we have an instance of the distinction between bourgeois morality and Socialist morality. To the first it is 'immoral' to live in a marital relation without having previously subscribed to certain legal formalities. . . . To the second . . . to live in a state of unlegalised marriage defileth not a man, 'nor woman neither.' There are some persons even who need enjoining to deny themselves the pleasure of asceticism and the smug self-satisfaction they derive from it. . . .

"Enforced monog my and its correlate, prostitution, is the great historical antithesis of civilization in the sexual sphere, just as mastership and service is in the economic sphere, or as God and nature in the speculative sphere, or as sin and holiness in the sphere of ethics generally, etc.

"Socialism will strike at the root at once of compulsory monogamy and prostitution by inaugurating an era of marriage based on free choice and intention, and characterised by the absence of external coercion.

"In this, as in other departments, the modern man, immersed in the categories of the *bourgeois* world, sees everything through them. For him, therefore, there exists only legalized monogamic marriage and prostitution, both of which are based essentially on commercial considerations. The one is *purchase*, the other *hire*. He cannot see the higher and only really *moral* form of the marriage-relation which transcends both, and which is based neither on *sale* nor *hire*. Prostitution is immoral as implying the taking advantage by the woman of a monopoly which costs her no labour for the sake of extorting money from the man. But the condition of legal marriage — maintenance does the same.

"If it be asked, is marriage a failure? the answer of any impartial person must be — monogamic marriage is a failure — the rest is silence. We know not what the new form of the family the society of the future, in which men and women will be alike economically free, may evolve, and which may be generally adopted therein. Meanwhile, we ought to combat by every means within our power the metaphysical dogma of the inherent sanctity of the monogamic principle."

What plainer declaration could be made against the monogamic family? — And Bax is the leading "philosophic reasoner and exponent of socialist theory and doctrine." How, now? Shall socialists be given the political power with which to put their theories into universal practice? This is not the opinion of one man; but the logical conclusion from the false premise of their philosophy — their basis of "economic determinism."

. Certainly, it is impossible for Bax and his fellow socialists to see where the "nobility and loftiness comes in" when considering questions above their mental horizon. But it is quite clear that they comprehend the "lively imaginations and bohemian temperaments" which look upon sex relationship as a development of the physical organism, merely. Most assuredly, one who concisely holds to the materialistic concept of life is unable to realize that "monogamic chastity" is the highest ideal of sex relation. God has ordained one ideal higher than that, virgin purity.

Note this "Prostitution is immoral as implying the taking advantage by the woman of a monopoly which costs her no labor for the sake of extorting money." Prostitution is immoral because it implies the taking of money without labor. Not because there is a command to woman, from the Most High, to live a life of purity, that happiness and honor may attend all her days. Now listen to this reflection from the socialist philosopher which makes all married women prostitutes, also. "But the condition of legal marriage— maintenance — does the same." There is no sacred thing under the touch of these vile hands — all is brutalized and degraded by socialist philosophy.

But we must note one important fact. It is clearly in view that Bax acknowledges that the only basis for the present form of marriage is to be found in religion. Hence the opposition to the church. For outside the influence of religion no moral law can be adduced that will establish, maintain and perfect the sacred institution of the monogamic — the natural family — the God-given family.

From page 114 of "Outlooks From a New Standpoint" we take further testimony that socialism is "hell's lowest vomit." Read it carefully; bearing in mind the while that this is the application of socialist principles to the present-day conduct of men and women — that here is given the ethical standard of a political party which dares to ask of respectable American citizens their suffrages.

"Now, a man may justly reject the dominant sexual morality; he may condemn the monogamic marriage-system which obtains to-day; he may claim the right of free union between men and women; he may contend he is perfectly at liberty to join himself, either temporarily or permanently, with a woman; and that the mere legal form of marriage has no binding force for him.

"Suppose that in Russia or elsewhere, a sudden and urgent demand for material resources for party purposes arose, and that much hung upon its being immediately satisfied. Suppose again, that, as a last resort, a female member of the party were without any hypocritical pretence to sell her body to raise the money. Would not this be a commend-able act? Given the elimination of the mystical theory of the sexual relation, I should say yes. Prostitution for private gain is morally repellant. But the same outward act done for a cause transcending individual interest loses its character of prostitution and acquires a new content."

Let us make a close at home application of this reasoning — Suppose there were a carpenters' strike on for an eight-hour day — Consequently there would be a good opportunity to propagate the doctrines of socialism — But the socialist party were in sore need of funds to carry on their campaign — It would be in no wise immoral, provided it were done with-out hypocrisy, for any woman in the party to sell her body, giving the money to the party for the purpose named — After all it is not the selling of one's body that makes one a pros-titute, but the purpose for which the money is used. In the good cause of socialism it would be a virtue, not a vice?

Now, we should like an answer (not a mere denial, for we have presented you with the data by which you must stand, if still you claim to be a socialist) from the women of the socialist party. Do you desire to give over the control of this great nation to the keeping of a movement advocating such unholy sentiments — such mawkish standards? More, I insist, than the satisfaction of "lively imaginations and bohemian temperaments" is needed to constitute happy living, even though idle bread and butter were served from off golden plates.

The following appears on the front page of "The Social Democratic Herald," Milwaukee, June 13, 1903.

"A FOUL SLANDERER."

"Father Sherman, the degenerate son of old Tecumseh, repeated his assault on Socialism at Racine last week under the auspices of a Roman Catholic society, that ought to blush for being behind such an outpouring of untrue and filthy allegation. Sherman is certainly not a scholar, and he showed himself a superficial fellow. The meanest part of his assault was with regard to Socialism and the marriage relation. His charge that the Socialists believe in loose morals is a miserable slander, one that can only come from a man with a foul mind.

"Only a low whelp would persist in such a slander, in the face of the repeated denials of the Socialists themselves, in the face of their literature on the subject and in the face of the moral standing in the community of the socialists themselves. This lie about the attitude of the Socialists toward marriage is kept up for only one reason, and that is, that filthy slander is considered by a man of Father Sherman's calibre an effective weapon to use against Socialism among the less enlightened members of his church. But he defeats his own ends, nevertheless. When such people find that he has been lying to them they will even come to mistrust his religious teaching."

Turning to the next page, of this issue, one may find a double column advertisement of "Books on International

Socialism", on sale at the office of the "Social Democratic Herald"; many books from which I have quoted in this work. Is the "Social Democratic Herald" innocent? Or is it convicted of blatant bluffing for the good of the cause?

Of Enrico Ferri, who is the editor of the socialist daily paper of Italy "The Avanti", and member of the Italian Parlement, "The International Socialist Review" (Chicago, April, 1903) says, he (Ferri) is "The foremost exponent of Socialism now living." He is associated with Lombroso in his school of criminology. Ferri's principal work is "Socialism and Modern Science", printed in Italian, and translated into French, German, Spanish, Dutch and Servian. It was also translated into English by Robert Rives La Monte, New York, 1900. "The International Socialist Review," February, 1901, speaking of this book, says:

"Since the translation of Marx' Capital there has been no greater contribution to the socialist movement of the English speaking world than is afforded by this work. Under the title "Socialisme et Science Positive" it had already become one of the classics of the French, Belgian and Italian movement. . . The book is a perfect arsenal of ideas for socialist writers and speakers, and must form a part of the equipment of every well-armed socialist."

In this book (Socialism and Modern Science) one may find "economic determinism" run mad, nothing but bread and love, by which he means sex passion, remain when life is sifted to its last analysis. On page 48 Ferri says:

"When in a family financial affairs run smoothly and prosperously, harmony and mutual good-will prevail; as soon as poverty makes its appearance, discord and struggle ensue."

This is not true—it assumes that happiness is conditioned upon the quantity of bread and butter in the larder. Certainly finance determines whether one shall live in an overcrowded tenement or in a mansion, if in the city, or in a substantial farm house or in a little wooden shanty if in the country. But thanks to the good God finance is not the prime factor in determining whether "harmony and mutual good will prevail" within the several degrees of domestic poverty, or abundance. "Harmony and good-will" may spring from one of two sources. It may be the good nature of "old Tillie" or it may be the result of self discipline, the conquering of selfishness, ambition and the other vices to which the human flesh is heir. Of course being merely a negative—a materialist—philosophy socialism could not be expected to take cognizance of the positive self-attainment which comes from obedience to religious law. The dumpy good nature which comes from a full belly, and the sex vanity which is pleased with fine apparel is not of the same stuff as the scanting of one's meal that the children may have sufficient food and the cheerful surrender of the good clothes to the one who needs them the most. Certainly the "harmony and good-will" which is born of purely material pleasures will flee out of the window when poverty comes in at the door, but it is as moonlight to the sunlight in the heart of the conscious man— In one word, the one is nature and the other is grace — That is to say, the "harmony and good-will" worth the having comes by obedience to the will of God.

If wealth be sufficient cause of "harmony" as is alleged by Ferri. I would ask these "modern scientists" how it happens that so much disharmony and lack of good-will exists among the rich? Are the rich happy and are the poor miserable? No, verily. Happiness, that elevation of the spirit which is the fruit of religion alone is found with the poor and it is found with the rich — God is no respector of persons. But. alas, so also is discord and misery found alike with the rich and with the poor. "Elevation is not conditioned upon location."

Another question to socialists is also pertinent. Do you think finance would guard the happiness of your household if your mother, wife, daughter or sister were to carry out the socialist code of morals — if in answer to a "sudden and urgent demand for material resources for party purposes arose and she were to sell her body to raise the money"? No? I believe a personal taste of "hell's lowest vomit" would soon bring you up with a round turn, to the realization that finance is not the sure cause of "harmony and good-will."

Here is more of Ferri's "materialistic science."

"It may be said these two fundamental instincts of life — bread and love — by their functioning maintain a social equilibrium in the life of animals, and especially in Man.

"It is love which causes, in the great majority of men, the principal physiological and psychical expenditure of the forces accumulated in larger or smaller quantities by the consumption of daily bread, and which the daily labor has not absorbed or which parasitic inaction has left intact.

"Even more — love is the only pleasure which has a universal and equalitarian character. The people have named it 'the paradise of the poor' and religions have always bidden them to enjoy it without limits — 'be fruitful and multiply' — because the erotic exhaustion which results from it, especially in males, diminishes or hides beneath its pall of forgetfulness the tortures of hunger and servile labor, and permanently enervates the energy of the individual; and to this extent it performs a function to the ruling class." ("Socialism and Modern science.")

"This is their last ditch! Nothing could pass beyond the bounds of this insult. Is this command to be fruitful and multiply given alone to the poor? Answer you vilifiers of sacred order. Study the Word of God and note the frankness with which lewd and lustful conduct is condemned. It was for lewd practices that the Sodomites were wiped from off the face of the earth. — The sons of Abraham were commanded not to spill their seed upon the ground. Marriage was elevated to a sacrament by Christ in fulfillment of the Mosaic law given by God. Then contrast the customs of pagan Rome, where marriage was looked upon as an irksome restraint, and was little resorted to. The passions being indulged by intercourse with female slaves. Then follow the contrast in ideals and in practices, in the nations that were overcome by the Christian Religion. Then look at this insult passing current within the socialist movement which alleges that sexual excesses were, aye were and are, encouraged by the religious to hide "beneath its pall of forgetfulness the tortures of hunger and servile labor."

"Pray consider the facts in the case. Look at the command to be "fruitful and multiply" with the pure eyes which behold in marriage a sacrament. Think, if you would know its meaning, of the loving sex restraint self-put upon a man to protect the wife of his heart from his approaches during the period of gestation — through the period of nursing. Think what it means to sacrifice the sexual desires to the end of maintaining marriage as a sacred institution and then read the command to be "fruitful and multiply" with the pure light of love, rather than with the lustful eye which reads into it the opportunity for the "erotic exhaustion," of which Ferri treats. Or for that refined damnation, which passes under its several "scientific" names, of setting up the sex fluids and translating them into "idealistic pleasures." To be fruitful and multiply is the clean, the simple command of God to man, it deals not with substitutes, but goes straight to the moral core. Use the sex organs for one purpose only — that of procreation, within the sacred bond of matrimony — outside that bond — adultery is a deadly sin and a crime to the integrity of the state. I say the devil cannot paint a blacker picture in vilification of the religious effort of the ages to purify the lusts and institute chastity amongst men. Nor can the devil encroach upon the standards of sex morality with more seductive garb than that of science."

And what have scientists to offer towards the perfection of the marriage state? Prof. Flint says with truth that:

"From the time of Plato to the present day the constitution of the family has been a favorite subject of socialistic speculation. . . .

"All the schemes of Family organization proposed by socialist theorists in the course of the last two thousand years and more have been of a kind which, had they unfortunately been adopted, would, instead of improving the world, have done it incalculable mischief. They have been reactions from actuality, not without some soul of truth and justice in them, yet so extreme and unnatural that carrying them into effect, far from purifying and elevating the Family, would have degraded it, and brutalised the community. And Socialism has in this direction made hardly any progress. Babel and Lafargue have not got beyond Plato and Campanella. Socialist critics of what they call 'the bourgeois Family' or 'mercantile marriage,' can easily point out various imperfections prevalent in modern domestic life; but when, granting their criticisms not to be without more or less foundation, we ask them how they propose to get rid of, or at least to lessen, the evils which they have indicated, they have virtually no other answer to give us than that they would introduce evils far worse — absorption of the Family in the community, free love, the separation of spouses at will, transference of children from the charge of their parents to that of the State." ("Socialism," Robert Flint, Professor, University of Edinburgh.)

August Babel, the leader of the Social Democratic party in the Reichstag, led the socialist parliamentary fight against the tariff bill, which was introduced at the last session. Socialists accredit to him more than to any other socialist in Germany the increase in the vote polled by the Social Democrats in the June election. Babel was first elected to the North German diet from Glauchen Meeran district, Saxony, in 1867. In 1871 he was sent to the Imperial Parliament, and with brief exceptions he has remained a member ever since. 179

Babel has been associated with the editorship of "The Berlin Vorwaerts," the leading socialist daily of Germany. Chief among his literary productions is "Woman, of the Past Present and Future." It is considered the text book on the woman question, from a socialist standpoint. In the introduction to this book, of which there have been thirty-three editions in Germany alone, there is to be found this passage: "I request readers to regard the following statements as the expression of my personal opinions." Of course this may have been prompted by the spirit of democracy; which prompted him to protect the party from taking a position upon which it had not voted. — It may have been modesty, or it may have been vanity in him, — claiming the first right to such a remarkable misconception of historic data. However that may be, Babel's "personal opinions" are an integral part of the socialist garment. Not to be torn out of its warp and woof without rending the coat asunder.

The Rev. Carl D. Thompson, a socialist lecturer of the West, is presumably somewhat restive under its dogma — somewhat ashamed to meet its text, which from cover to cover is an attack not only upon the marriage bond but upon all else which the religious hold sacred.

· Rev. Mr. Thompson presents Babel's statement with one of his own, — which is expected to shield the individual socialist who feels the need of protection. "Babel had a perfect right, . . . to set forth his views as he did, whether they were a part of Marx's or not." Certainly, yes. But there is not a shadow of doubt that Marx and all other "scientific" socialists agreed, and still agree, with this book; for they have most industriously circulated it in propagating the socialist doctrine.

"This book contains Babel's personal opinions"? Good. The question is, are Babel's opinions, written down in "Woman," socialist opinions? Emphatically, yes.

"Science and Health," "A Key to the Scriptures,"

presents the personal opinions of Mrs. Mary Baker G. Eddy. But "Science and Health" also embodies the opinions of the members of the "Church of Christ Scientist." Therefore "Science and Health" is of much more weight in propagating the dogmas of this sect than would be the merely personal opinions of "Mother Eddy." For it embodies the collective opinions of the cult at which the Rev. Mary Baker G. Eddy stands at the head. Just so it is with "Woman." There is no quarrel on the score of its being the personal opinions of Herr Babel (very vile opinions they are) and there is but the faintest quarrel, made here and there by one who really has no affiliation with socialist doctrines, as to whether the socialist party have made this socialist leader's opinions into socialist dogma. Therefore "Woman, of the Past, Present and Future" no longer represents merely the personal opinion of a great leader of the party, but it embodies the collective opinion of the International Socialist Movement.

Of course there is this difference — one is the key to the "science" of health — while the other is the key to the "science" of sex. One denies everything but spirit, while the other denies everything but matter. — (Would these two halves make one whole?)

We quote from "Woman."

"Marriage is the basis of the family, the family is the basis of the State; if you attack marriage you attack society and the State and undermine both," exclaim the advocates of the present "order" of things. Certainly, marriage is the basis of social development. But we must ascertain which form of marriage is the more moral, or, in other words, more likely to conduce to the advantage of humanity in all its phases, a marriage founded on the bourgeois idea of property, and therefore compulsory, with its many attendant evils and mostly imperfect realization of its object, a social institution beyond the reach of millions, or a marriage founded on the free, untrammeled choice of love, *such as is only possible in a Socialistic society.*"

Here we have the stock phrase of the socialists, "Marriage is based on the bourgeois idea of property," that marriage is a development incident to industrial relationship and we have the socialist forecast, that because love evolves out of free economic relations, love marriages are "only possible in a socialist society." Love is nothing more nor less than animal sex sensation become conscious of its sensations. Look on this picture and then on this. Love is a quality impressed by the hand of God upon the human soul. It brings out the purity of its glowing colors in obedience to the chaste laws which God has ordained. Evolution in either case, which do you, reader, prefer?

"The part played by Church and State in the sacred ceremony is far from creditable in more respects than one. However certain the State official or the minister of the Church may be that the bridal pair before him has been brought together by the dirtiest of tricks, however apparent it may be that there is not the smallest compatibility between the two . . . . All of this is of no consequence to the representative of Church and State, it does not concern him; it is his business to bless the matrimonial bond, and the blessing on the part of the Church is all the more solemn the larger the sum paid for the sacred act." ("Woman," Babel.)

Neither the church nor the state assumes the authority of passing judgement upon the compatibility of the persons entering into matrimony. But the religious requirements are "that both parties . . . . be in a state of grace when they contract the sacrament of marriage, for two reasons, 1st, because they themselves administer the sacrament and 2ndly, because they receive the sacrament."

Consistency thou art indeed a jewel! Would the socialists within the "free society" search into the compatibility of their fellows who bed and board together?

"Thus are human beings chained together; the one becomes the slave of the other, and is forced, in the fulfillment of matrimonial duty, to submit to the most intimate embraces and caresses of the other, which she possibly detests more than blows and abuse.

"Now I ask, is not such a marriage — and the number is great — worse than prostitution. The prostitute is at least to a certain extent free to withdraw from her shameful trade; she has, at least if she is not the inmate of a brothel, the right of refusing the embrace of a man whose personality repels her. But a wife is sold into the hands of her husband, and must endure his embraces though she may have a hundred causes to hate and abominate him." ("Woman" Babel.)

Does it follow that the awful state pictured is the result of poverty? Is this a case of "economic determinism?" Is it not rather a case of sin? And shall the whole structure of civilization fall because some men and women, many men and women, live in sin and are chained together."

The truth of the matter is that socialist idealism is modeled on "The Ode to the Prostitute" and so fascinated with its deformity are they that everything is measured by its hideous standard. It is the two opposing poles which attract attention — beauty and deformity — with the abnormal vision deformity is the yard-stick by which all things are measured. W. S. Lilly, writing on this point says, "You would abolish pauperism by making all men paupers, so would you abolish prostitution by making all women prostitutes."

"After society has entered into exclusive possession of all the means of production, *the equal duty of all to labor, without distinction of sex, will become the fundamental law of the Socialist community*." ("Woman," Babel.)

All motherly instincts are to be smothered within the socialist's economic machine. Women will no longer be the mistresses of the homes, in fact there will be no homes,—but women will have equal opportunity, with men, to work.

"In the new community woman is entirely independent, no longer subjected even to the appearance of supremacy or exploitation; she is a free being, the equal of man.

"Her education is the same as that of man, except where the difference of sex makes a deviation from this rule and special treatment absolutely unavoidable; she develops all her mental and physical powers and capabilities under natural conditions of existence: she can select such fields for her activity as her wishes, tastes and faculties may direct. She works under exactly the same conditions as a man. Having performed her share of social labor in some branch of industry, the next hour she becomes educator, teacher, or nurse, later on she devotes herself to art or science, and afterwards exercises some executive function. She enjoys amusements and recreation with her own sex or with men, exactly as she pleases and occasion offers.

"In the choice of love she is free just as man is free. She wooes and is wooed, and has no other inducement to bind herself than her own free will. The contract between two lovers is of a private nature as in primitive times, without the intervention of any functionary, but it is distinguished from the primitive contract by the fact that the woman no longer becomes the slave of a man who obtained her as a gift or by purchase, and can cast her off at his pleasure.

"Human beings must be in a position to act as freely, where their strongest impulse is concerned, as in the case of any other natural instinct. *The gratification of the sexual impulse is as strictly the personal affair of the individual as the gratification of every other natural instinct.* No one has to give an account of him or herself, and no third person has the slightest right of intervention. Intelligence, culture and independence will direct and facilitate a right choice. Should incompatibility, disappointment, and dislike ensue, morality demands the dissolution of a tie that has become unnatural and therefore immoral." ("Woman," Babel.)

"I fear forever: Milan and Naples have
  More widows in them of this business making,
  Than we being men to comfort them."

To sum up this picture of woman's future under socialism: —

1st — She will have an equal chance with men to work. — Moreover all women must work in some one branch of the "social industry." Under the "vile system of capitalism" woman may spend quiet happy days at work in her home with her children. For those women who work in shop or factory the trade unions are forcing equal industrial standing of women with men.

2nd — After work, woman may take a turn as teacher or nurse for an hour or so, and then devote herself to art or science. The socialist regime offers this at the cost of her motherhood and her womanhood. Under "the hell of capitalism," should hes ambition be high enough, without the sacrifice of her home or her honor, she may carve out for herself a distinguished career.

3rd — She will be free to woo or be wooed — it is more befitting the sex basis of socialism to say she is free to pair or be paired.

4th — She may enjoy herself with her own sex or with the other sex. Certainly this does differ from to-day. For she is forbidden by the moral law, which she may not now, as under socialism, be "free" to violate without disgrace, from selecting a new husband every little while if she were to happen to take it into her head.

5th — She will then have that new thing "free will," which of course is evolving under the law of "economic determinism" and will come into vogue when the capital belongs to the people collectively. Socialists see a vast improvement in the quality of their "free will." It is not God-given and therefore there is no moral law which brings along with it personal responsibility. Their particular brand of "free will" consists in the license to enter into sex associations "without the intervention of any functionary."

It is necessary that we listen not merely to high, but to the highest authorities within the socialist movement upon matters of such vital import to human welfare. Matters which are presented for political action to American citizens.

The work which forms the basis of the International Socialist Movement comes jointly from the pen of Marx and Engels. Upon these teachings socialism must stand or fall.

Frederick Engels, whose position on the family we shall present, is the father of the "materialist basis of history" from the socialist standpoint. He was the life long friend and co-worker of Karl Marx. From 1844 to the time of Marx's death, their work is so interwoven that one shares equal credit with the other. — They are known in socialist circles as the fathers of "modern scientific revolutionary socialism." Together Marx and Engels wrote the "Communistic Manifesto;" which socialists consider "the most important political document ever issued." It has a much larger international circulation than any other pamphlet socialists issue.

Engels edited the first English edition of "Capital." He also edited the second and third volumes of "*Das Kapital.*" Among his numerous publications are "Socialism, Utopian and Scientific," "The Condition of the Working Class in England in 1844," and "The Origin of the Family." This latter book was worked out from rough notes of Marx, after his death.

"The People" (New York, Jan. 12, 1900), referring to these men says:

"Among the men whom the conditions of the nineteenth century raised up as mouthpieces of the proletarian revolution, two stand pre-eminent — Karl Marx and Frederick Engels. Their lives were closely united from the beginning of their friendship in 1844 to the day of Marx's death in 1883.

They were so intimately connected in their activities that the work of the one can hardly be considered separately from that of the other."

"They sharpened the sword for us and taught us how to use it. Marx and Engels are the spiritual (a strange designation for atheist philosophers) leaders of the international proletariat.

"Their writings laid the scientific foundation upon which socialism is built. From their work proceeded the clear knowledge which divided the modern social democracy from the dreams of the Utopians." ("Frederick Engels, His Life, His Work and His Writings," Chicago, Ill., 1899).

In "Socialism, Utopian and Scientific" Engels lays down the boundaries within which socialist governmental functions will be confined. It counsels the free marital association between men and women, no intervention of Church or state. It would create, what socialists and anarchists term, a "free family." We ask your careful reading of the following quotation that you may see that free love is to reign triumphant within the socialist co-operative commonwealth.

"With the seizure of the means of production in the name of society . . . The interference of the state in social relations becomes superfluous in one domain after another, and falls of itself into desuetude. The place of a government over persons is taken by the administration of things and the conduct of the processes of production. The State is not 'abolished'— It Dies Out."

No state, for patriotism is "a curse!"
No family, for love is "free!"

From "The Roots of Socialist Philosophy," by Frederick Engels (1903) we take this:

"Feelings of affection between man and man, and particularly between members of the two sexes, have existed as long as mankind has. Love between the sexes has been cultivated especially during the last eighteen hundred years and has won a place which has made it, in this period, a compulsory motive for all poetry. The existing positive religions have limited themselves in this matter to the bestowal of complete consecration upon the State regulation of sexual love, and might completely disappear to-morrow without the least difference taking place in the matter of love and friendship."

What may this mean? "Is it but the knack for slippery writing which gives us a statement and a contradiction of it in the same paragraph? — During the Christian era love has won a higher place in the lives of men; because of the moral qualities — charity, justice, love, wisdom, faith and hope — taught and practiced by the religious. But for all the work — the long and devoted effort to elevate the race — the Church and the State might be broken down to-morrow "without the least difference taking place in the matter of love and friendship?" So say these materialist philosophers, when speaking plainly to the issue. Let us ask, is the environment which cultivated — which purified — human affection no longer necessary to support and advance it? Have human love and friendship climaxed at the top notch of perfection? Is there nothing left to strive for? With mere "sex fondness" as their only guide to conduct, would not men and women fall under its debasing standard? — If men do not go forward will they not move backward?

"Thou shalt love the Lord thy God with all thy heart — and thy neighbor as thyself. This is the Law. The husband and the wife are made one flesh — This is the Law, which has made itself felt during all these 18 hundred years. And it follows that personal and social obligation have hung like a millstone about the neck of the unfaithful. Were the knowledge darkened from the mind of man, perdition would catch each fleeing soul.

"We must insist, that from the beginning the Law is

Perfect — and we must further insist that human perfection is the nearer and yet nearer approach to the Perfect Law."

But let Engels speak?

"We must either despair of mankind, and its aims and efforts, when we see all our labor and toil result in such a mockery, or we must admit that human society has hitherto sought salvation in a false direction; we must admit that so total a reversal of the position of the sexes can have come to pass only because the sexes have been placed in a false position from the beginning." ("Condition of the Working Class in England in 1844.")

We must certainly despair of mankind if civilized nations fall into the socialist slough of despond.

"If the reign of the wife over the husband, as invariably brought about by the factory system, is inhuman, the pristine rule of the husband over the wife must have been inhuman too. If the wife can now base her supremacy upon the fact that she supplies the greater part, nay, the whole of the common possession, the necessary inference is that this community of possession is no true and rational one, since one member of the family boasts offensively of contributing the greater share. If the family of our present society is being thus dissolved, this dissolution merely shows that, at bottom, the binding tie of this family was not family affection, but private interest lurking under the cloak of pretended community of possession." ("Condition of the Working Class in England in 1844.")

But the family of "our present society" is not being thus dissolved, save that portion of it which falls under atheistical teachings, and succombs. To such the toil and labor of the atheist has resulted in a mockery — black as the devil. To declare that the religious effort to elevate the family relationship has proved a mockery is the result of a distorted vision — the inability of the "socialist mind" to see the advance which the race has made. Were socialists to understand the difference between the Perfect Law and the necessarily imperfect (because human) demonstration of it, many things, which now lie in darkness, would be revealed to their minds. — I pray their hearts may be opened to the light.

We shall enter into a somewhat extended examination of "the Origin of the Family," which may be correctly viewed as the joint production of Engels and Marx. Of this work Karl Kautsky has the following to say:

"In the summer of 1884 Engels published his work on the 'Origin of the Family, of Private Property and the State,' in which he carried out what Marx himself had planned. He gave to the public the investigations of Morgan, and at the same time enlarged upon them. Morgan, in his pre-historic studies, had arrived at the same materialistic conception of history which Marx and Engels had reached in their historical investigations. The orthodox knowledge of the time sought to suppress Morgan as they had previously tried to do with Marx. It was necessary not only to save him from threatened oblivion, but also to fill in the historical gaps in Morgan's investigations; to fit these into the frame of the Marx-Engels materialistic conception of history and to blend in one uniformly developed series the pre-historic and historic. Nothing less than this is accomplished in this book." ("Frederick Engels, His Work, and His Writings.")

All scientific socialists, writers and speakers, follow the lines laid down in this book. It is the criterion by which the truth or falsehood of socialist doctrine is made known.

The socialist publishers of this book say.

"This book, now for the first time offered to English readers, is one of the most notable works of the man who shares with Marx the honor of being the first to formulate the principles of modern Socialism. It is a work which no student of social science, whatever his opinions may be, can afford to overlook. It is moreover a powerful argument for Socialism, showing as it does how our present social forms have resulted inevitably from economic conditions, and how the changing conditions will as inevitably develop new forms based on common ownership of the means of production. To those who have at heart the emancipation of women this work of Engels will be a revelation, showing them at once the real causes of the wrongs now suffered by women and the one way of escape."

"The Appeal To Reason," in its "special religious edition" (Gerard, Kansas, Feb. 21, 1903), recommends the "Communist Manifesto" and "The Origin of the family" as text books from which to gain the understanding of the socialist position on marriage.

"This book has long since been translated into nearly every civilized language except English, and thousands of American readers will enjoy and profit by it as soon as it can be brought to their attention.

"For the student of social science "The Origin of the family" is of great importance because it gives in condensed form the actual results of the investigations of the last half century into the beginnings of the marriage relation. It is no mere grouping of facts, but the data are dealt with by a hand that can use them. Thus the book is as useful to the Socialist propagandist as to the student. Any reader who masters this work of Engels will be rid, once for all, of the complacent notion that things have always been as they are, and therefore must always remain so. He will also find himself better able to understand the complicated problem which must soon be faced of adjusting the relations of husband and wife, parent and child, to the radically different economic conditions which are near at hand." ("International Socialist Review," Chicago, Sept. 1902.)

The following endorsement is from "The Comrade" (New York, November, 1902).

"One of the most important issues of that excellent Standard Socialist Series is "The Origin of the Family," by

Frederick Engels, now for the first time translated into English by Ernest Untermann. This book, first published in 1884, has been translated into almost every European language and has long been regarded as one of the "classics" of Socialist philosophical literature. That it had not been heretofore accessible to English readers is surprising, and too much cannot be said in praise of the publishers who have supplied the movement with an admirable translation.

"It was, so Engels informs us, the intention of Marx himself to publish a work pointing out the importance and value of Morgan's investigations, and he left exhaustive critical notes prepared with that intent, so that in a manner this little work contains the blended efforts of those three intellectual giants, Morgan, Marx and Engels. There are the original researches of Morgan, the critical acumen of Marx and the added information of Engels upon the Celts and Germans. Need anything else be said to commend it to the reader?"

Next, we present the encomium of the "International Socialist Review" in the October number (1902). For we desire to make it clearly apparent that this book is of supreme authority in the socialist movement, as against any moral revolt that an individual here and there may have upon this subject.

"This book has long been known as one of the great socialist classics and has been translated into almost every other language than English. It is in many senses a supplement to Marx's Capital in that it begins at the very origin of things whose climax and latest developments are described in Capital.

"   .   .   .   .   The book is really one of the two or three great socialist classics and now that it is in English it must find a place in the library of every one who hopes to master the real fundamental philosophy underlying socialism."

We shall make "The Worker" speak for itself. Referring to Frederick Engels' "Origin of the Family" and another socialist classic it says, "These will be among the most important additions to the literature of Socialism in the English language since the translation of 'Capital.'" (July 13, 1903.)

This quotation was taken from the edition which appeared seven days before "The Worker" with blooming editorial audacity challenged the "Catholic Light" to cite one speech or written article in support of the declaration that socialism is an attack upon the home, the family and the church. Later on, October 12, 1902, "The Worker" again endorses the "Origin of the Family" by saying,

"An English translation of this great Socialist classic has long been needed and many Socialists will now for the first time have an opportunity to read and profit by it."

Still later, possibly forgetting its challenge to produce evidence on December 21st, 1902, "The Worker" publishes four columns of extracts from this book, beginning with the following statement.

"THE ORIGIN OF THE FAMILY, PRIVATE PROP-
ERTY AND THE STATE. By Frederick Engels.
Translated by Ernest Untermann. Chicago, Ill.

"Like 'Capital,' the 'Communist Manifesto,' and 'Socialism, Utopian and Scientific,' this book is one of the great classics of Socialist literature. It has already been translated into every other civilized language, and the translation into English is as necessary and valuable as it is belated.

"This work of Engels is based on the discoveries set forth in the 'Ancient Society' of the American, Lewis H. Morgan, which was published in 1877. Morgan had, to a certain extent, discovered for himself the materialistic conception of history originated by Marx and Engels. Marx had planned to write such a work as this one which his friend Engels completed after his death.

"The work is one which will be of absorbing interest to all students of social science who have not read it in the original, and the depth and keenness of the reasoning of Morgan, Engels and Marx combine to provide an intellectual feast for the student."

We now come to the "classic" itself. "The Origin of the Family."

SAVAGERY.

"1. Lower Stage. Infancy of the human race. Human beings still dwelt in their original habitation, in tropical or subtropical forests. They lived at least part of the time in trees, for only in this way they could escape the attacks of large beasts of prey and survive. Fruit, nuts and roots served as food. The formation of articulated speech is the principal result of this period. Not a single one of all the nations that have become known in historic times dates back to this primeval stage.

"Although the latter may extend over thousands of years, we have no means of proving its existence by direct evidence. But once the descent of man from the Animal Kingdom is acknowledged, the acceptance of this stage of transition becomes inevitable." (Pages 27 and 28.)

This is easy! What one don't know he may fancy he knows. But before one can take the first "scientific" step, at this point, he must plant his foot hard down upon his "living imagination." One must some how or other span the gap which "science" most confidently assumes the race to have passed. As this is the place for links, why not complete the chain by placing Heackel's "Sir Linkship, Pithecanthropus Erectus of Jarva" in the ditch, and so fill up the gap?

"Not a single one of all the nations that have become known in historic times dates back to this primeval stage." Certainly not, and this fact should teach "scientists," who are supposed to deal with knowledge, a little modesty in making assertions which are not supported with data in proof. Humanism as a deduction from animalism is all very well as a philosophy — as an intellectual toy, but as science it is no better than a brass monkey.

Taking the socialist philosophy as his basis one might with some show of reason conclude that the monkey is descended from the man. To be sure this has no better claim to science than the support of the newspapers which report

PROF. HAECKEL TO HAVE REVERSED THE THEORY OF DARWIN.

"Paris. — 'L'Autorité' says Professor Haeckel, the German scientist and professor at Jena University, while traveling in Java recently, in search of the missing link, discovered striking evidence that monkeys are descended from man, and not man from monkeys.

"Professor Haeckel, according to the paper, says that children, when lost in the forests, adopt monkey habits."

This is not so strange, for some men appear to be of close kin to monkeys, who are not lost in the woods.

Certainly, one must accept atheistic conclusions when once their materialistic premise is proven, but until such time as the "descent of man from the Animal Kingdom" shall have been proven it is the wise — not to mention the pious course, to stand by revelative knowledge which has never yet failed man as a faithful guide. Until the missing link is found socialist philosophy is a rope of sand — aye, it is more, a blasphemy against God.

In "Tactics of Infidels," which could as well be named tactics of socialists, the Rev. L. A. Lambert deals with the same take-it-for-granted basis.

"LAMBERT. When will the infidel understand that he is not the accepted judge of the nature of mature manhood? When will he understand that man began his career on this planet in mature manhood and not in infancy? When will he learn that the egotism of assuming that manhood is more mature at present than it was four thousand years ago is puerile nonsense or a miserable begging of the question? When will he learn that snarling at everything sacred, as a rabid cur snaps and snarls at straws, is no evidence of sense or manhood? In a word, when will he get into his skull that if his brains had never developed there would still be brains enough in the world to get along with? What has infidelity or scepticism ever done for the world of mankind? We look over the surface of the earth in vain, and through all time in vain, for any such evidences of its beneficent tracks. Its past leaves no monument to be honored; its present is destructive of morality, social order and liberty; its disciples are proud, self-conceited and egotistic; it pilfers the results of the labors of honest workers in the field of knowledge and the fruits of Christian enlightenment, and unblushingly parades these stolen properties as its own; it talks of love for mankind with lips white with hate; of mercy now, but when it had the power, as in the French revolution, it proved that it had it not; it talks of honor, when its principles leave no reason for its existence; of woman while it strips her of all real dignity and leaves her no more than a female animal; it talks of virtue, while in its code the word has no meaning. Spectre-like it moves down the ages with Christianity, gibing and gibbering as monkeys in the equatorial regions bar and interrupt the advances of the civilized explorer. It enjoys the fruits of Christian civilization as the barnacle or parasite enjoys the vigorous health of a stronger organism, or as a tubercle lives on the human lungs. It is an intellectual disease."

A logical deduction drawn from a false premise does not hold with a man of truly scientific mind. Your animalism-humanism having no proof behind it, is fairly termed false. While an analyzation of your minute deductions from which you build up your anti-monogamic conclusions is unnecessary.

We shall deal only with the vital points of socialist philosophy. Points which directly assail those fundamental principles and institutions which religious men — men of high mind, hold as the very corner-stone of civilization.

"Monogamy was the first form of the family not founded on natural, but on economic conditions, viz. : the victory of private property over primitive and natural collectivism." ("Origin of the Family," page 79.)

This is clearly in direct hostility to the revelative law. To declare that monogamy is not the natural form of the family is to deny that perfect design of the family which God created and to cast contempt upon religious truth. What higher form of marriage could be designed — all marriages are recorded in heaven ; and that which God hath joined together, let not man put asunder.

If socialists were to present a higher ideal, it certainly would be worthy of grave consideration. But the fact of the matter is, they present no form whatever ; their programme consists in the destruction of monogomy. The natural, inevitable form of the family if there is to be one. This perfect ideal form is imaged in the heart of every true man and pure woman, and it is not to be torn asunder by the vandal hand of irreligious, of unscientific philosophy.

Imagine the love scene in which you promise to be true to the love of your heart's desire until — well, perhaps the next moon.

Of course, if monogamy is the first form of the family founded upon unnatural conditions, one must conclude that the herding of men and women, the promiscuous, the punalunan, or the consanguin family was the natural form, founded upon natural conditions. But, having an *if* to start with, against which there is proof, one may drop this point from a scientific examination of this data.

That economic conditions and economic ambitions play a part in the make-up of many marriages is well known.

But that the monogamic family was founded upon property, as socialists assert, is quite a different proposition.

Socialists allege that the desire of man for "children that could be his offspring alone and were destined to be the heirs of his wealth" was the economic condition which introduced monogamy. No doubt many men have married for this reason. But what has that to do with the simple, patent fact that the natural family is one man, one woman and their child. Not the child of another man or woman, but these three persons that as a family are one. Whether the union of the man and the woman, which resulted in the establishment of the family, were from pure or from mixed or from impure motives, has nothing to do with the origin of the family. However greatly it have to do with the happiness of the family.

"Monogamy—does by no means enter history as a reconciliation of man and wife and still less as the highest form of marriage. On the contrary, it enters as the subjugation of one sex by the other, as the proclamation of an antagonism between the sexes unknown in all preceding history. In an old unpublished manuscript written by Marx and myself in 1846, I find the following passage: 'The first division of labor is that of man and wife in breeding children.' And to-day I may add: The first class antagonism appearing in history coincides with the development of the antagonism of man and wife in monogamy, and the first class oppression with that of the female by the male sex." ("Origin of the Family," page 79.)

You are right, "monogamy does not enter history as a reconciliation of man and wife." Monogamy enters history as the design of Almighty God in peopling the earth with his children. If the design be kept pure grace and happiness abound, but if the design be befouled

> "barren hate,
> Sour-ey'd disdain, and discord, shall bestrew

The union of your bed with weeds so loathly
That you shall hate it both: therefore take heed,
As Hymen's lamps shall light you."

And you are wrong, you cannot see by the foul light which blurs the lines between the time and care bestowed upon rearing children; and the work of producing wealth. One belongs to the purely human world and the other to the economic world. You are not only wrong but your philosophy is disgusting.

"The modern monogamous family is founded on the open or disguised domestic slavery of women, and modern society is a mass composed of molecules in the form of monogamous families. In the great majority of cases the man has to earn a living and to support his family, at least among the possessing classes. He thereby obtains a superior position that has no need of any legal special privilege. In the family, he is the bourgeois, the woman represents the proletariat. In the industrial world, however, the specific character of the economic oppression weighing on the proletariat appears in its sharpest outlines only after all special privileges of the capitalist class are abolished and the full legal equality of both classes is established. A democratic republic does not abolish the distinction between the two classes. On the contrary, it offers the battleground on which this distinction can be fought out. Likewise the peculiar character of man's rule over woman in the modern family, the necessity and the manner of accomplishing the real social equality of the two, will appear in broad daylight only then, when both of them will enjoy complete legal equality. It will then be seen that the emancipation of women is primarily dependent on the reintroduction of the whole female sex into the public industries. To accomplish this, the monogamous family must cease to be the industrial unit of society." (Origin of the Family," page 90.)

Your reasoning is too far fetched. It assumes the cause

of man's superior position in the home to be because the monogamic family is founded economically; the man being the bourgeois and the woman being the proletariat. This fallacy will appear in broad daylight when once the real equality of the sexes is understood. How, although equal, the innate quality, the positive structure of the man puts him naturally at the head of the family. And it always will, despite the big words which would make this gabble stand for science.

Were it not for the home work of the women it would be impossible for men to carry on the industries necessary to civilization. The work of men and women complements each other. Many a man who has arisen to a high station in life frankly owes his success to the power behind the throne. Upon the principle that the support of the throne is as powerful as the throne itself may history correctly be read. Then may one understand the equality of man and woman. Although being equal, the positive structure of the one and the negative structure of the other forms the contrast necessary to social activity.

After the regular dose of "scientific" balderdash, the socialist remedy is again put forward; destroy the monogamic family and "re-introduce the whole female sex into the public industries." It requires a "socialist mind" to make this appear possible, not to say desirable. One has but to study the cause of failure of the communistic colonies, to become acquainted with the fact that the familiarity of the sexes is the chief cause of their disruption. It would be well to take particular note of the sex experiences of the communities organized by socialist idealists. There may be found a miniature demonstration of the disintegration that would overtake the "free society" of the socialists' programme.

Turning to pages 85 and 86, "The Origin of the Family" proceeds.

"Civil matrimony in our day is of two kinds. In Catholic countries, the parents provide a fitting spouse for their

son as of old, and the natural consequence is the full development of the contradictions inherent to monogamy : voluptuous
hetaerism on the man's part, voluptuous adultery of the
woman. Probably the Catholic Church abolished divorce
for the simple reason that it had come to the conclusion,
there was as little help for adultery as for death. In Protestant countries, again, it is the custom to give the bourgeois
son more or less liberty in choosing his mate. Hence a certain degree of love may be at the bottom of such a marriage
and for the sake of propriety this is always assumed, quite in
keeping with Protestant hypocrisy. In this case hetaerism is
carried on less strenuously and adultery on the part of the
woman is not so frequent. But as human beings remain
under any form of marriage what they were before marrying,
and as the citizens of Protestant countries are mostly philis-
tines, this Protestant monogamy on the average of the best
cases confines itself to the community of a leaden ennui,
labelled wedded bliss. The best mirror of these two species
of marriage is the novel, the French novel for the Catholic,
the German novel for the Protestant brand. In both of these
novels they "get one another : " in the German novel the man
gets the girl, in the French novel the husband gets the horns.
It does not always go without saying which of the two deserves
the most pity. For this reason the tediousness of the German
novels is abhorred as much by the French bourgeois as the
"immorality" of the French novels by the German philistine. Of late, since Berlin became cosmopolitan, the German novel begins to treat somewhat timidly of the haeterism
and adultery that a long time ago became familiar features of
that city.

"In both cases the marriage is influenced by the class environment or the participants, and in this respect it always
remains conventional. This conventionalism often enough
results in the most pronounced prostitution — sometimes of
both parties, more commonly of the women. She is distin-

guished from a courtisane only in that she does not offer her body for money by the hour like a commodity, but sells it into slavery for once and all. Fourier's words hold good with respect to all conventional marriages: "As in grammar two negatives make one affirmative, so in matrimonial ethics, two prostitutions are considered as one virtue." Sexual love in man's relation to woman becomes and can become the rule among the oppressed classes alone, among the proletarians of our day — no matter whether this relation is officially sanctioned or not."

Is this a chapter from one of these "French novels"? No indeed, it takes the "socialist mind" to turn this indecent, this insulting matter with its false conclusion; and its last drop of deadly poison, into the greatest of great work — into "socialist science."

It is entirely clear to the careful student, who can see things above and things below, that the attitude of the Catholic Church upon marriage and divorce is the power which above all else has maintained the integrity of the family. If socialists were to pull down the blinds of prejudice and bitterness and pull open the blinds of religious enlightenment and faith, they would be enabled to see the purity of the psychological influence which this institution throws around the family. They would be better able to appreciate the progress made towards perfecting that unit (the monogamic family) which is the unit of the state. — Even with their vision which distorts all things, Socialists know very well that religion is the bulwark of the family and that the family is the bulwark of the state. Hence their simultaneous attack upon these three institutions.

We shall take from first hand sources a statement upon the family. Quoting from the doctrine of that world-wide faith; which numbers over 230,000,000 members; which for centuries has stood as an impregnable fortress in promotion of and in defence of the monogamic family, against which the attacks of men and of governments have beat in vain.

"Catholic Belief" by the Very Rev. Joseph Faá Di Bruno, D, D. bearing the Imprimatur of John Cardinal Mc-Closkey and Henricus Edwardes, Card. Archiep. Westmonast.

"Matrimony, or Marriage, is the conjugal union of a man and a woman who are naturally and legally fit to marry.

"It has been raised by Christ to the dignity of a sacrament, and is a bond to be dissolved only by death.

"The marriage state has many responsibilities, many difficulties to meet, many burdens to bear, and many temptations to overcome.

"It is the teaching of the Church that legitimate matrimony between baptized persons can never be a mere contract, but is also always a sacrament. Though not defined as a point of faith, it is more generally held that the ministers of this sacrament are the contracting parties themselves, when by word or outward signs they mutually accept each other as husband and wife.

"The words which the Priest pronounces upon the contracting parties — "I join you together in matrimony, in the name of the Father, and of the Son, and of the Holy Ghost," are only intended to acknowledge and solemnly ratify the sacred engagement just effected by the contracting parties. The other prayers which he recites afterwards serve to implore more abundant blessings upon the couple just married.

"Hence it follows that both parties ought to be in a state of grace when they contract the sacrament of marriage, for two reasons, 1st, because they themselves administer the sacrament, and 2ndly, because they receive the sacrament.

"As the union of Christ with the Church cannot be broken, so the bond between husband and wife is indissoluble. There is no cause that can justify, or power upon earth that can authorize the breaking of a legal and true marriage-bond between Christians after the marriage has been consummated.

"Separation, except by mutual consent, is forbidden. For grave reasons, it is sometimes permitted to the innocent party to live separately, but this separation would only im-improperly be called divorce, as in such case the marriage-bond is not broken, and neither party can marry again during the lifetime of the other ; if ever, therefore, the word divorce is used, it is understood to mean only *a separation from bed and board;* but *divorce*, properly and strictly so called, in the sense that a divorced person may re-marry during the lifetime of his or her respective partner, is forbidden by the Law of God : and there is no reason that can justify, or authority on earth that can sanction it.

"Society in general, and Catholics especially, ought to be most thankful to Jesus Christ for having established this inviolable sanctity of marriage, by which numberless scandals, family strife and miseries, are prevented, family happiness more universally secured, and the weaker sex and children greatly protected.

"If in some particular case this law may happen to be burdensome, especially to persons who have not been wanting either in prudence in the choice they made, or in justice and kindness towards their partners, this hardship to the few is small compared with the immense good derived from this law by society at large.

"The sufferer must not on account of his special grief revolt against God, but bear patiently this, like any other trouble, and adore the general dispensation of the Creator and Lord of nature.

We further supply some historic data from the pen of James Cardinal Gibbons in "The Faith of our Fathers : "

(Matrimony.)

"The Catholic Church, following the light of the Gospel, forbids a divorced man to enter into second espousals during the life of his former partner. This is the inflexible law she first proclaimed in the face of Pagan emperors and people, and which she has ever upheld, in spite of the passions and voluptuousness of her own rebellious children.

"Henry VIII., once an obedient son and defender of the Church, conceived, in an evil hour, a criminal attachment for Anne Boleyn, a lady of the queen's household, whom he desired to marry after being divorced from his lawful consort, Catherine of Aragon. But Pope Clement VII., whose sanction he solicited, sternly refused to ratify the separation, though the Pontiff could have easily foreseen that his determined action would involve the Church in persecution, and a whole nation in the unhappy schism of its ruler. Had the Pope acquiesced in the repudiation of Catherine, and in the marriage of Anne Boleyn, England would, indeed, have been spared to the Church, but the Church herself would have surrendered her peerless title of Mistress of Truth.

"When Napoleon I. repudiated his devoted wife, Josephine, and married Marie Louise, of Austria, so well assured was he of the fruitlessness of his attempt to obtain from the Holy See the sanction of his divorce and subsequent marriage, that he did not even consult the Holy Father on the subject.

"A few years previously, Napoleon appealed to Pius VII. to annul the marriage which his brother Jerome had contracted with Miss Patterson of Baltimore. The Pope sent the following reply to the Emperor; 'Your majesty will understand that upon the information thus far received by us, it is not in our power to pronounce a sentence of nullity. We cannot utter a judgment in opposition to the rules of the Church, and we could not, without laying aside those rules, decree the invalidity of a union which, according to the Word of God, no human power can sunder.'

"Christian wives and mothers, what gratitude you owe to the Catholic Church for the honorable position you now hold in society! If you are no longer regarded as the slave, but the equal of your husband; if you are no longer the toy of his caprice, and liable to be discarded at any moment, like the women of Turkey and the Mormon wives of Utah; but if you are recognized as the mistress and queen of your household, you owe your emancipation to the Church. You are especially indebted for your liberty to the Popes who rose up in all the majesty of their spiritual power to vindicate the rights of injured wives against the lustful tyranny of their husbands."

Kindly listen again to "the fathers of socialism." Marx and Engels have the following to say as to what may be anticipated about the re-adjustment of sexual relations after the downfall of capitalism:

"We are now approaching a social revolution, in which the old economic foundations of monogamy will disappear just as surely as those of its complement, prostitution. Monogamy arose through the concentration of considerable wealth in one hand — a man's hand — and from the endeavor to bequeath this wealth to the children of this man to the exclusion of all others. This necessitated monogamy on the woman's, but not on the man's part. Hence this monogamy of women in no way hindered open or secret polygamy of men. Now the impending social revolution will reduce this whole care of inheritance to a minimum by changing at least the overwhelming part of permanent and inheritable wealth — the means of production — into social property. Since monogamy was caused by economic conditions, will it disappear when these causes are abolished?" ("Origin of the Family," page 91.)

At this point the author would again ask, is not this evidence sufficient to show that the socialist party coming into the control of the political power of these United States would use that power to disrupt the family life of this great nation? This is a question which is most vitally answered at the ballot box.

Your question is *naïve!* And your logic is inferentially good. But since the word *since* is all the rock you have to stand upon, your promise is weak — it is as flabby as a dish rag.

"Since" monogamy was not caused by economic conditions it does not change with the change in economic conditions. And so consequently it will not be abolished however many economic causes (or results either) may be abolished by socialists or by anybody else. Being a Divine institution: having already withstood the change of the three great industrial epochs, it will last until the human race perish from off the face of the earth.

Of course it would be correct to say that we are approaching a social upheaval in which monogamy will disappear. That is to say, it would if the socialist parties gain control of the civic power throughout the civilized world and should socialist philosophy completely dominate men's minds — But God is not mocked!

The contempt in which marriage is held by socialists is displayed in the following low-lived statement, taken from "this social classic."

"And if strict monogamy is the height of virtue, then the palm belongs to the tapeworm that carries a complete male and female sexual apparatus in each of its 50 to 200 sections and passes its whole lifetime in fertilizing itself in every one of its sections." (Page 39.)

This is plain enough to be clearly understood by the most unlettered "proletarian." It were well for public safety that it were read to him as coming from the highest possible authority standing in the front rank of socialist literature:

"With the transformation of the means of production into collective property the monogamous family ceases to be the economic unit of society. The private household changes to a social industry. The care and education of children becomes a public matter. Society cares equally well for all children, legal or illegal. This removes the care about the 'consequences' which now forms the essential social factor—moral and economic — hindering a girl to surrender unconditionally to the beloved man. Will not this be sufficient cause for a gradual rise of a more unconventional intercourse of the sexes and a more lenient public opinion regarding virgin honor and female shame? And, finally, did we not see that in the modern word monogamy and prostitution, though antitheses, are inseparable and poles of the same social condition? Can prostitution disappear without engulfing at the same time monogamy?" ("Origin of the Family," pages 91–92.)

The cat is well out of the bag — not even the tip of her tail is concealed. Here is a clear statement of what may be expected as the practice of the socialist society relative to sex relation.

1st — When the capital of the country is owned by the people collectively the present form of the family ceases.

This is skilful, it shakes off the moral responsibility of abolishing the family by covertly denying moral responsibility.

2nd — The private household, the home, becomes a social industry (whatever that may mean). Being no families, communal relations take their place. That is to say, a " free family " will be in evidence. — No domestic love! No mother's love! No father's care!

3rd — Society will care for all children, "legal and illegal." "Legal" children evidently refers to the possibility of one pair of the human animals breeding more than one child. For the destruction of all law relating to the "administration of persons" having long since taken place, children cannot rightly be said to be legal or illegal. Marriage being sunken in the social cesspool, all the words of moral import will have passed into oblivion.

4th — Children will be fatherless — Possibly they may,

in years to come, be told who their mother was — but it is not likely.

5th — The "consequences" which a girl now encounters should she enter into illegitimate sex relationship will be abolished. Consequently sexual intercourse will be unconventional — like flies which cross themselves in the air.

6th — Virgin honor and female shame will gradually disappear and later become extinct phenomena, because of economic progress, you know.

7th — Monogamy and prostitution will disappear. For, say Engels and Marx, are they not the result of the same social conditions? Certainly not! You mistake the stage of enactment for the cause of the actions. Monogamy and prostitution are both in evidence within the present society. But one is caused by obedience to the law of God and the other is caused by disobedience to Divine law — socialist philosophy to the contrary notwithstanding.

8th — Then comes the negative of the question, put negatively, of course. Can prostitution disappear without engulfing monogamy? The meaning is, and it may be brought out in Yankee fashion by asking another question, Can monogamy disappear without engulfing the distinction which exists between it and prostitution? W. S. Lilly has given the correct answer, socialism "would abolish prostitution by making all women prostitutes. However, let us meet the question directly, Can prostitution disappear without engulfing monogomy? Yes! By the elevation of sexual desires, under the purifying influence and the self-discipline of religious environment; by the perfection of the family and by the sacrifice of sexual passion society may advance to that desirable stage— Socialist philosophy, not to say practice, is a stumbling block to this progress — with its specious arguments and its intoxicating idealism.

A "new element" — individualized "sex love" — is to be born, when once socialism prevails. In the place of marriage, which to hundreds of millions of men and women is a sacrament, this "new element" will come in. Instead of a "state of grace" being necessary, mere "sex fondness" will take its place in the sacred union.

"Here a new element becomes active, an element which at best existed only in the germ at the time when monogamy developed: individual sex love." ("Origin of the Family," page 92.)

"Hence the full freedom of marriage can become general only after all minor economic considerations, that still exert such a powerful influence on the choice of a mate for life, have been removed by the abolition of capitalistic production and of the property relations caused by it. Then no other motive will remain but mutual fondness." ("Origin of the Family," page 98.)

"Mutual fondness" will be the only motive for marriage — a very correct term to designate the socialist substitute for love of wife, of children and of home. "Mutual fondness" evolved from "economic determinism" will throw women upon the dirt heap, while men will wallow in the mire of sex degradation. Words which bring a stench to the nostrils alone suffice to paint the sea of corruption which the socialist philosophy, by the use of the political power, would launch our ship of state upon.

Socialists have nothing to offer but an excess of liberty — license. "License they mean when they cry liberty."

"What we may anticipate about the adjustment of sexual relations after the impending downfall of capitalist production is mainly of a negative nature and mostly confined to elements that will disappear. But what will be added? That will be decided after a new generation has come to maturity; a race of men who never in their lives have had any occasion for buying with money or other economic means of power the surrender of a woman; a race of women who have never had any occasion for surrendering to any man for any other reason but love, or for refusing to surrender to their lover from fear of economic consequences. Once such people are in the world, they will not give a moment's thought to what we to-day believe should be their course. They will follow their own practice and fashion their own public opinion about the individual practice of every person — only this and nothing more." ("Origin of the Family," page 109.)

This! from the book which "The Worker" says is "as necessary as it is belated" in the propagation of socialist doctrine. — And, too, while the ink of its challenge to Bishop Quigley to produce one word of evidence in socialist literature hostile to religion, is still wet on the page.

"However, those peculiarities that were stamped on the face of monogamy by its rise through property relations, will decidedly vanish, namely, the supremacy of men and the indissolubility of marriage. The supremacy of man in marriage is simply the consequence of his economic superiority and will fall with the abolition of the latter.

"The indissolubility of marriage is partly the consequence of economic conditions, under which monogamy arose, partly tradition from the time where the connection between this economic situation and monogamy, not yet clearly understood, was carried to extremes by religion. To-day, it has been perforated a thousand times. If marriage founded on love is alone moral, then it follows that marriage is moral only as long as love lasts. The duration of an attack of individual sex love varies considerably according to individual disposition, especially in men. A positive cessation of fondness or its replacement by a new passionate love makes a separation a blessing for both parties and for society. But humanity will be spared the useless wading through the mire of a divorce case." ("Origin of the Family," page 99.)

In a most flattering four column review of this book on Dec. 21, 1902, "The Worker" uses the above quotation in full. — One could easily have found these words against religion — for the advocacy of free love is most hostile to religious principles. — But we must set the brazen impudence of "The Worker" down to the score of socialist tactics,

Under socialism the indissolubility of marriage will vanish. — Indeed! this must be so, for under socialism marriage itself will be unknown.

Socialism postulates that marriage and divorce are both evolved by economic conditions. Except where monogamy has been "carried to extremes by religion." That is to say, socialists assert that the safeguarding of the family by religion has been an abnormal demonstration. We would submit this matter to the women of America; and we are sure that they would stand with good Queen Katherine.

With the negative twist given to logic "socialist minds" would show that ecclesiastical law must fall. For love, asserts religion, is the basis of marriage. Then to be moral, say these logicians, marriage should last only so long as love lasts. But the difference is as far as foul black is from pure white in the connotation of the word love. Religion would write lust where the socialist cult writes love. — How long will socialist love last? Why, until "sex fondness" has exhausted its force. "The duration of an attack of individual sex love varies considerably according to individual disposition." When the sex flame is burnt out "its replacement by a new passionate love makes a separation a blessing." Blessing? a strange word in the mouth of an atheist. A blessing comes by the grace of God. Not by the glare of sex flames. It would be more fitting were socialists to say that separation stimulates sex depravity, for it gives the next opportunity to indulge a new "sex love." Science will be unhindered by moral responsibility, for "humanity will be spared the useless wading through the mire of a divorce case." In place of American homes, this is given as the ideal socialist breeding farms.

FREE LOVE.

We shall conclude this chapter with quotations from Dr. A. Shäffle's book, "The Impossibility of Social Democracy." Dr. Shäffle, Austrian Minister of Finance, is the author of "The Quintessence of Socialism." Although this book is in opposition to socialism, it is circulated by them as of value to their propaganda, being a clear and concise statement of the socialist position. We educe this fact in proof that Dr. Shäffle has a thorough acquaintance with his subject.

"It is my opinion . . . . that the firm family bond between husbands and wives, parents and children, is not destined to destruction, but rather to a more perfect development: every loosening of the bond would tend only to the emancipation *of the man from the woman*, to the loss for the weaker sex of some of their strongest supports, to their abandonment by men, to a relapse into a Hetærism in the highest degree derogatory to feminine dignity. But if it is true that the stability of the family bond is so indispensable for the highest development of civilization, it follows that the great majority of women as a rule are not, or at least not primarily, suited to be productive laborers outside the walls of the home. They are and will remain wives and mothers, integral parts of a stable family unity, and will still have in the man their lawful head — with due limitations imposed by custom, by private law, by administrative, punitive and corporate justice — and their protector and representative as against the world without.

"The office of family life, namely, the propagation of the species, must be regarded from two sides — first, as it effects the whole nation through the renewal, increase, and improvement of the population, both quantitative and qualitative, and next as to what it means for the personal happiness of all individuals. The fundamental question, therefore, which Socialism raises is whether on the existing level of civilization the progress of family development is to follow the same lines as hitherto, whether this kind of progress is the best for the healthy movement of population and for the sum of individual happiness within the whole nation. According to the answer which is given to this question, will it be determined whether we are to agree with or to refuse and oppose certain extreme views as to the family which are held by various Social Democrats. By these extreme views I mean, first, the substitution for a stable marriage-tie of a system of temporary unions, whether terminable by notice or not binding at all, or Free Love in this sense, and secondly, the more or less complete substitution of State education for family education.

"If husband and wife belong to one another for life and have themselves to care for their own children, instead of forming fugitive unions and then delivering over the children to the national educational institute, there will be greater prudence exercised in contracting marriage.

"The 'reform' of the family in the direction of 'free love' and 'equal' State-education, has a significance not only for the preservation and renewal of population, but also, and this in a higher degree than almost any other question; for the *personal happiness of individuals*. Let us examine a little more closely on this side also the family life of Social Democracy, and first the main feature in it, namely, '*free love*.'

"What then would be the result upon the happiness of the people, if there were no longer any binding marriage-union, if marriage were to become a contract which could at any time be entered into or dissolved, and that was not in any sense binding? The great majority of the weaker sex lose the assurance of support of the stronger, and the adjustment of the inequality of the wage earning power between the sexes, which to-day is accomplished by the stable marriage union, would be lost, without the woman's being able to gain any more through her emancipation than she already posesses to-day through the man, or can earn by her own capacity.

An immense proportion of the happiness engendered by the love of husband and wife, parent and child, would be destroyed, and the true and purely human nobility of the office of propagation be lost; or at the very least, all this happiness would be constantly threatened and never in any degree secure.

"It is true we are told that things would for the most part remain as they are, and marriage unions would still for the most part remain constant: free love would only be called into play for the loosening of unhappy marriages. Then why not let the stable marriage-tie be the rule, with separation allowed in cases where the marriage-union has become morally and physically impossible? Why not have at least the existing marriage-law as among Protestants? But the whole statement, even if made in good faith, will not stand examination.

"What then is an 'unhappy' or relatively a 'happy' marriage? No one is perfect, and therefore, not a single marriage can ever hope to be entirely 'happy.' First love must always yield to the sober reality, after the cunning of nature has secured its end for the preservation of the species. In the indissoluble life-union of marriage, with the daily and hourly contact between the inevitable imperfections of both parties, there necessarily arise frictions and discords, which, if severance is free, will only easily give rise to the most ill-considered separations from the effect of momentary passion : and all the more readily if the one party have begun to grow at all tedious to the other, or pleasant to a third party. The very essential advantage of the stable marriage-tie is just this, that it secures the peaceful adjustment of numberless unavoidable disagreements, that it prevents the many sparrings and jarrings of private life from reaching the public eye, that it allows of openness on both sides, and avoids the possibility of pretence, that it induces self-denial for the sake of others, that it insures a greater proportion of mutuality in both spiritual and physical cares for the general run of wedded couples; in short, that for the majority of cases at least a relative possibility of wedded happiness is attainable. Therefore the indissoluble marriage-tie must still remain the rule, and separation the exception, confined to cases where its persistence becomes a moral impossibility. But it is clear that if once the emancipation of woman made it general for her to step out of the home into public life, and if once the bond of common love and common care for the offspring were loosened, or even weakened, frequent marriage changes would very easily become the rule, and permanent unions only the exception. The training in self-conquest, in gentleness, in consideration for others, in fairness, and in patience, which the present family and wedded relations entails, would also be lost in the entrance of all into public life outside the home. The gain to separate individuals in point of sensual gratification through fugitive unions, would be very far from outweighing the loss of the ideal good attainable by man, and by man only, through the channel of marriage.

"Neither would 'free love' be even sure to exterminate prostitution, although this has been claimed for it. Those individuals who were least in request, and even others, more favoured would be tempted, even with 'certificate money' of the popular State, to take and give payment for love not freely bestowed. But even free marriage, without any question of payment, might to a great extent, and probably would, cause the level of sensual intercourse to fall to the coarse sensuality of prostitution. It is therefore not possible to link the question of prostitution to the abolition of the stable marriage-tie.

"It is no less certain that existing marriage rights and married life are susceptible of further improvement, but this is not to say that the problem of their personal, moral, industrial and social amelioration will be solved by facilitating for every one the breaking of the marriage-tie; we may rather look to restoring, perfecting, and generalizing the external and moral conditions of the highest possible happiness in binding unions. This can be done without Social Democracy, and cannot be done with it. The new Hetærism of Free Love reduces man to a refined animal, Society to a refined herd, a superior race of dogs and apes, even though all should become productive labourers, and spend a few hours daily in manual labour. "

Homeless Children.

"Look how he laughs and stretches out his arms,
And opens wide his blue eyes upon thine,
To hail his father: while his little form
Flutters as wing'd with joy. Talk not of pain !
The childless cherubs well might envy thee
The pleasures of a parent."

BYRON.

THE children? Yes, there will be children under socialism, but they will be orphaned ! The community will
the father and mother of them all — the home will have been
absorbed by the "household industry": And the infants will
have been turned out to grass in the pasture of the nursery
farm. For it must be realized that when women are "free,"
domestic industry will have become a "social industry."

As a preparation for this great change from home, to
the social barracks and the infant farm, the children of to-day
are to be educated in the "Socialist Sunday School."

Since time began it has been recognized that the early
teachings set the seal to the future character of the man.
Hence the command, Honor thy father and mother in the
days of thy youth. Hence also the care with which religious
principles are instilled into the child's mind by devotedly
religious parents — Nothing is so important as this.

It is necessary, from the socialist point of view, to destroy the foundation upon which moral recognitions rests, in
order to prepare the mind for taking hold of socialist philosophy and practice. For the double purpose — first of preventing the children of socialists from receiving religious instruction on Sunday — as would be somewhat likely to happen —
and second, for the purpose of instilling the materialistic
doctrine of socialism into the children's minds, socialist Sunday schools are being organized throughout the world.

The socialist Sunday schools of Glasgow, Scotland, publish a monthly magazine called "The Young Socialist." This magazine is owned by the Glasgow Socialist Sunday-School Union, and it is gotten out in the interest of the socialist children of the country — and the English speaking world. This organization in ("Aims and Objects of the Socialist Sunday-School Movement" Glasgow and District, Scotland) thus sets forth its views.

"As the sea's tumult affects and moulds the pebbles on the shore, so current conceptions of Society affect the teaching and outlook of those not yet beyond the borders of life. The importance of capturing the child mind has been recognized by the Churches, and Sunday Schools are common all over the country. It is time that Socialists also realised the far reaching effects of early impressions on the youthful mind, and rallied to the work of organizing and spreading Socialist Sunday Schools. Such Schools have been started in various parts of the country. Their basis is unsectarian. The teaching given deals with the economic causes of present day social evils, while a love of goodness is implanted by all reasonable means. The object aimed at is to guide the child's mind and activities, so that the Socialist convictions may be built up naturally and firmly, that there may not be a great deal to unlearn in later life."

"Socialists should, in the interests of their children, take their full part in starting and supporting Schools for many reasons. Children are taught contrary to the wishes of Socialist parents at ordinary Sunday Schools, so cannot wisely be sent there. They learn comparatively little merely running about and, if taken to meetings of grown-up Socialists, the lectures are not suited to their years and knowledge. The only way out is to encourage, by all means, the growth of Socialist Sunday Schools."

Because "children are taught contrary to the wishes of Socialist parents at the ordinary Sunday schools"! Therefore the Socialist Sunday school must be organized. " Their basis is unsectarian."

This position, to a superficial mind may seem entirely fair. But in reality it is the assumption of a superior position Schools devoted merely to the teaching of the three R's may truly be said to be unsectarian in character. But when a school enters the departments of philosophy, history, ethics and morals it must take a position either for or against religious revelation. No half-way house can be found, for the weaklings to rest within, between the two schools of philosophy, which are as old as the hills.

It is innocent, to say the least, to parade as unsectarian, that Sunday school whose avowed purpose is to pour into children's minds, in diluted doses, the " class conscious socialist doctrine." The "Socialist Sunday School" is a strictly sectarian organization. It is an atheist Sunday school, and nothing but the atheistic doctrine may properly be taught there.

The socialists of many cities in this country, taking pattern after their " comrades " across the water have been busily engaged in starting socialist Sunday schools. They have been especially active during the past two years. Several of the weekly socialist papers have what is known as a children's column, for spreading this work.

The chief center for the socialist Sunday school in this country is located in Chicago. A series of " Socialist Sunday School Lessons," by May Wood Simons — the American leader of the children's movement — is being published in "The Chicago Socialist," official organ of the Socialist Party. The objects are stated as follows :

"The Socialist school has two ends or objects to accomplish — first to familiarize the children with the ideas of Socialism — second to train in them the power to think. In short in this last thing the Socialist school must attempt to accomplish for the working man's children what the public schools are doing so imperfectly, enable them to become independent thinking personalities.

"We should recognize that the work of a teacher must be that of an interpreter, of a mediator who stands between the child and the environment and who because of his knowledge of society, past, present and future and of nature, is able to interpret the environment to the child." "Chicago Socialist," July 4th, 1903.

The July 11th lesson is on the "Inorganic and Organic Worlds." The teachers are instructed to inform the children that "each living thing is a product of past environments the first but becomes a part of the second."

Here we find the socialist key with which to unlock their atheistic Sunday school door. The school through whose agency the child is to be taught that he owes his existence to past environment, that he has been evolved from what Engels calls his "fish ancestors." That probably the pithecanthropus erectus was his first upright forefather. Hence his environment — not he — is responsible for his character. Hence, also — some day — a long way off — when "economic determinism" shall have forced into the hands of the working class the tools of production there will be evolved a "Social will," which will be "free." Then and not until then will the individual man be morally responsible for his own acts. For it must be remembered that to the socialist mind no God exists; Who fashioned with His Almighty hand every living thing after His own Perfect Design — Who crowned all His wondrous creation with that noblest creation, man. — God is a myth which must fade away under the scientific teaching of socialism. There is no command upon the socialist Sunday school scholars to love God — to honor and obey their parents — no command to walk humbly before God and to keep His laws.

We here present the first lesson of the socialist Sunday school in contrast with the first part of the lesson "on the end of man " from the catechism. One teaches that free will is to be evolved by a socialist environment; the other, that God endowed man with free will from the beginning.

THE NATURE OF LIFE.

Lesson one.

1. The extent of scientific knowledge of the origin of life.

2. In the lowest forms of life it is difficult to distinguish between plant and animal. For example we read in biology of one of these simplest forms of life called meridion circulare which examined under a powerful microscope is seen to multiply by dividing itself; each part developing into a new individual.

3. Lowest form of life consists of one cell, hence because it is made up of a single physiological cell it is called unicellular.

In animal life these unicellular organisms are called protozoa, in plant life they are known as protophyta. As far as unicellular organisms are concerned whatever is true of the growth and development of protozoa is true of protophyta.

4. A protozoon like cells in general has a nucleus and it multiplies by a process of discontinuous growth; that is the cells divide and the separate parts start as distinct physiological units.

5. A gradual differentiation takes place and multicellular organisms appear called in animal life metazoa, in plant life metaphyta.

6. Multicellular organisms consist of a plurality of physiological cells modified to subserve different functions in the economy of the plant or animal.

Central thought — Life means change — change of environment into things to support life." ("The Chicago Socialist," July 4th, 1903.)

LESSON FIRST.

Q. WHO MADE THE WORLD?

A. God made the world.

Q. WHO IS GOD?

A. God is the Creator of heaven and earth, and of all things.

Q. WHAT IS MAN?

A. Man is a creature composed of body and soul, and made to the image and likeness of God.

Q. IS THIS LIKENESS IN THE BODY OR IN THE SOUL?

A. This likeness is chiefly in the soul.

Q. HOW IS THE SOUL LIKE TO GOD?

A. The soul is like God because it is a spirit that will never die, and has understanding and free will.

Q. WHY DID GOD MAKE YOU?

A. God made me to know Him, to love Him, and to serve Him in this world, and to be happy with Him for ever in the next.

Q. OF WHICH MUST WE TAKE MORE CARE, OUR SOUL OR OUR BODY?

A. We must take more care of our soul than of our body.

Q. WHY MUST WE TAKE MORE CARE OF OUR SOUL THAN OF OUR BODY?

A. We must take more care of our soul than of our body, because in losing our soul we lose God and everlasting happiness.

Q. WHAT MUST WE DO TO SAVE OUR SOULS?

A. To save our souls we must worship God by faith, hope, and charity; that is, we must believe in Him, hope in Him, and love Him with all our heart."

These lessons forcefully exemplify the opposite teachings of socialism and the church. We leave them to the judgment of mothers and fathers who are responsible for the teaching given to their children. Asking this question, as you must take your choice, which do you think is conducive to the best interest of the children? The one leads them into disregard for religion and morals; into free love ideals and practices: the other to the love of God, and the fear of disobedience to His moral precepts; to the recognition of the sacredness of marriage.

At the convention of the National Educational Association, held in Boston, July, 1903, the foremost subject under discussion by the 35,000 teachers assembled was the "necessity of increasing the moral power of the schools." Not only the teachers of the public schools and the professors of our colleges, but also the general public, are realizing more and more, as the years go by, that the "formation of character," "The development of the will" (Topics discussed at this convention) cannot be advanced by mere pedagogy. This national issue does not alarm the socialists. They see in this fact a satisfactory evidence that their materialist philosophy is filtering down into the minds of the youth; which makes them ready converts to the socialist party. Therefore socialists are not seeking a remedy for this laxity of morals and degeneracy of the will. — They are putting forward the "Socialist Sunday School" to promote that which even the general public are beginning to deplore. They would augment these tendencies with the study of atheistic philosophy — with the theory that the "class struggle" moulds the characters of men.

In an interview with the "Boston Post," January, 1903, the socialist party member of Brockton, Mass., school committee gives her opinion (in correct line with socialist teachings) that children should be taught the "class struggle;" that socialist books should be introduced into the schools as text books. In a word, with the school boards under social-ist control, the children are to be taught that the industrial con-flict between the capitalist and the working class is "irrecon-cilable." That they must with the " spirit of class conscious-ness " (which generally leads to class hatred) oppose the capitalist class and overthrow them, thereby revolutionizing the existing social order. While socialists hold out dazzling but vague ideals of ease and plenty as the fact of future en-vironment — their teachings as to the design is nil. Their writings commonly end with the confession that a constructive programme is lacking. The following, from Engels, is a good example of their style. After tearing down the religious institution of the family he goes on to say : " What we may anticipate about the adjustment of sexual relations after the impending downfall of capitalist production is mainly of a negative nature and mostly confined to elements that will dis-appear." ("Origin of the Family," page 100.)

August Babel, the German leader of international social-ism, with the ambition to introduce teachings along the lines which the socialist sunday school lessons are now following, issues the following condemnatory statement on the subject of education :

"Thus we find modern society as helpless with regard to the question of education and training as with regard to all other social questions. What are its resources? It calls for the stick and beats, preaches religion in every shape, and founds reformatories regulated by a religious spirit to receive the worst elements. Having done this, its pedagogic wisdom is at an end." ("Woman in the Past, Present and Future.")

This shows that there are no places in which religious or moral teachings prevail but socialists would enter to de-stroy. Are these seducers of sex virtue to be trusted with the teaching of the children?

Mothers and fathers now listen to what socialists think fit training in virtue for your children! We quote from

Edward Carpenter's "Love's Coming of Age," (Chicago, Ill., 1903). This book is recommended by the leader of the socialist sunday schools in her publications.

"Each youth or girl should personally see enough of the other sex, at an early period, to be able to form some kind of judgment of his or her relation to that sex and to sex-matters generally.

". . . . the doing away with the absurd superstition that because Corydon and Phyllis happen to kiss each other sitting on a gate, therefore they must live together all their lives, would soon mend matters considerably. Nor would a reasonable familiarity of this kind between the sexes in youth necessarily mean an increase of casual or clandestine sex-relations. But even if casualties did occur they would not be the fatal and unpardonable sins that they now — at least for girls — are considered to be. Though the recognition of anything like common prematrimonial sex-intercourse would probably be foreign to the temper of a northern nation; yet it is open to question whether society here, in its mortal and fetichistic dread of the thing, has not, by keeping the young of both sexes in ignorance and darkness and seclusion from each other, created worse ills and suffering than it has prevented, and whether, by giving sexual acts so feverish an importance, it has not intensified the particular evil that it dreaded, rather than abated it." (Page 100).

"In both man and woman . . . . we find a distinct tendency towards the formation of this double unit of wedded life (I hardly like to use the word monogamy on account of its sad associations) — and while we do not want to stamp such natural unions with any false irrevocability or dogmatic exclusiveness, what we do want is a recognition today of the tendency to their formation as a natural fact, independent of any artificial laws.

"It might not be so very difficult to get quite young people to understand this — to understand that even though they may have to contend with some superfluity of passion in early years, yet that the most deeply-rooted desire within them will probably in the end point to a permanent union with one mate; and that towards the end they must be prepared to use self-control against the aimless straying of their passions, and patience and tenderness towards the realization of the union when its time comes. Probably most youths and girls, at the age of romance, would easily appreciate this position; and it would bring to them a much more effective and natural idea of the sacredness of marriage than they ever get from the artificial thunder of the Church and the State on the subject." (Page 97).

Comment seems hardly necessary when the issue is so clear between virtue and vice. So clear before one's view is the parting of the ways — one towards happiness and holiness — the other towards misery and corruption. Which would you choose, mothers and fathers of this great nation, that your children be given the knowledge of chaste conduct to meet temptation when the high blood of youth is set in motion by sex attraction? Or the let-alone-policy which relies upon familiarity of the sexes at an early age to inform them as to fitting sex conduct? Please to remember that under socialism there will be no religious instruction to give them at once high idealism and self discipline. Will you rely upon "sex fondness" and free intercourse to give your girls and boys the opinion that a "permanent union with one mate" is desirable, although behind it a dozen broken fancies with casualties may live to haunt that "permanent union" with their consequences?

But let us leave the teachings and practices for children and ask the Declaration of Independence to kindly step one side while we introduce "The greatest political document ever issued," "The Communist Manifesto." It speaks authoritatively on all socialist questions. It is not so difficult, to those who understand its negative tongue, to gather its meaning.

"Do you charge us with wanting to stop the exploitation of children by their parents? To this crime we plead guilty.

"But, you will say, we destroy the most hallowed of relations, when we replace home education by social.

"The bourgeois clap-trap about the family and education, about the hallowed co-relation of parent and child become all the more disgusting, as, by the action of modern industry, all family ties among the proletarians are torn asunder, and their children transformed into simple articles of commerce and instruments of labor." ("Communist Manifesto.")

The socialist method of reasoning is not to prove its own case, but to throw off the scent by exaggerating existing evils, to the end of developing "socialist minds." Here we find the holy relationship of parents and children called "bourgeois clap-trap." Here also the "socialist mind" is made to see things out of proportion.

It is true that some parents have through greed, drunkenness or irreligion "exploited their children." But is this the rule? Have the great mass of mothers and fathers lost their love for their children or their sense of obligation to them? Certainly not! The sacrifice and devotion of parents, high and low, shame your ill conclusions. It is too true, one of the crimes of modern industry is that it employs thousands of children in the mines, the mills and factories, who ought to be at school under mental and moral training. And it is too true that parents as well as employers are ready to sacrifice their children to the greed of Moloch. But your conclusions that "all" family ties are thus torn asunder among the "proletarians" is a far stretched falsity of socialist reasoning, of which a German friend once said "it rymes vel aber it dond reason."

But what remedy do you socialists offer to "stop the exploiting of children by their parents?" Why, you would put them into the factory for educating community children. You would deprive them of their natural association, of the care of father and mother. You would replace — no ! you cannot "replace home education," you would substitute "social education" for the home training. Fathers and mothers would do better to throw their children to the protection of the wolves, than to place them in the hands of " an administration of things," which seeks to convert the home into a "social industry."

The "manifesto" declares for "the abolition of all right of inheritance." This is good evidence that socialists aim to break down all traces of family life. H. M. Hyndman, who follows the "manifesto" style of reasoning, says that "Marriage for life and responsibility of the parents for the children born in wedlock, is almost at an end even now . . . and must result in a widely extended communism." (Historical Basis of Socialism, page 453.)

This international leader of socialism has lost his perspective. He sees the coming of his ideal rather than the fact. For responsibility of parents is not coming to an end, unless the race is coming to an end — were socialists universally elected to the seats of power the doom of the race might well be sealed.

"Property in children would cease to exist, and every infant that came into the world would be born into full citizenship, and would enjoy all the advantages, whatever the conduct of its parents might be." (Morris and Bax, page 298, "Socialism, its Growth and Outcome.")

What clap-trap is this? How may infants be born into citizenship? Citizenship implies manhood — not the immature state of childhood. It implies rights and the power to enforce one's rights. How may infants lodged in the "household industry " protect their rights of socialist citizenship? The child's rights as a member of civil society are necessarily recognized and also protected by its parents or guardians — or by the foundling society — until such time as it shall have attained its majority. And until it shall have arrived at the age where its five senses shall perfectly co-ordinate, it may not be said to reason as to its rights or duties — it is in the care and power of its parents. Big talk which has a pleasing sound but no sense is a specialty with socialist philosophy. — God protect us from the "household industry" and the "full citizenship," which socialism would thrust children into. I am confident that the poorest of mothers under this "capitalist system" would prefer their scanty home with the control of their infants to the seductive offers of "full citizenship" for infants.

Woman will be "entirely free" under socialism, "her household and children, . . . cannot restrict her freedom." Certainly not, she will have no home and her children will belong to the community.

"The compulsory marriage is the normal marriage in bourgeois society, the only 'moral' union of the sexes, and every other sexual union is, from this point of view, under all circumstances, immoral. This is quite consistent. The bourgeois marriage is a consequence of bourgeois property. This marriage standing as it does in the most intimate connection to property and the right of inheritance, demands 'legitimate' children as heirs; it is entered into for the purpose of obtaining them, and the pressure exercised by society has enabled the ruling classes to enforce it in the case of those who have nothing to bequeath.

"But as in the new community there will be nothing to bequeath, unless we choose to regard household furniture as a legacy of any importance, compulsory marriage becomes unnecessary from this standpoint as well as from all others. This also settles the question of the right of inheritance which socialism will have no need to abolish formally.

"Woman is, therefore, entirely free, and her household and children, if she has any, cannot restrict her freedom, but only increase her pleasure in life." ("Woman," Babel.)

It will be noted that Babel, true to the dogma of socialism, opposes the right of inheritance. In the name of liberty, socialists wishing to pull down, and trample under foot, every essential mark of family life, would prevent the exercise of this most natural — one may say divine right — of inheritance. For it is past reason that the community has a natural, a moral right to enter the home of the individual, to take from him the wealth which is designed as a legacy to his issue.

Socialism has no moral vision — no spiritual insight — therefore it has only to consider economic causes. Economic action caused marriage, and further economic action will undo marriage. Socialists declare "Monogamy arose through the concentration of considerable wealth in one hand — a man's hand — and from the endeavor to bequeath this wealth to the children of this man to the exclusion of all others. . . . . Now, the impending social revolution will reduce this whole care of inheritance to a minimum." ("Origin of the Family.") It is very simple to the socialist mind, to abolish the right of inheritance. But as the exercise of this right lies securely at the base of society it is safe to say that while men may be sporadically prevented from leaving their property to their children, this inherent right can never be abolished.

In this case as in all others socialist philosophy covers over the infamy of its proposals by an appeal to economic evolution, to "science."

"With the transformation of the means of production into collective property the monogamous family ceases to be the economic unit of society. The private household becomes a social industry. Care and education of the children becomes a public matter. Society cares equally well for all children, legal or illegal." ("Origin of the Family," page 91.)

In further comment upon socialist infringement of human rights, to the lovers of true liberty; to the lovers of home; to those conscious of rights and duties towards children; to those who love their country we commend the following simple and yet powerful declaration of Leo XIII.

THE STATE MAY NOT ABOLISH NOR ABSORB PATERNAL RIGHTS.

"The idea, then, that the civil government should, at its own discretion, penetrate and pervade the family and the household, is a great and pernicious mistake. True, if a family finds itself in great difficulty, utterly friendless, and without prospect of help, it is right that extreme necessity be met by public aid; for each family is a part of the commonwealth. In like manner, if within the walls of the household there occur grave disturbance of mutual rights, the public power must interfere to force each party to give the other what is due; for this is not to rob citizens of their rights, but justly and properly to safeguard and strengthen them. But the rulers of the State must go no further: nature bids them stop here. Paternal authority can neither be abolished by the State nor absorbed; for it has the same source as human life itself; "the child belongs to the father," and is, as it were, the continuation of the father's personality; and, to speak with strictness, the child takes its place in civil society not in its own right, but in its quality as a member of the family in which it is begotten. And it is for the very reason that "the child belongs to the father," that, as St. Thomas of Aquin says, "before it attains the use of free-will, it is in the power and care of its parents." The Socialists, therefore, in setting aside the parent and introducing the providence of the State, act *against natural justice,* and threaten the very existence of family life." Encyclical letter on "The Condition of Labor."

Under such a regime of desolation as socialism presents either mothers would pine and die for the want of their children or the love of mothers for their children must come to an end. Or shall one paint the revolting scene where socialist females are so wrapped up in pluming their feathers for the changing sex pleasures that children will be gladly passed over to the "social industry."—As did Rousseau, one after another, pass over his five illegitimate children to the Foundlings' Hospital. Yes, "sex fondness" may breed children like rabbits, for they may be thrown upon the "social industry" for motherly affection and fatherly care.

William Morris has pictorially portrayed the ideal woman under "the collective ownership of the means of production and distribution."

In "News From Nowhere," Clara, the socialist mother, "got it into her head that she was in love with someone else." Giving her children to the care of her friend Hammond (I fail to see how they escaped the social industry) left Dick to live with her new sex partner. After a year had gone by, and this flame burnt out, she took it into her head to return to Dick, her one true love. Morris does not inform us whether she had a child while she was away. But, no matter, what difference would it make in the "new society" if a woman were to have half a dozen children by as many fathers so long as she is "free?"

In "The Comrade," New York, March, 1903, the editor in reviewing John Graham Brooks' latest publication "The Social Unrest" says,

"On page 273 our author says: "It is true that many artists call themselves Socialists in their hot reaction against this same commercial tyranny; but I have rarely seen one who was not in his ideal, anarchist, like William Morris, and not properly Socialist." This absurd view of Morris is so utterly unwarranted that its longevity is surprising. No less surprising is it to find one so clever as Mr. Brooks repeating it. The spirit and purpose of Morris were far from anarchism. A brief illusion as to "non-parliamentary methods of conquest" does not make a man an anarchist. I will not now attempt to convince Mr. Brooks of the absurdity of his estimate of Morris by extensive citation, though that were easy. Upon another page will be found a hitherto unpublished letter which, I venture to think, ought to convince Mr. Brooks that, "in his ideal," Morris was far from anything like anarchism."

We give the letter referred to; which very conclusively proves the contention both of Mr. Brooks and of the editor of "The Comrade." As regards their attitude upon sex and family relationship socialism and anarchism are as like as two peas.

"This letter, now for the first time published, has been placed at our disposal by Mrs. Sharman to whose husband, the late Rev. William Sharman of Preston, England, it was written sometime in 1886-87. Mr. Sharman was a Unitarian minister and he and Mrs. Sharman were among the earliest members of the old Socialist League. (Editor.)"

"*My dear Sharman:* I believe I shall be about on the 28th. I shall be pleased to see you at my house if you can come; but let me have notice. As to the matter of education, it is after all a difficult one to settle, until people's ideas of the family are much changed; but in the meantime here is the problem: How is it possible to protect the immature citizen from the whims of his parents? Are they to be left free to starve his body or warp his mind by all sorts of nonsense, if not, how are they to be restrained? You see that one supposes in a reasonable community that experience will have taught the community some wisdom in such matters; but the parents may, and probably will, lack this experience. Well, then, hasn't the young citizen a right to claim his share of the advantages which the community have evolved? Must he be under the tyranny of two accidental persons? At present the law says yes, which means that the young citizen is the property of the two accidental persons.

"Putting myself in the position of the immature citizen, I protest against this unfairness. As for myself, being the

234

child of rich persons, it did not weigh heavily on me, because my parents did as all right people do, shook off the responsibility of my education as soon as they could; handing me over first to nurses, them to grooms and gardeners, and then to a school — a boy farm I should say. In one way or another I learned chiefly one thing from all these — rebellion, to wit. That was good; but, look you, if my parents had been poorer and had had more character they would have probably committed the fatal mistake of trying to educate me. I have seen the sad effects of this with the children of some of my friends.

"On the whole, experience has shown me that the parents are the *un*fittest persons to educate a child; and I entirely deny their right to do so, because that would interfere with the right of the child as a member of the community from its birth to enjoy all the advantages which the community can give it. Of course, so far as grown people are concerned I quite agree with your view of complete freedom to teach anything that any one will listen to. But for children I feel that they have as much need for the revolution as the proletarians have. As to the woman matter, I do not think Bax puts it unreasonably in his article [an article had appeared in the *Commonweal*, Morris' paper, to which Mr. Sharman had taken exception], though I have heard him exaggerate that in talk and have often fallen foul of him. By the way, you must try to write something for us. Let me know what you think of it.

"Mind you, I don't think this change in the family (or in religion) can be done by *force*. It is a matter of opinion and must come of the opinion of people free economically. I rely on the stomach for bringing it about.

"Yours fraternally,

"William Morris."

The editor of "The Comrade" after rummaging among

the socialist archæological excavations brings forth this piece
of Morris art; in which is pictured the socialist-anarchist
ideal of parental relation (or rather non-relation) to children.
But surely he fails to show in what respect it differs from the
well known position of anarchism on this point.

This letter clearly questions the right of parents (whom
Morris perhaps with the license of "art" terms "two accidental persons") to educate their children. It is correct socialism — it is correct anarchism and it is correct atheism to
deny to fathers and mothers their God given rights — however the petty detail of their doctrines may differ. The sad
result of Morris' parents' method of farming him out to nurses,
grooms and gardeners may have grown in him the noxious
weeds of socialist free love doctrine. If so, parents are
thereby very clearly demonstrated to be the fittest persons to
educate their own children. Surely Morris was not an anarchist of the bomb using variety, he stood with the Social
Democratic Federation of England, for the control of political
power — the modern method of masquerading atheism. In
the last paragraph of this letter he says: "Mind you, I don't
think this change in the family (or in religion) can be done
by *force*. It is a matter of opinion and must come of the
opinion of people free economically. I rely on the stomach
for bringing it about."

Here we have mere animality as the basis for progress
towards the socialist regime. This is well — for when the
perfection of the animal man is clearly seen to be the be all
and end all of socialism, it will become sharply distinct from
that desirable human progress which leads ever on to the
purer air of human sensation, of human recognition, of human aspiration.

The stomach placed above God was the cause of the
pagan degeneracy of Rome.—The importance of the stomach,
minus religion, family life and love of children, with socialism full fledged into communal governments will send men

and women with plentiful stomachs to wallow in the slime and slush of sex degeneracy.

William Thurston Brown, in "The Socialist Spirit" (May, 1902), exclaims with spirit:

"Where is there a minister in good standing to-day who has a faith at all comparable with that of William Morris?"

I myself know those who have faith above that which appeals to the stomach to move the race towards more equitable modes of industrial relationship, but they are in "good standing." If, however, there be one so irreligious as to believe that the monogamic family should be abolished; that "parents are the unfittest to educate children"; that it is wise to place them in the social industry, his place is by the side of the Rev. Mr. Brown in the socialist movement, and very soon he will fall out of "good standing" — very properly so.

With the assumption that "reason" in religion is an unusual quality and quantity, Bax augments the teachings of Marx, Engels and Morris with the following plea for "Reason" to be forcefully taught in place of religion; that is to say, parents should not be allowed to control the religious education of their children. With the increasing political power socialists are becoming bolder, they have been waxing hot and hotter over the question of "liberty of conscience," and with "the fathers" the lesser lights are agreed that "the vampire, bourgeois liberty of concience, must — be impaled, before true liberty of conscience can become a healthy living reality."

"Liberty of conscience" is, again, another of the glib phrases so neatly rolled off the tongue, and which are supposed to crush an opponent against whom they are invoked by their mere intrinsic weight. This, too, as employed by the ordinary Freethinker and Radical, is often but a vampire, a semblance of a reality which has ceased to be. The typical British "Freethinker" would regard with horror, as a violation of that sacred idol "liberty of conscience," any attempt under any circumstances to prevent the infusion into minds incapable of judgment of doctrines which he would admit to be injurious morally and perhaps even physically. His sheet-anchor is argument and reasonable persuasion. But let us take a case. A child or person, intellectually incapable either naturally or through ignorance, or both, comes under the influence of the Salvation Army or the worst kind of Catholic priest, it matters not which, is terrified by threats of the wrath of God into "conversion," becomes the slave of General Booth or the "Church," is warped morally and mentally for life, and in the worst case possibly driven to religious mania. There's the result of liberty of conscience. The *bourgeois* Freethinker, hide-bound in this abstraction, is quite sure of the fact that, though the form of liberty is there, it does but enshrine the reality of slavery; that it is a liberty to deprive others of liberty. It would be intolerance, forsooth, to suppress the Salvation Army, he will tell you; liberty of conscience demands that the Salvation Army and every other body or individual shall have the privilege of enslaving the minds of the young or the ignorant of threats or cajolery, of fooling them to the top of their bent. Against this the only weapon he permits himself is argument or persuasion. He forgets that argument is only a reliable weapon when employed against argument, *i. e.*, against a doctrine avowedly based on reason, and against one which makes its appeal, not to reason, but to faith, fear and ignorance, argumentative persuasion must be a broken reed. The freedom to hold and propound any proposition, however absurd, as a theory to be judged of, and accepted or rejected at the bar of Reason, is quite another thing from the liberty of the "hot gospeller," who claims to hold a speculative pistol to the ear of ignorant and weak-minded people by threatening them with damnation if they reject his teaching. The one is of the essence of real liberty, the other is the vampire of a dead liberty of conscience which was only living and real when it was opposed to the positive power of the representatives of dogmas over men's persons and lives. As Gabriel Deville (a leading French Socialist) well puts it, "The aim of collectivity is to assume liberty to each, understanding by this the means of self-development and action, since there can be no liberty where there is the material or moral incapacity of consciously exercising the faculty of will . . . to permit by religious practices the cerebral deformation of children is in reality a monstrous violation of liberty of conscience, which can only become effective after the proscription of what at present passes muster for religious liberty, the odious licence in favor of some to the detriment of all. The vampire, *bourgeois* liberty of conscience, must in short be impaled, before true liberty of conscience can become a healthy living reality." ("The Religion of Socialism." "Some Bourgeois Idols, or Ideals, Reals, and Shams." Ernest Belfort Bax. Pages 113, 114, 115.)

You know, the little boy said the Puritans came to this country to worship God as they pleased and to make everybody else do the same — It is only a question of power whether socialists who fail to worship God "compel everybody else to do the same." Any sort of tactics that will gain adherents and win votes — then the deluge.

As the last testimony from socialists as to their opinion on the question relative to children we shall again present Bax, who has the brute courage to stand the odium of seeing his "illicit equation" in cold type. From the "Outlooks from the New Standpoint" (page 151), we take the following ;

"There are few points on which the advanced Radical and the Socialist are more completely in accord than in their theoretical hostility to the modern legal monogamic marriage. The majority hold it, even at the present time, and in the existing state of society, to be an evil. Yet, strange to say, they, most of them, contract these legalized monogamic unions. The excuse being the stigma on offspring and

other inconveniences. That there is considerable inconvenience in any other course cannot be denied. It cannot be
denied that this is largely because persons who profess to be
otherwise emancipated, and who ought to know better, pander to the current views by adopting an ostracising attitude
towards at least the female side of the illicit equation. They
defend their action in rather lame fashion, urging the conveniences of current society and the general desirability on
grounds of expediency of legal forms."

"The reverence of the bourgeoisie for the monogamic
principle now rests almost entirely on the fact, that he objects
to being exposed to the danger of having to put his hand in
his pocket for the maintenance of his neighbour's children.
This is the real core of ' *la morale bourgeoisie.*' "

Bax can always be counted on, with true English frankness, to state the socialist position. Socialism stands against
the monogamic form of marriage, he says so, and therefore
he scoffs the idea of legal marriage even to-day. Which form
he claims is complied with by socialists and radicals mainly
to prevent the stigma on offspring. Bax is a thoroughly
"emancipated" socialist. He does not "pander to the current views." With the stomach-eyes of socialism, he declares
that the remaining reverence amongst the bourgeois is mainly
due to the fear of having to pay for maintaining one's neighbors' children. — Of course this last hold upon the "conventional morality" will disappear under socialism. For the
children will be placed in the " social industry " — the collectivist nursing factory.

We appeal to the mothers and fathers, to your hearts and
to your heads; To the young men and women who one day
hope to take your places as the honored parents of pure
homes, to study with care the attitude of the socialist parties
as to the family and the care of children; that you may be
prepared to do battle in defence of the home, the family and
the citizenship of our country. When socialists eloquently

inveigh against poverty and the fear of poverty (which God knows to be distressing) the sympathy of your hearts must be held in check that you may with cool deliberation supply your minds with the knowledge of socialist principles which lie behind these fervid pictures, and for which their propaganda is made. With a knowledge of what socialism truly is, you may yet turn those who are not yet thoroughly corrupted with its specious philosophies back again to moral ideals, to a life of honor to their country and their God. My hope is and my effort is to supply the knowledge that shall set your hearts on fire with the task of awakening those who are now entranced with the glamor of socialist doctrine. Having felt its fatal spell I would show the carrion beneath its red folds. To those who support the socialist propaganda within the councils of the trade unions I would have them realize, when the socialist breath is hot with promises of economic freedom, there lurks behind the doctrine which would rob the child of his mother's love, and the pride of his father's heart. To those who vote the socialist ticket I would say that while they paint the glowing picture of "free men and free women" in the socialist commonwealth there lurks behind this glitter the stench of broken virtue, the awful chasm of sin.

In bringing this chapter to its conclusion we present a statement from Dr. A. Shäffle, who in "The Impossibility of Social Democracy" clearly sums up the socialist position quite in line with our convictions.

"The second fundamental change to take place in family relations, . . . would consist in the substitution of State education for family education."

"I say advisedly, "substitution" of State education side by side with and supplementary to family education obtains already to a very large extent in our own day. We are both of us in agreement with the generally received opinion that public institutions for education and training are seasonable, and are worthy of every encouragement and improvement.

Especially where family life is threatened by the factory system, women and girls have a just claim to public care and protection. The protection of children, also, by means of the Crêche, the Boys' Home, and other kindred institutions, is also probably only the beginning of a far-reaching system of family protection at the cost of national production, for these exceptional cases where home education is of necessity lacking. But with none of this are we concerned here.

"The question in presence of extreme Social Democracy, is rather this: whether family education must entirely give way to public education and the general Orphan Asylum and general Foundling Home, whether the children shall become modern horde-children, whether their parents would only see them or be able to play with them in the 'many hours of leisure' to be secured them by the Social State, or whether the parents shall keep their children with them as hitherto, preserving a community of life with them and exerting a determining influence upon their upbringing.

"Cloak it as you will, there is no disguising the fact that in the Social Democratic Commonwealth which demands equal and universal Popular Education, the public training would not simply supplement family upbringing, it would of necessity weaken and ultimately supersede it. The children almost from their birth and cradle, would be the children of the nation, not of the family.

"This system of education, this tearing out of the second chief ingredient of the indivisible living unity of the inmost family circle, robs the overwhelming majority of the people, whose well-being it is designed to secure, of the highest and purest form of happiness, and of that very form which differences of outward circumstances down to the very lowest conditions almost entirely fail to touch: this happiness would be sacrificed to envy. This same system would appreciably weaken the desire of parents to work hard and to leave behind them a large legacy to the future of both public and private wealth, and hence would seriously damage the collective prospects of accumulation of the means of production. Further, it would tend either to make parents indifferent to the lot of their children, which would be prejudicial both to the child's happiness and to its good upbringing, or to set the parents constantly in arms against the organs of public education.

"Even were our children to be laid in State cradles from their very birth, ... no State education can avail to produce equality. It would destroy the love of parents for their children, and of children to their parents, and by sapping all the springs of individuality would prevent all possibility of an individualizing system of education on the part of the State. The universal setting aside of family nurture in favor of State nursing is inconceivable. Even in the bee-community the nurses who are at the same time the only female workers, who kill the gallant males and bring up the children of one royal universal mother, are at least sexless individuals; but in the social state this is physically and morally impossible, nor would it be democratic or on principles of equality. Now since even with free love children would still come into the world unalterably unequal, the inequalities in their development would still repeat themselves, and possibly even increase, under a system of public education. We shall never succeed in either making all men *virtuosos*, or in making them all *mediocre*. Moreover, an exclusively public education could never accomplish what parental training allied to public education, can do. The parental upbringing of the children is a no less indispensable and necessary part of family life than the rule of permanent marriage-unions. Such marriage-unions indeed derive their second fundamental justification from the importance and necessity of parental upbringing."

Two Socialist Leaders.

"ROMEO
    Come bitter conduct, come unsavory guide!
    Thou desperate pilot, now at once run on
    The dashing rocks thy sea-sick, weary bark!"

"HAMLET
    The instances, that second marriage move,
    Are base respects of thrift, but none of love."

    "I'm going home to get into a hammock with
    my children around me and stay there for one solid
    month."

                     JOHN MITCHELL.

PRINCIPLES find their embodiment in the relationships of men and in the institutions which they build.

Socialism is international in its scope; the principles it seeks to overthrow are world wide in extent, while those which it would institute know no state boundaries. Socialists cannot demonstrate their principles until, at least, a nation is fully under their domination.

What one can see, however, of socialist principles, is in miniature. Relations which will consequently be universal under the regime which is advocated. We shall cite two cases of the personal application of socialist philosophy, one national and the other international.

Were we to set our search light upon the immoral and illegal sex association of some of the "class-conscious" socialists in many centers in which they congregate and propagate their doctrine, it would astonish not alone those who vote the ticket but many of the members of the organization — the greater number of which never enter into its inner council, nor become acquainted with socialist philosophy, — for the very simple and sufficient reason that socialism, as superficially understood, relates merely to the "labor movement."

Socialist sophistries and double dealing are on no question more in evidence than on that of marriage. Socialists advocate a new society in which the sex association of men and women will be maintained without let or hindrance of state or church. It follows that many socialists, although they hold to the doctrines so plainly brought out in our chapter on Free Love, are constrained for politic reasons to marry, and some are quite vulgar enough, in the interest of socialist propaganda, to parade their "legal association" (one may be sure there was no ceremony at the altar) as "proof" that socialists believe in marriage. While others being bolder or less politic, or less responsible to society, having no regard for the "present marriage system," and consequently feeling under no moral obligation to live up to its civil or religious mandates — or rather scorning the slavery of being tied to one man or woman for life, live as they please, declaring that one's body is one's own to do with as one pleases.

The two illustrations of socialist free love philosophy which we shall present have been before the public gaze; they are here given as woeful illustrations of that which would by dominating a socialist society inevitably destroy it, were it once erected.

The author would refuse to bring before the public eye the view of these cases for motives of a personal character. But the baneful cause of socialism may not be so clearly seen as by the awful light of tragedies upon the hearth stone. I may say that although having been active for years in the socialist party I have never made the personal acquaintance of either of the persons referred to. Nor shall the cry of "dishonoring the dead" or of "scandal" cause me to waver a hair's breadth from the necessary course outlined.

The acts of public men and women are by right open to

public inspection. Acts of a character not above reproach: acts of those who advocate the destruction of moral standards should be opened up to view that the unwary may not be led into the traps that are set for them. The motives which prompt this chapter rest on these grounds. In fact the motives that prompt this book are impersonal, they are civic, a love and regard for the advance of my countrymen; especially the hope of improving the present conditions which press heavily on the wage-workers; the desire that civic harmony on the high plane of democracy shall one day be the common life of man. These are the reasons for this work.

Karl Marx's daughter, Eleanor, was the most prominent woman socialist ever known to the movement. She was an able linguist; acting as interpreter at the international socialists' conventions; translating reports of the socialist and labor movement throughout the world for the "International Workingmen's Association," and its press. She translated many socialist works of great importance to the movement; such as Lissagaray's "History of the Commune of 1871," from the French. And Phechenoff's "Anarchism and Socialism."

Eleanor worked untiringly for the interests of socialism. Her motives, from all that is known to the writer, were above question. Those who knew her personally say she possessed a charming personality. But Eleanor imbibed the teachings of her father! Her life was wrapped up in her father's philosophy. She believed in "economic determinism," in atheism, in free love. To her, her father's doctrine was more than belief — It was bone of her bone and flesh of her flesh; she was a class conscious socialist — and, alas, she practiced what she preached. Here lay her sin — here she fell. We trust, God in His infinite mercy will take the sufferings of her last unhappy days, and the terrible conclusion of her life, as an atonement for the evil she committed — Betrayed as she was by the false teachings of her own father.

Wilhelm Liebknecht, late leader of the German Social

Democracy — a close personal and political associate of Karl Marx and his family, says of Eleanor, "To write a history of her life — I should have to write the history of the international working class movement!"

One may become specifically acquainted with Eleanor's views on religion and on the sex question from her review of the first English edition of August Babel's book, "Woman; of the Past, Present and Future." We quote:

"That a work dealing so thoroughly and ably as Babel's with such immense questions as woman's social position, the relations of the sexes, marriage, prostitution, population, must be of the greatest value to all socialists and to all students of social science, is self-evident. But to English Socialists such a work is doubly valuable, for we have to fight, not only the usual prejudices and opposition of the governing classes, but also the hypocrisy of a Bible-reading nation still imbued with the early Christian fear and hatred of the nature of woman (as the embodiment of all evil and temptation) which would forbid every open reference to either subject. The ordinary English *bourgeois* will tolerate, indeed enjoy, an indecent innuendo or doubtful allusion; but he will turn away in virtuous horror from a frank and serious discussion of serious questions, and feel a thrill of moral indignation at an earnest and scientific examination of them. Hence in England the most determined champions of Woman's rights rarely deal with the all-important marriage question, and when a woman is brave enough to do so she has to do it anonymously, besides assuring the world that she *is* "respectable." Socialists in England—especially we *women* Socialists—are, then, deeply indebted to our comrade, August Babel, for his brave and noble work. . . . .

"Babel's treatment of the marriage question is admirable. Of course the virtuous Philistine of all classes will be profoundly shocked." (Vol. 1, No. 6. "The Commonweal.")

In the early 80's, before Marx's death, Eleanor made

the acquaintance of her father's friend, Edward Bibbings Averling, a once prominent leader of the Secularist Society of Great Britain. Having been forced to resign from this atheist organization he devoted his time to the socialist movement. Later he became one of its ablest champions. Dr. Averling gained an international reputation through the translation of "Das Kapital" into English — and from the large circulation of his books. He was also an "economic determinist," an atheist, a free lover. The quality of his work may readily be judged by noting the quotations in the foregoing chapters of this book.

Eleanor and Averling fell in with each other's views, believing in an "unconventional intercourse of the sexes" and in the other socialist ideals so plainly exposed in our chapter on Free Love ; they lived together as man and wife. It was current gossip that Averling had a wife, living in the city of London, at the time he began his association with Eleanor. The author not being fully acquainted as to the truth of Dr. Averling's marriage, will consider the question in hand quite apart from this point in the case. Save to call the reader's attention to the socialist dogma upon this point — the fact of having a wife would in no wise prevent the new association : — For when "mutual fondness" ceases, a separation and "its replacement by a new passionate love is a blessing" to all concerned.

It was well known to Marx, and to the other leaders and also to the socialist movement generally that his (Marx's) daughter Eleanor and Dr. Averling were living together in accordance to socialist sex philosophy.

Together they worked in the socialist movement. In 1886–87 they made a fifteen weeks' tour of the United States under the auspices of the Socialist Labor Party.

To come to the climax, Averling's "individual sex love" ceased — Eleanor's "fondness" remained unbroken. — Being utterly devoid of faith — Her purely physical ideal snatched from her by the hand of blind fate — With love for Edward, she filled a vial with poison — with disgust for the world she drank it to the dregs, dying a martyr to what socialists call "freedom."

Edward B. Averling, filled with the unrest of an irreligious spirit — sex crazed — soon after Eleanor's suicide — he died.

The press reports of Miss Marx's suicide were sent throughout the world, despite the socialist efforts to suppress the news.

Very few comments were made in the socialist press about the affair. It was a blow they gladly would have smothered. Neither was the death nor the life work of this faithful and untiring woman, and martyr to the socialist cause scarcely mentioned. Eleanor Marx's loss to the socialist movement was great. — But to speak much of her worth they dare not! There stood the spectre of her sex life and its awful end. To speak in disapproval of her association with Dr. Averling would be a condemnation of the well-known principles of socialism relative to the family; therefore silence as to the tragedy — silence as to her due credit — was the policy best calculated to make political progress in these United States — And to what end — Why, God forfend — to the end of submerging the nation in this vortex of sex sin by setting up their ideal, the "free family." The lid of hell may well come off and the damned dance free, at the project.

If so faithful, so able, so brave a woman to do their vile hests meet with so little honor at the hands of those who call her sin virtue, what treatment may lesser women expect at their red hands if once they hold the nation's power. It were well for socialist women to consider.

Even the "Social Democrat" of London, England, Eleanor's home, had very few words to say.

The following quotation is taken from its papes: "Apart from the *merely* legal tie, Eleanor Marx was truly and devotedly his wife in every sense." The italics are ours. But for that weak, that fatal word *merely* what a different tale might have been told. The contempt for the divine — the civic life of the family — the defiance of all institutions, secular and sacred, lead, naturally, to such scenes as were enacted by this ill-fated and faithless couple.

The public have especial interest, even the right, in the knowledge of the lives of public men and women — more particularly when a radical departure from the prevailing manners and customs is counciled. This knowledge of Eleanor Marx was furnished by Mrs. Caroline Corbin, under the caption "Are Socialism and Home Life Antagonistic?" in "Labor and Capital" (April, 1903):

"I have been a faithful student of Socialism for thirty years. I have read many books on the subject, have carefully watched its public action and read all the declarations and programmes of its various congresses that I could discover by careful search in that time. I have conversed with some eminent European advocates of the system with the express purpose of elucidating this very point, as to whether Socialism would recognize civic or Christian marriage, and I have failed to discover a shred of evidence that it would do so.

"MISS MARX'S VIEWS. — On the contrary, I have found in the utterances of such men as Hasenclever, Hyndman, Bebel and many others abundant evidence that the declaration of Eleanor, daughter of Karl Marx, made in my presence and in that of more than a score of witnesses besides — and I may add repeated in almost identical terms by one of my recent critics — sums up the whole teaching of the Socialistic system of this subject.

"Miss Marx said, as stated in the Chicago *Tribune* Nov. 14, 1886, by an impartial witness:

"'*Love is the only recognized marriage in Socialism, consequently no bonds of any kind would be required. Divorce would be impossible, as there would be nothing to divorce, for when love ceased, separation would naturally ensue.'*

"Miss Marx was at that time traveling in this country with Dr. Averling, the intimate friend of her father, Karl Marx, and the translator into English of his chief work, 'Das Kapital.' She passed as Mrs. Averling, although the real wife of Dr. Averling, an ageing and invalid woman, was living in London. When at her death a few years later Dr. Averling discarded Miss Marx and married another woman, the tragic story of the suicide of the sometime 'free wife' was heralded in the leading newspapers of England and America."

This recent article by Mrs. Corbin has forced this matter into view within socialist circles. In answer to it we cull the following from a socialist editorial — and, too, this other also from a socialist editorial. — We submit them side by side as a sample of socialist tactics:

"As regards Mrs. Corbin's statement that Eleanor Averling lived with Dr. Averling as his wife without being married to him according to recognized forms, I have often heard this stated as a fact, and I presume it is true. But what of it? What has Eleanor Averling got to do with the principles of Socialism? The question that confronts us as sane men and women is not what Eleanor Averling did or did not do, but, shall we have industrial freedom or industrial slavery?" ("The Coming Nation," Red Hill, Mo., May 23rd, 1903.)

"Father Sherman well knows that society to-day is honeycombed with immorality, yet he passes this by with evident approval, and then tries to make the Socialists appear immoral *by reciting the oft-denied story about* Eleanor Marx." ("The Social Democratic Herald," Milwaukee, Wis., June 13, 1903.)

Socialism: the Nation of Fatherless Children.

One socialist acknowledges the immoral relationship — and then throws its readers off the scent by suavely asking, "What has Eleanor Averling got to do with the principles of Socialism?" — with "industrial freedom or industrial slavery"? This interrogation may spring from ignorance, or it may be a sample of socialist tactics in embryo. If it be the former, then is it an assumption for so illy informed an editor to sit in a socialist sanctum. If it be the latter, then it is evidence that the editor has not yet the fully developed "socialist mind." For a well developed "socialist mind" lies right out to "down" an antagonist. Let us rather believe that the editor of "The Coming Nation" does not see the connection of Eleanor Marx's association with Edward B. Averling with the principles of socialism. He will be better informed when he shall have studied this book, which is meant to give just this necessary education. A fully informed person knows that Eleanor's life was a miniature demonstration of the "free marriage" which is to be the rule under the "free society" of socialism.

The editor assumes that "industrial freedom" and "socialist principles" are synonymous terms — Nothing is falser! Industrial freedom, barring the "socialists' minds" amongst us, from the universally accepted standpoint connotes an improved (a vastly improved, if you please) social condition for the middle and lower industrial classes over their present means of living. But not a change in the existing social order from a basic point of view — Not a revolution. While the phrase "industrial freedom" in the mouth of a socialist editor means (or ought to mean) a state of affairs which is brought about by a revolution — by the distinction of the family, the church, and the state. Industrial freedom, in common parlance, is consequent upon the elevating influence of the family, the church and the state; while in the socialist tongue "industrial freedom" is consequent upon getting rid of the family, the church and the state — and all the other things mentioned in our last chapter — One method leads to chaos, the other expands and perfects.

What Edward Averling "did or did not do" would not be of interest to us, were it not for the fact that he embodies the ideals of an organization which seeks the suffrages of our citizens. We would do much that his individual life might not become the pattern for the life of all the people.

As for the second of these editorials, the editor of the "Social Democratic Herald" is better versed in socialist tactics. He simply throws the untrained reader off the scent by engaging his mind with sentiments of discredit to Father Sherman.

In the same issue "The Coming Nation" again takes up the discussion of Eleanor Marx.

"Mrs. Corbin bases her assumption that 'home life' — and by that she means the sacred marital relation existing between husband and wife — would be abolished, on the statement of some half dozen Socialists. Mrs. Corbin should bear in mind, as should all others who are considering this phase of the question that a Bebel, a Hyndman, a Hasenclever, count but one, and their influence and ideas would extend just to the extent that the rest of society accepted them."

Oh no! You are mistaken, my dear socialist editor, they count three, not "one"! And when you add the authority of Marx, Engels, Bax, Ferri, Carpenter, Herron, Oscar Wilde and hundreds of others — when you add the dozens of socialist editors the only one that is left is the misinformed Red Hill editor.

How fitting it is for socialists to practice their tactics on Independence Day. It brings in sharp contrast its opposition to the sound principles of free government. On July 4th, 1903, "The Social Democratic Herald" issues a second characteristic editorial on the Marx-Averling case. Under the atheistic caption "The Church and the Money Bags" it says:

"As to Mrs. Corbin and her filthy insinuations against the Socialists we hardly feel called on to reply. Only a woman of filthy mind could persist in her slanders when all the evidences go to disprove them."

The editor then proceeds in socialist tactical fashion to condemn the evils of low wages and the hard conditions of the working class and adroitly closes without answering Mrs. Corbin's questions, and by giving the "socialist minds" the socialist method of self-defense, in making propaganda, namely, slander.

"Mrs. Corbin's articles referred to above are filled with untruth, distorted utterances of Socialists used to bolster up her foul insinuations, and slanders of people now dead, and hence unable to defend themselves — notably Eleanor Marx. Mrs. Corbin is certainly a low-minded woman."

This is really in defense of Eleanor's work for socialism — it is no doubt deemed necessary to keep in the good graces of the "international working class," who have no qualms of conscience about accepting her life as correct, after the socialist pattern.

When the women of this country realize the danger which confronts the home, — when they become aware of this cuttle fish that swims in our civic waters, — when they learn the immoral standards which rest on socialist principles (which the life of Eleanor frightfully examples), then the service of Mrs. Caroline Corbin, who is by socialists called "low-minded," will be rightly valued — Then will the socialist movement be nearer its end.

The issue must be met! Socialists may answer, guilty. Or they may be proven guilty by the conspiracy of silence.

1st. Were not Eleanor Marx and Edward Bibbings Averling leaders of the socialist movement?

2nd. Are not their books circulated as means of propaganda within the international socialist movement?

3rd. Did not Eleanor Marx and Dr. Averling live the sex life as advocated by socialist teachings?

These are the questions which concern the public weal — for the reason that socialism has organized a political party to enforce its principles. — The socialist editors need not think to escape by lying, it only proves guilt — For which, Heaven forgive them — irresponsibility is in the marrow of atheistic bones.

We now turn to a more recent, a national example of the immoral practice of socialist philosophy. We will examine the conduct of one of the foremost among the class conscious socialists of America, George D. Herron.

The socialist movement of the United States, since the year 1900 probably owes more of its progress to this leader than to any other person in the socialist party. In 1899 a split took place in the Socialist Labor Party. The larger division set up its headquarters at Springfield, Mass. The Social Democratic Party, under the leadership of Eugene V. Debs, had headquarters at Chicago, Ill. By duplicity and diplomacy a union of the two organizations was effected.— And to George D. Herron, the present Socialist Party largely owes its existence. The national convention of July, 1901, effected socialist unity (which at the present writing is severely strained and gives signs of splitting). The first move which greatly facilitated unity was the election of Mr. Herron as chairman. The second point of reconciliation was his "compromise immediate demands." The Socialist Labor division having stood for the complete overthrow of the planks in the platform which by socialists are known as "immediate demands." Thereby signifying that those measures are not properly a part of socialism, but only the means of organizing a political party and getting elected to office.

In reporting the doings of this convention "The Worker"

says, "The selection of Herron as temporary chairman was unanimous and satisfactory to all parties, . . . he steered the convention through some threatening breakers during the opening and most trying hours of the convention."

In 1902, subject to the call of the Paris International Congress of Socialists, each country, by referendum vote, elected two secretaries to represent the organized socialists of their respective countries on the International Committee, with headquarters established at Brussels, Belgium. This secretaryship is the highest office within the gift of the United States' socialists. It places the incumbent in the forefront of the international movement. These secretaries are the only authorities recognized in international correspondence. By the referendum vote George D. Herron was elected to serve this country over all other nominees for the office.

Mr. Herron has made the largest financial contributions to the socialist movement within late years. Not only has he contributed hundreds of dollars to the organization directly; but also through the "Socialist Fellowship" he has given largely to the support of socialist editors, secretaries and speakers.

We have in previous chapters presented quotations from the pen of Mr. Herron, which are proof positive that he is a "class conscious" socialist and an eloquent and able expounder of socialist principles.

George D. Herron was a Congregationalist minister; with a some time pastorate in Burlington, Iowa. Mrs. E. D. Rand, a wealthy member of his pastorate, becoming infatuated with the work of Rev. George D. Herron, established for him a "Chair of Applied Christianity" at Grinnell University, Iowa.

The establishment of this chair was specifically for the purpose of "developing a social philosophy and economic from the teachings of Jesus, or the application of his teachings to social problems and institutions." Finding that his teachings were in conflict with the demands of Grinnell University Dr. Herron was forced, by the authorities, to resign, and the chair was abolished.

One year before his ordination as a minister of the Congregational Church Dr. Herron married Miss Mary Everhard of Ripon, Wisconsin. Five children were born of this union, four of whom are now living.

From the time his "chair of Applied Christianity" was endowed, Miss Rand, the daughter of the lady who financially created the chair, became his "constant companion." Later the ladies and Dr. Herron traveled together in foreign countries — Herron supporting himself by the bounty of Miss Rand and her mother. Finally becoming thoroughly inoculated with the sex virus of socialism, Dr. Herron left his wife and four children: Pressed his wife to sue for a divorce. Stopped the detail of the court procedure by giving his children some of Miss Rand's money — And turned a new page by marrying Miss Rand.

John Spergo, editor of "The Comrade" just after the divorce case, writing of Dr. George D. Herron said:

"Those of us who gather . . . in the dingy editorial rooms of the Commonweal, feel that this man will come forth out of the fire of persecution to be the greatest leader of the American Socialist movement. The unanimous call, weeks afterward, that he preside at the opening of the the great 'Unity Convention' bears witness to the growth of that feeling.

". . . his famous sermon on 'The Message of Jesus to Men of Wealth,' brought him fame and revealed to America the fact that a greater than Emerson had arisen; greater than Emerson, because of the greater soul-passion which moved him and the greater truth of his message.

"On his return from his European tour in 1900, Professor Herron made a notable declaration for uncompromising Socialism at a mass meeting held in Chicago by the Social-

Democratic Party — the first meeting in the Presidential Election campaign — when he confessed that for eight years he had been voting for the candidates of the Socialist Labour Party. Since that time he has thrown himself heartily into the work of the party, and his later writings show that his emancipation from the bonds of ecclesiasticism is complete. A clear, cultured thinker, equally powerful with voice and pen, he has laid all his magnificent powers upon the altar of the class-conscious revolutionary Socialist movement of the world." (New York, September, 1901.)

It certainly will be interesting to put the case of George D. Herron before the Congregational Church in contrast to his standing in the socialist party at this time.

"The council called by the Congregational church of Grinnell, Ia., to advise concerning the church membership and ministerial standing of Mr. George D. Herron convened at Grinnell, June 4. Of the thirteen churches invited, ten were represented, all strictly of the vicinage, with the single exception of Burlington, where Mr. Herron was formerly pastor. The council organized with the choice of Rev. J. W. Cowan of Newton moderator, and Rev. R. L. Marsh of Burlington scribe.

"The following statement was presented by the committee representing the church:

"STATEMENT OF THE COMMITTEE TO THE COUNCIL.

"The committee appointed by the First Congregational Church of Grinnell, in accordance with the resolution adopted at the Grinnell Association held at Baxter, Io., April 30, 1901, for the purpose of calling a council to advise as to what shall be done with reference to the ministerial standing and church membership of George D. Herron, have communicated with Mr. Herron in regard to the calling of a mutual council.

.   .   .   .

"It has been made to appear by the recent divorce proceedings between Mr. and Mrs. Herron at Algona, Ia., and his subsequent marriage to Miss Rand that his relations to and treatment of his wife and children have been such as are, to say the least, unbecoming a Christian minister. There is evidence that may be presented to the council with reference to the devotion of Mrs. Herron to her husband and his beliefs, his teachings and his interests, also with reference to the divorce proceedings and the manner in which they were brought about. There is evidence that the divorce proceedings, while brought in the name of Mrs. Herron as plaintiff, were, in fact, instituted by Mr. Herron and against the wish and protest of Mrs. Herron.

"Since March 21, 1901, at which time the divorce was granted, Mr. Herron has married Miss Carrie Rand, a lady with whom he has for the past nine years been on terms of intimate acquaintance. This conduct on the part of Mr. Herron seems to be at variance with the teachings of Christ as recorded in Matt. 19: 8, 9; Luke 16: 18.

"If the council so desire the committee can introduce evidence tending to substantiate the statements herein contained.

"Mr. Herron has sent to the committee a communication in the nature of a defense, which will, at his request, be submitted to the council.

"At the request of the council, the committee suggested what evidence was at hand that would tend to confirm the facts presented in their statement. The witnesses called were E. M. Vittum, pastor of the Congregational church of Grinnell, Prof. Charles Noble, Mrs. R. G. Cole, Miss Edith Denise and Prof. Clara Millerd, members of the Iowa College faculty, Mrs. Jesse Macy, Mrs. J. H. T. Main, Mrs. Charles Noble and Mrs. H. H. Robbins, members of families connected with Iowa College, and Miss S. E. Parker, who had been employed frequently as a dressmaker in the Herron home.

"The testimony tended to show that Mrs. Herron began helpful service for her husband while they were together in Ripon College, reading his lessons for him when his eyes were weak, and that she had continued to show the same self-denying care during their married life. She completed her college course — though Mr. Herron did not finish his — and was considered one of the finest students, well-equipped to be the companion of a literary worker. Five children were born to them, of whom four are living. Mrs. Herron has been a faithful and hard-working mother, taking upon herself many of the home cares usually shared by a husband. She was always solicitous for her husband and for his comfort. When visiting or receiving calls her conversation was almost sure to turn to him and his work. When he was present in the home everything was planned for his comfort and convenience. Mrs. Herron was much interested in her husband's work, believing that he was a man with a special "mission." And so far as could be gathered from her conversation and public utterances, she was in full accord with his teaching. During his long absences from home she went into society but little, spending much time in reading the books he recommended and taking up new studies in order that she might be able to enter into his life as much as possible.

"During the last few years, when it became apparent that Mr. Herron was seeking companionship and affection elsewhere, Mrs. Herron showed no signs of resentment or jealousy — so far as her neighbors could judge — but only the burden of sorrow and tried to retain her husband's love by serving him more faithfully. The statement of Miss Parker that 'she did everything but breathe for her husband' when he was at home raised a smile in the council, but it was the expression of an honest conviction.

"Mrs. Herron had said little about divorce except under the seal of confidence, but enough was known to convince the council that she was an applicant for divorce only in a technical sense, not consenting to become such until fully convinced that it would be impossible to maintain the integrity of her home.

"Mr. J. P. Lyman, chairmain of the church committee, presented a certified copy of the court records in the divorce proceedings, showing that the petition for divorce, the answer and the decree were all filed on the same day at Algona, Ia., while Mr. Herron was in New York city. The petition alleged that 'the defendant without cause or excuse deserted this plaintiff and refused to longer live and cohabit with her as her husband,' also that he 'has been guilty of such cruel and inhuman treatment as to seriously impair her health and to endanger her life.' In his decision the judge declared, 'The court finds for the plaintiff and finds that the allegations of her petition are true.' A divorce was granted, giving to Mrs. Herron the custody of the four children. This was on March 21, 1901. Evidence in the form of a business letter signed 'Carrie Rand Herron' was produced to show the truth of the published reports that Mr. Herron had already contracted a second marriage with the woman who had been on such terms of intimate association with him for at least nine years.

"The council adopted the following as the result of its deliberations.

"The Finding of the Council."

"At a council held in the First Congregational Church of Grinnell, June 4, 1901, to consider the right to church membership and ministerial standing of George D. Herron, the following findings were rendered:

"1. That the charge of immoral and unchristian conduct is sustained by the findings of the court which, at Algona, on March 21, 1901, granted a decree of divorce to

Mary Everhard Herron from her husband, on the grounds of desertion and inhuman treatment.

"2. The same charge is further sustained by evidence presented to this council, showing that George D. Herron's manner toward the wife who consecrated her life to the effort to make him happy, relieve him of care and aid him in fulfilling what she believed to be his high calling, has been that of unfeeling and selfish indifference and, at least since 1896, of studied neglect, culminating in a heartless desertion and the final tragedy of divorce.

"3. The same charge is still further sustained by confessions contained in the paper written by Mr. Herron in his own defense and read to the council. In this paper he denies the right of society to sanction or undo a marriage tie between man and woman and presents a view of the conjugal relation, of fatherhood and the home which is abhorrent to enlightened Christian sentiment, and which confirms the council in the opinion that this action of George D. Herron is simply the criminal desertion of a worthy wife and devoted mother by a man who has deliberately falsified his marriage vows.

"In view of these findings it is

"Resolved (1), That we recommend to the Grinnell Association that the name of George D. Herron be dropped from its roll of membership.

"Resolved (2), That we recommend to the First Congregational Church of Grinnell that the name of George D. Herron be dropped from its roll of membership.

"Resolved (3), That we express our conviction that George D. Herron has forfeited all right to be known by the churches of our faith and order as a minister of the gospel, and that he is by vote of this council deposed from the Christian ministry." ("The Congregationalist," June 15, 1901.)

Comment on the proceedings of the council seems to us entirely unnecessary. Suffice it to say, amen to their efforts to maintain the integrity of the family against the world-wide encroachments upon it by atheism in one or another form.

"The Congregationalist and Christian World" (Boston, June 15, 1901.) gives voice to its sentiments in the following editorial — Its high quality deserves the commendation of all right-minded men and women. We quote:

· DR. HERRON AND THE INTEGRITY OF THE FAMILY.

"We have chronicled from week to week the important facts relating to Dr. Herron's divorce and the successive steps in the procedure against him on the part of the church at Grinnell, Ia., and the local Association, with both of which he was connected. We preferred to reserve editorial comment until the highest ecclesiastical court known to Congregationalism had spoken, and until any evidence that Dr. Herron or his friends might adduce should be given to the public. Now that the decision of the *ex parte* council of last week, advising expulsion from the church and the Association and deposing him from the ministry, and now that the letter Dr. Herron sent to the council are in our hands, it is proper to speak plainly.

.   .   .   .

"What we now say arises from no desire to extend or prolong interest in this tragedy. During the last ten years, in which Dr. Herron has posed conspicuously as a social reformer, we have repeatedly spoken as charitably of him as our consciences would permit, and more than once we have given him the freedom of our columns in which to champion his peculiar views. We have never expected that he would make any large or permanent contribution to the cause of social reform, but we had hoped that his work as an agitator might, perhaps, serve some good use in the progress of mankind toward a better social order.

"But even Dr. Herron's prominence in the religious world would not justify extended comment upon his present lapse were there not to be drawn from it and the antecedent circumstances certain wholesome lessons for all who have witnessed and sorrowed over it. Reduced to its final terms this recent chapter in his life is but the old story of infatuation, unfaithfulness and desertion. He has put away a loyal and devoted wife in order to take to himself another woman. That is the whole of the matter. The naked, terrible fact does not appear any less reprehensible though one may consume reams of paper in trying to justify it.

"Dr. Herron's letter is worth reading, simply that one may see what a man with his back to the wall, defying all the delicate and noble instincts of human society, can say in his defense. No man ever put more effort or eloquence into an apology for his conduct. An affluent vocabulary, an uncommon deftness in argumentation, a misguided ethical passion and a gratuitous assumption of personal martyrdom are all brought into requisition to buttress his position. But the flimsy structure of his laborious logic falls the moment that the solid fact that he has tired of his wife and given himself to another woman touches it. There never has been in civilized society but one verdict upon such conduct. There never will be. There never can be so long as sane men dwell in a universe such as we understand ours to be.

"The essential viciousness of Dr. Herron's position is its unrestrained individualism. The right of a man to order his life purely to further what he fancies to be his own largest welfare is forever balanced by his right and duty to relate it to society in such a way that he will fulfil all reasonable obligations to others, and particularly to those most intimately connected with him. To disown the claims of the social order is nothing short of consummate selfishness, however much such behavior may be disguised in beautiful phrases.

"Nor is it the educated and well-to-do elements of society only that are visiting their disapproval upon him. We doubt if anywhere there is sterner judgment of him than in the humble cottages of the working people, whose special champion he has professed to be.

"The one general lesson to be drawn relates to the ethical equipment of the reformer. Here was a man who not only denounced the existing social and industrial order, but claimed to discern the will and spirit of Jesus Christ more accurately than most of his fellow-Christians. If there was any subject in regard to which Jesus taught explicitly, it was the marriage relation. He

departed from his usual custom of enunciating general principles
and laid down a specific law touching the reciprocal obligation of
a man and woman when they have been joined in the holy bands of
wedlock. To claim to understand and interpret the teachings of
Christ in general and then depart from them at a point where he is
most insistent and most specific involves a man in such a flagrant
inconsistency that his influence as a teacher is forever gone. Certainly when he deliberately transgresses so plain a law he forfeits
a right to designate his teaching as Christian or to be himself considered in any way a loyal disciple of Christ. That is why so many
persons are justly feeling today a certain personal grievance against
Dr. Herron. They have looked to him for guidance respecting
what might bring about a more Christian social order, and he plays
them false at a point where unfaithfulness is most disastrous.

"The family relation, as Prof. F. G. Peabody finely says, is
given not to make life easier, but to make life better. It is conceivable that into what once promised to be a happy, harmonious
comradeship there may come elements of friction and disunion.
But whenever such a situation has arisen the bravest, most Christ-
like men and women of history have borne it as true hearts always
bear the will of God when it ordains for them pain and sorrow.
Under the discipline of disappointed hopes they have grown sweet
and strong. Rather than do defiance to a divinely established
order, and strike one more blow at a foundation principle of wholesome human relationships, they have gone forward along their appointed way until God gave them release.

Those who are agitating and laboring in the field of what is
technically known as social reform should heed this warning. Social
reform involves a challenge of prevailing standards of morality in
various directions. Unless the social reformer keeps the very flower
and fragrance of his character, his moral challenge becomes a
mockery.

"We are put into the world primarily, not to agitate in behalf
of single tax or of co-operative industry or a socialistic commonwealth, but first of all to be good husbands and wives, fathers and
mothers, sons and daughters, brothers and sisters. No degree of
activity and apparent success in efforts looking to the public welfare can atone for lack of fidelity and tenderness in these primary

human relations. The family always has been and always will be the sphere in which men get their best discipline and their largest growth. Not until a man is trying to do his utmost to fulfil the obligations imposed by kinship with others ought he to venture out into the wide field of action in which the general good of society is the object sought. Fortunately, we are not without men and women who are loyal both to the family and to society and who are serving both with unflagging zeal. From such persons as these and from them alone will proceed the impulses that will lift the world's burdens and right its wrongs."

We now submit the communication of Rev. G. D. Herron to the Congregational church council, which was printed in the "International Socialist Review."

LETTER TO GRINNELL CHURCH COMMITTEE.

NEW YORK, May 24, 1901.

" To the Committee appointed by the Congregational Church of Grinnell, Iowa, to call a council of churches to inquire into my ministerial standing and church membership.

" Brethren — I received your request that I join with you in calling a council to inquire into my standing as a minister and as a member of your church. I could not join with you in this call, nor do I feel it essential that I should. You are a body of Christian gentlemen, seeking to do what you believe to be your whole duty, and the council called by you will be as impartial, and as eager to do what seems to it right, as if I had joined in the call. I could not hope to include a friendly church in the council; for, however sad the reflection on myself to say so, I have no friend that I know of in the Congregational Church or ministry of Iowa.

" When I turn from the desires of a father's heart to what is best for the children themselves, I think their choice of their mother would be wise; for they will have a good mother, and the life of a man given to the socialist revolution cannot fail to be more or less the life of an outcast, as the revolution intensifies and arrays a ruling class against a working class in a final issue and crisis.

" In this connection, I would like to say that I do not see why

266

the matter of adequate financial provision should have been made a basis of complaint or discussion. Certainly, it was the right and duty of the mother of these children to accept such provision, in simple justice to herself and them, as it was my privilege and duty to provide to the utmost. As to what friends enabled me to do this, that is a matter into which the public has no right to inquire, so long as those concerned are satisfied.

"As a council, you are acting in defense of what you believe to be the sacredness of the family institution, against which I am to you an offender. In order that your action on this point may be complete, let me say to you that I do not believe that the present marriage system is sacred or good. It rather seems to me to be the destruction of the liberty and love and truth which make life sacred and worth living. If love and truth are the basis of morality, then a marriage system which makes one human being the property of another, without regard to the well-being of either the owned or the owner, seems to me to be the very soul of blasphemy and immorality. The family founded on force is a survival of slavery, and one of the expressions of the slave-principles on which our whole civilization is built. It is a mode of the superstition which thinks it good for human beings to own each other, and good for the race to have all its sources and tools of life owned by the few who are strong and cunning enough to possess them. The ethics of the legally and ecclesiastically enforced family make it possible for a man to live a life of monstrous wrong, of ghastly falsehood, even of unbridled lust, and yet be highly moral according to the standards by which we are judged. The same standards condemn and disgrace the purest expressions of comradeship, if they cross the conventions or forget the decrees of custom. Free and truthful living is thus made a tragedy, to have overwhelming and revengeful retribution added unto it, while slave-living and falsehood may be rewarded with world-blessings and ecclesiastical canonization. I thoroughly believe in the vital and abiding union of one man with one woman as a true basis of the family life. But we shall have few such unions until we have a free family. Men and women must be economically free — free to use their powers to the fullest extent — free from the interference of legal and ecclesiastical force, and free to correct their mistakes, before we can have a family that is noble, built on unions that are good. Lives that are essentially one, co-operative in the love and truth that make oneness, need no law of state or church to bind or keep them together. Upon such, the imposition of force is a destruction and a blasphemy. On the other hand, no law in the universe has a right to keep together those who are not vitally and essentially one. It is only in freedom that love can find its own, or truth blossom in the soul, or other than a slave-individuality unfold. It is the business of society to see to it that every child is surrounded by the full and free resources of a complete life; it is the business of society to see to its own fatherhood and motherhood of every child, as well as to hold every parent responsible; it is the business of society to know every child of woman as a free and legitimate child of God, and welcome it as an inheritor of the reverence and resources of the earth; but it is not the business of society to unite or separate men and women in the marriage relation. Love must be set free and liberty must be trusted, if noble and beautiful homes are to spring up to make the earth a garden of truth and gladness. The coercive family system is filling the earth with falsehood and hypocrisy, misery and soul-disintegration, and is perpetuating the morality of slaves and liars. In times past, men have thrown away their lives in protest against what seemed to them tyranny and wrong. There is a new world coming whose way can be made ready only by those who will throw away their good names, and accept, perhaps, everlasting disgrace, as the price of their protest.

"And if I willingly accept all the obloquy and retribution which church and society may visit upon me, in making a protest against a system that seems to me destructive to all true morality, and to the very citadel of the soul's integrity, then my protest has earned its right to be heard.

"It seems useless and hopeless to speak to religious or moral custodians about the agony of the soul for self-revelation; about the increasing and intensifying struggle of man to outwardly express what he inwardly is. Our morality is so altogether based on appearances, on calculated action, and has so little to do with truth or reality, that the spectacle of a man trying to be simply honest with the world, in order to be honest with his soul, causes him to be taken for either a criminal or a mad-man. Under our social system, no one says what he really thinks, or lives out what he really is. Our sayings and doings, or the things we do not and say not, are guided by the desire to be respectable, to be approved; hence action and thought are alike dishonest, and without freedom or beauty. Our religion and conduct, our customs and good names, our international diplomacies and business successes, deal with chances and appearances; they are a matter of the dice, and not of the soul. Civilization, with its network of falsehood and suspicion, of retribution and revenge, is a sort of world-conspiracy against the soul's integrity and against individuality. Yet the right of a single soul to fully and freely express itself, to live out and show forth all the truth about itself, so that it need have within itself no hid thing, but be naked before the universe and not be ashamed, is infinitely more important than the whole fabric of civilization. The travail of the soul to become honest, the struggle of man to come to himself, is far more vital and revolutionary, more menacing to what we call civilization, than any questioning of the marriage system, or the questioning of any institution. You may be sure that when the son of man rises out of the common life, tnere will not be left a shred of any kind of institutional bond, and there will be no sentinels on the walls of the soul's possibilities."

Speaking of Miss Rand, Mr. Herron says: "When publicly placed in a position where I must either affirm or deny the unity of my life with hers, or else evade the interrogation, I can be truthful to the world in no other way than by establishing the fact of this unity. After this storm of savage and senseless wrong has broken upon her, after the world has taken everything it values from her, after all she has given and lost, after she has been the source and inspirer of so much of such work as I have done, after I have lived for so many years because she has lived also, after she has dedicated my life to the socialist cause of freedom, for me to leave her to face the world alone, or to wait an hour after she would permit me to announce her to men as my wife, would be for me to commit spiritual suicide, and to try to deceive the world in order to win for myself some place or work in it, or some fragment of faith from it. If this confession of life is evil to you, and to all the world, then let it be evil; if to any one on the earth it is good, to that one let it be good. If free and truthful living be the final outcome of things, then the outcome will vindicate us.

"In conclusion let me say, out of justice to you as to myself, that I shall not misrepresent your action, nor put it on other than your own grounds. I shall not represent you as dismissing me for socialism or heresy, or for my attacks on the church. I have nowhere and at no time used language indicating this, and every such word attributed to me has been newspaper forgery. I am dismissed from the church and its ministry for what you consider to be conduct unbecoming a minister and a gentleman. And your view of the life I have lived, with such service as I have tried to render, only seems to you to confirm your judgment, to which must be added the voluntary testimony of this letter. So I shall accept my dismissal in the terms in which you give it, and I shall not try to evade the consequences of your decision. I shall not again speak as a minister of the church, nor seek its fellowship, nor act as its representative, nor use its language. If anything I may hereafter do or say shall be of service to any one or to any cause, it shall be done or said with the clear understanding that the church is free from any responsibility for such service, and that I am disowned by the church because of its judgment upon my life and character."

(Signed) Faithfully yours,
GEORGE D. HERRON.

Can anyone of high moral standards fail to approve the action of the Congregational Church in dismissing this blasphemer; who, still posing as a professor of "Applied Christianity," insults the institution of the family with this free love communication? Mr. Herron may well be questioned: If it be better for your children to be fatherless, upon your sickly sentimental reason that "the life of a man given to the social revolution" is "the life of an outcast," by what system of logic do you morally enter into marital association with a possible mother?

We must differ with you, professor of applied Christianity; it does concern the public as "to what friends enabled" you financially to settle your divorce suit! You are a public man — you seek the civil power for the political party of which you are the leader. It is of public interest that you enter into association with a woman who destroys the happiness of a wife (her sometime household friend), and four children are made to blush with shame at the honored name of father. We, the public, have the right and the duty to inquire from whence this Judas comes. For the especial reason, if none other, that you and your new wife have the audacity to insult the institution of the family. — No, the crime cannot be covered with thirty pieces of silver.

Mr. Herron's letter was quite at home in the socialist press. Reading it, one may well imagine he were reading a chapter of Engels, Marx, Babel, Bax or other socialist classics. We are quite familiar with the thought expressed by Mr. Herron, that "men and women must be economically free . . . free from the interference of legal and ecclesiastical force, and free to correct their mistakes, before we can have a family that is noble, built on unions that are good."— And yet it is quite the fashion, by a slight o' hand, to protest against socialists being called free lovers. Socialism gains the, I may not say moral, support of many radical men who have not yet propagated the socialist doctrine from a party standpoint. — This outside force greatly aids in maintaining the standing of socialists, of the Mr. Herron type, with the rank and file of the membership of the organization. — The workingmen, many of whom are led to believe that socialism is merely a part of the labor movement, the most consequential part. More and more these intellectually cultivated but morally degenerate "gentlemen" are finding their political home within the socialist movement.

Divorced from religious teachings, the minds of many persons are hopelessly confused by materialism in its manifold guises. The assertion that men *perforce* obey their class interests robs weak minded men of the sense of moral responsibility. "He can't help it, it is the way of his class!" is a good sample of the current application of socialist doctrine. Fatalism is thus made to hide moral offences — financially as well as sexually. Many a socialist secretary-treasurer has appropriated the party's money to his private uses — these offences are excused upon the plea of economic condition — the want of economic freedom. Possibly if Mr. Herron had been "economically free" he would never have gone to visit the Holy Land hand-in-hand with friendship betrayed by lust. Only to think of it! treading the paths of sacred feet; of Him who raised marriage to the dignity of a sacrament! Nothing less than moral degeneracy could have made the emotion of these visits less than tragic. Possibly economic freedom would have been the prop to aid this man in living an honorable life.

Listen to this sick sweet talk — listen to this hero who left a poor wife and took one with money: "For me to leave her (Miss Rand) to face the world alone would be for me to commit spiritual suicide." No, he could not leave Miss Rand alone — but his wife, whom he had said had been his "living conscience," he could leave; not quite alone, for his four children were left fatherless with their deserted mother. Is not this vile cant? Is it not much too sweet to be wholesome? "She (Miss Rand) has dedicated" his "life to the socialist cause of freedom," He has added to the mess of "hell's lowest vomit." This is what he calls "applied Christianity." Many such applications would quickly leave a nation with fatherless children. Thank God, socialism has not gotten control of the civic power, to make a general application of its heathen philosophy which Mr. Herron insultingly terms "applied Christianity."

He says in "The Coming Nation" (March 28th, 1903):

"If it is a free land we are after, or a free religion, or a free family, or a wholly free society, we shall find it at the other side of socialism, or along the socialistic way."

Mr. Herron has not waited for socialism, he has established a "free family" along the socialist way. Mr. Herron speaks much of freedom — "free land," "free family," "free society." It was with abstract cries that the French Revolutionists sought to overthrow the Church, the State and the Family. It is with abstract cries that the "pest of socialism" stalks forth to incite the downtrodden poor to mutiny and to rage.

But, Professor Herron, this is not a personal matter — Principles find their embodiment in persons, your conduct is the fitting expression of socialist principles. With the knowledge of socialist principles, we stand ready, with voice or pen, to prove with undeniable evidence that your communication to the Congregationalist Church, and your conduct relative to it, is strictly in conformity with the philosophies enunciated by the founders and by the promoters of modern socialism. Not that we think you are unaware of the fact but because the camp followers of socialism are not so well informed — neither are the general public.

Under the caption "A Socialist Wedding" the "International Socialist Review (Chicago, July, 1901) prints a report of the wedding of George D. Herron to Carrie Rand, written by Leonard D. Abbott, a leading New York socialist, which is in part as follows.

"We were gathered together, we of the inner circle of comradeship, on the last Saturday evening in May. Outside our doors the rain beat down, but within the mellow light fell on a room decked by the skill of the craftsman and aglow with the art of the painter. The fragrance and blossom of spring flowers seemed to transform our rooms into a fairy garden; and the strains of a primitive love-melody, as they drifted to us were full of mystery and beauty.

"Our comrade, George D. Herron, arose, care-worn and sorrowful as one who has passed through the Valley of the Shadow of Death, yet strong-hearted and gladsome withal; and beside him stood Carrie Rand, clad in pure vestal white and bearing lilies-of-the-valley in her hand. 'We believe, friends, in fellowship,' he

said, 'and because we believe that fellowship is life we have asked
a few of you to let us share with you the fellowship and sacrament
of the unity of life which we wish to now announce to you. For
many years this unity of life has made us one in fact, but now we
wish this unity to become manifest unto the world, and it is to
announce to you this marriage of our souls, which is to us a reality
before the foundation of the world and which we can conceive of as
having no ending, that we have asked you to kindly come together
to-night.' Miss Rand responded: 'This is the day and hour which
we have chosen to announce to you and the world our spiritual
union, which is a fact in the heart of God.'

"The host of the evening, Dr. Charles Brodie Patterson, editor
of 'The Arena' and 'Mind,' next made a brief address. Dr. Patterson was followed by the Rev. William Thurston Brown, of Plymouth Church, Rochester, whose 'Annunciation Service' was a
poem in prose. It seemed entirely fitting that this tried and true
comrade, whose best labor and thought for many years has been
given to the socialist cause, should be here to participate in the
dedication of these two lives to the socialist movement. He said:

"I cannot but feel — as all of us must to-day — the impotence
of words fittingly to express or announce to the world that which
this occasion means. This is the time and place for the muse of a
poet, the speech of a god; the office of priest or magistrate were an
intrusion here. Better than all would it be if the fact of which we
here are conscious might be announced to the world in the sweet
strains of some wordless music.

"But since these dear friends and comrades have honored me
with the task of speaking for them a word of annunciation concerning this sacred consummation of their life, I joyfully respond. And
the one word which above all others impresses itself upon me as
suggestive of that which brings us here is the old word 'sacrament.'
I know it comes to us from the buried years a-drip with blood and
moldy with superstition; and yet, it is a human word, and through
it throbs the yearning and struggle and climb of a race. It names
an age-long groping after truth — a gleam of the divine — a rift in
the clouds disclosing the glory that bathes and interpenetrates the
universe. That which calls us here to-day is a sacrament. Not in
any conventional sense, but in the elemental significance of the

word — a significance which reflects the mind and being of the Eternal and the Infinite.

"Nowhere has the religious institution so nearly approached the frontiers of vital truth as in conceiving marriage to be a sacrament. But nowhere has it departed so far from all that is divine and ennobling as in supposing that any word of priest or prelate can be sacramental. Neither statute nor official, civil or religious, can ever create this sacred thing. Neither has it the smallest sanction to give to that which is sacred, if at all, by the supreme fiat of a pure and perfect love. The divine is not in legislature or council, church or state. It abides forever in human life. Human life alone incarnates God — and laws and civilizations are tolerable only in the measure of their recognition and service of that life.

"We are not here to establish a relationship which otherwise would not have been. We are not here to inaugurate or consummate a marriage. No words of ours or any one's can add to or take from the truth and solemnity of the sublime fact of a reciprocal love uniting soul to soul by a sanction in presence of which all human enactments seem profane and impertinent, for this is the supreme sacrament of human experience. There is something about it which transcends all other things and proclaims its inherent divinity.

"Nor are we here to lend our countenance to that divine event of which it is our privilege to be witnesses. That which is essentially and elementally true gains nothing from the sanction of individuals or states or nations. We are not here to perform a sacrament, but to receive one — to honor ourselves and enrich all that is best in us by sharing somewhat in the truth and beatitude of these dear friends.

"We are here to-day to announce to the world the oneness of two human souls in a love that reflects and manifests and reproduces somewhat of the essence of that Infinite love which swathes and animates the universe. This oneness no more begins to-day than God does. It has no beginning and can have no end. The discovery of such oneness is the discovery of life — the laying bare the very soul of the cosmos. Time loses its meaning. There is no yesterday and no to-morrow in the married harmony and the joyous rhythm of two such souls. There is only an eternal now, and life rises above its narrow limitations and seems to merge in the All-living and All-loving. Let the fleeting years bring what they may, it cannot matter. Love holds all the years that have been or are to be. Its dominion is universal and its reign eternal. And it lives only to give itself in ever-abounding richness to the hungering needs of men.

"This is a day of joy — overflowing, unsullied, serene; a day of hope — clear, strong, inspiring; a day of faith — laying bare before the souls of men in love's clear light the realities of the eternal world. It is a day of courage and cheer. It has for the world only a message of freedom and fellowship. It anticipates the dawn of a higher life for all. It proclaims the sanctity and omnipotence of love. It asserts the elemental rights of man — the rights that blend with duty and irradiate the skies with hope and gladness.

"If I have any understanding of what this means, it is supremely a gospel. No note of peace or power or purity is wanting. These friends of ours announce to-day their marriage. They do so not primarily because our faulty human laws require it at their hands, but for a deeper and diviner reason. They do not assume that their life belongs to them alone — nor even that this supreme affection which has made them one, disclosed to them the face of God, and transfigured all this earthly life with His shining footprints, is theirs to hoard or hide. In asserting the limitless freedom and the boundless authority of love they but disclose the full-orbed liberty of the sons of God and anticipate a world's emancipation. They do not announce that they have now separated their life from the rest of the world. They announce a fuller, deeper, richer harmony with that divine life which is emergent in the unfolding aspirations of the world, than could have been theirs as separate individuals.

"Inasmuch, therefore, as George D. Herron and Carrie Rand are thus united together by the bond of a reciprocal love, I announce that they are husband and wife by every law of right and truth, and I bespeak for them the fervent benediction of all true souls and the abiding gladness that dwells in the heart of God forever."

Richard Le Gallienne was the first to speak:

"All the friends that Mr. and Mrs. Herron love," he said, "will love them forever, and will love them all the better because they have had the courage to stand up and say they love each other and that love is all the marriage they need. I feel very honored that I had the opportunity of being present·on this momentous occasion, and only wish that I had had longer notice, in order to have prepared an epithalamium worthy of its dignity."

" Two of the Social Democratic comrades spoke next, emphasizing the fact that the marriage meant, above all, more complete consecration to socialism. 'The peculiarly happy thing to me to-night,' said William Mailly, (now national secretary of the socialist party) 'is the knowledge that these two comrades of ours are working shoulder to shoulder in the world-wide movement for the emancipation of the toilers — a movement that is destined to usher in the universal life of leisure and love for all men.' "

" The last speaker was Franklin H. Wentworth, formerly editor of the 'Socialist Spirit.' 'Having shared the joy and sorrow, the trials and problems, of my two comrades here,' he said, 'it is perhaps fitting that I should say the last word on this occasion, and that this word should be a word of personal affection and comradeship. And yet I must confess that the feeling of joy which I have to-night relates not so directly to them as to the cause, in the service of which we are all enlisted. It seems such a mighty triumph of truth and sincerity in the world that the cause must be helped by this union. I believe that the high service of each will be helped by the fact of these two souls working side by side in mutual sustainment, united — yet free. I feel this strongly because of the strength and uplift which has come into my own life through my comradeship with my own true and noble mate. In the very fact that so large a number of persons as are here assembled can be inspired by the same ideal, I see a demonstration that the truth is beginning to force its way and dramatize itself in reference to every human institution. There seems in the gathering of such a company a hint of the dawning of the day when the spirit of freedom shall rule the world — freedom of the body, and freedom of the soul.

Now, in conclusion, there is a personal word I wish to say : I wish to pay a tribute of loving admiration to the woman who was already standing for human freedom when most of us here were children ; a woman who all her life long has been far ahead of her

time; who has steadfastly stood against all forms of hypocrisy and
organized wrong. In her girlhood life this woman was scoffed at
because she was an abolitionist — then the most bitterly hated of
all reformers. In her middle life she was jeered at first as a free
republican and afterward as a free trader ; and now in the time of
her age we find her standing bravely 'mid those who believe that
the world should take another step toward human freedom, namely
the socialists. In her girlhood she worked for the freedom of the
chattel slave, and then lived to see the world come halting after
her, accepting the truth she saw. And I believe there is no more
fitting prayer which I can offer in her behalf to-night, or which will
find a more appreciative response in the staunch soul of Mrs. Rand
herself than that she may be spared to witness at least the beginnings of the world's industrial emancipation.' "

" The gathering broke up, and finally, as a sweet benediction,
the bride herself took her seat at the piano and played to us for
awhile, pouring out her soul in the interpretation of one of Bee-
thoven's greatest sonatas. And as she played, the memory of a
ghoulish press, of human vultures, of slave-marriage, of cruel capitalism, was blotted out. We saw only the vision of the New Life of
Socialism, when the love that made this union holy shall be the .
only basis of marriage, and when this love, stretching out, shall
embrace the common life of the world."

It is the counterfeit which deceives ! It is the employment of holy words for impure uses which makes this devil
formidable. Contrast this event which is held up, by this political atheist force, as ideal before the public gaze ; with the
underlying facts in the case and the hideous skeleton will
come forth.

The "International Socialist Review" has correctly described it "*A Socialist Wedding.*" Socialist George D. Herron, the hero, the deserter of the marriage bond and the be-
trayer of the family, rises, out of "the Valley of the Shadow
of Death" to give poetic testimony of his guilt. "For many
years this unity of life has made us one in fact . . . .
it is to announce to you this marriage of our souls, which is

to us a reality before the foundation of the world." **Realities**
a little closer to the issue were needed to tie honor at home —
the reality of the woman he had deserted and the children he
had disgraced would have been a much healthier vision for
the contemplation of this sin-struck man.

The socialist heroine then arises and says: "We . . . .
announce to the world our spiritual union." What God hath
joined together let no man put asunder — this is the spiritual
Law. Woe be to them who desert this command of God,
flattering themselves that the petty passions of a day can endure against His Will.

The socialist, Rev. William Thurston Brown, arose to
dedicate these "two lives to the socialist movement," A most
fitting cause for the breakers of home and family! A most
fitting arena to display the disruption of faith born of materialist standards. "Priest or magistrate were an intrusion
here." Indeed it is ever out of sight of the representation of
the Law that license is committed. "This oneness no more
begins to-day than God does." This is the brazen tongue of
brass; it is the voice of tinkling cymbals.

The blasphemy of this "Socialist Wedding" is self evident. But it is veiled from the "socialist mind" by the
glamour of false gods, who are invoked in the most extrava-
gant language by the clerical collar socialists. A dishonored
union alleged to have been consummated "before the foundation of the world." — It is amazing that such intellectual
drunkenness can stand on its legs.

Let us look back a little. — After nine years of married
life Mr. Herron publishes a book with an acknowledgement
of moral helpfulness in language which, even at this period,
shows a lack of self control — a tendency to redundancy in
expression to say the least. "I dedicate this

A PLEA FOR THE GOSPEL

1892

to my wife MARY EVERHARD HERRON
who has been to me a living conscience."

Having exposed his "living conscience" to the mock of the world; a reflection were now worth while, whether the example set by those of the "privileged classes" in buying divorces is not the wickedest and most corrupting influence afloat upon this spiritually barren age?

"We privileged classes are wickedly insensible to the fact that, to the majority of human beings in what we call Christendom, the sensations of drink and sexuality are the only experiences which make life interesting; the only things that give anticipation and romance to life; the only sacraments of human fellowship, save the common misery and poverty." ("Between Cæsar and Jesus," George D. Herron, page 83.)

It were well to consider. Is it obedience to Cæsar — to atheism, to mammon, to sex sensation, in one word to socialism — which causes a man to leave a "living conscience?" Or would obedience to the one true God cause a man to shun such a course as the devil is said to shun holy water?

None but the vile will dance in the flickering light of "socialist weddings" when once American citizens are aroused to the fact that the socialist party under the war cry of "free land," "free family," "free society" lures the race to its own destruction.

On May 26th, 1901 — two months after George D. Herron's divorce — "The Worker" said editorially " . . . . some capitalist editors and preachers manufactured a scandal about Comrade Herron." This is merely the application of socialist tactics in his case. This is The Worker's way of manufacturing socialist sentiment, which later is expected to develop into "socialist minds." The "capitalist editors" did not make a scandal, it was The Worker's "Comrade Herron" who made the scandal. The "capitalist editors" have signally failed in opening this case up to public view. They have failed to realize that "Comrade Herron's" scandal was the socialist marriage philosophy put into practice—a little before the time, so with necessary hindrances.

There is no apology from the socialist press. On the contrary its defense is ample, it is even strenuous, and it is coupled with its complement a slap at marriage. And this, notwithstanding they still fight shy, at times and places very shy, of the term free love which directly tells the whole tale. We quote from the "Haverhill Social Democrat" July 2, 1901. In answer to the Haverhill Gazette, who takes George D. Herron to task for certain passages in his reply to the Congregational Church of Grinnell, Iowa.

"It is very doubtful, however, whether it was ignorance that prompted the editor to assert that the attack on the home by Herron is a fragment of European Socialism which the American exponents have hitherto declared they would not adopt. There is no such thing as European Socialism or American Socialism. There is only one kind of Socialism the world over—*international Socialism*, which means everywhere the same, among the Socialists of Haverhill as well as among the Socialists of a city of similar size in Germany, France, Belgium or England.

"Herron has been quoted by the capitalist press as saying that he does not believe that the present marriage system is sacred or good. We repeat the same. The truth cannot be avoided even when dealing with questions of a most delicate nature.

"What is there *sacred* in the modern home? Can anything be sacred which is based on a lie, or on impurity, or on ignorance?

"The marriage system to-day is based on impurity, on ignorance and on a big lie. People marry not for love; therefore modern marriage cannot be sacred."

"The Advance" the "Official Organ of the Socialists of the Pacific Coast" thus delivers itself in a tirade against the San Francisco "Call" for assuming that George D. Herron

and his followers have the habit of " viewing marriage loosely "
and " attempting to cancel the line that divides honesty from
dishonesty."

" The ' Call ' is rapidly winning for itself the proud distinction
of being the representative of capitalism *par excellence.* For un-
scrupulous falsification and contemptible, sneaking, underhanded
methods of personal attack is gaining a record that will make the
yellow sheets turn green with envy. When our Comrade George
D. Herron was divorced and re-married the "Call" seized with
ghoulish glee upon the misrepresentations of the news trust, the
Associated Press, gave an extra twist to the already distorted facts,
and indulged its hatred of Socialists in a fanatically venomous
attack on Herron. Since its first outburst of rage upon a man who
dared and dares to speak and live the truth, it has ceaselessly
searched for facts and alleged facts to throw discredit on the
Socialist movement."

Only to think of it! Herron and his mate are models
— they have dared and dare " speak and live the truth."

Mr. Herron may almost be said to have a personal organ
in " The Worker " (May 19, 1901).

"An Ovation given to Comrade Herron at his last lecture."

"The welcome received, came not alone as a tribute to the
man who has been on the firing line of the Social Revolution for
several weeks, the victim of a pitiless persecution by an unscrupu-
lous enemy, but also as an endorsement of the principles for the
promulgation of which he has undoubtedly been made to suffer. . .
If any man present doubted before the meeting that Comrade Herron understood scientific Socialism, his doubts must have been completely dispelled. There was no equivocation in the presentation
of the claims of the Socialist movement. There could be no com-
promising, no remedying, no reforming the capitalist system.
The movement could not tolerate patching up a bad system that
was wrong in its essence and its foundations, when Comrade
Herron summed up the case in these terse words : ' We don't want
to reform anything: we want to revolutionize everything,' he received his answer in a shout of approval from his listeners."

Mr. Herron had just come from the " firing line." That is, he had met the righteous protest of the people against his beginning to "revolutionize" society — his beginning by "revolutionizing" his own home — his own family. "We don't want to reform anything, we want to revolutionize everything." This illy considered statement gives him credit, credit from radicals — from skeptics — from positivists — from pantheists — from materialists — from socialists, but not from the common people, they are grieved at heart. They are too somewhat dazed at the blare, blare, blare of the brass trumpets, which shout glory, glory, glory : but having no relative shades of tone there are no contrasts — no consciousness of high and low — no knowledge of the Perfect Principles which because of human effort starting at the point unfolds more and more of civilization (in obedience to evolutionary law) towards human perfection.

"Society is progressive and continues to improve. Each century inherits from the past certain requirements, discoveries and improvements, and thus the sum of physical, moral and political benefits grows wonderfully."

The "socialist revolution" does not imply the improvement of society but — It would attempt the beginning of a new one. With a new design — with a design set in motion by "economic freedom." Blind force has fashioned the life of the race up to this point, now the "class conscious" socialists will lend a hand to the process by overturning the whole thing. — If something should not happen to prevent the ushering in of their prophecies.

What higher authority within the socialist movement of this country than "The Worker" could put the seal of approval upon one's understanding of scientific socialism? The seal of approval upon the disruption of the family as progress along the way?

And yet another stamp of honor is given to him whose

ears and eyes are closed to all but the sins which pollute and the folly which foolishness engenders.

"A PROPOSED CAPITALIST BOYCOTT."

"That there is a motive in the continual publication of false and malicious statements by the daily press anent Comrade George D. Herron must be apparent to even the most unsophisticated. That the motive is a dastardly one and worthy of its source is becoming plainer every day. The people who are carrying on this unjust and wicked crusade are not of those who could invite an investigation into their own private affairs with impunity, and their posing before the world as the conservators of public morals is as hypocritical and inconsistent as are all the pretensions of the corrupt and servile defenders and beneficiaries of the present system.

"The reason for the unanimity of action on the part of papers that otherwise appear to conflict in the political and theological views is not far to seek. We have before stated that the reason for it can be found in the fact that Comrade Herron has not only antagonized the organized church in its Christless attitude toward social problems and their solution, but because he has struck bold and deep at the foundation of social injustice, at the source from which the organized church draws its sustenance — the capitalist system of wage slavery.

"Confirmation for this statement is found in an article in "The Outlook" itself. Commenting in the usual strain upon Comrade Herron's marriage — a marriage morally and legally correct — it closes by saying:

"'The only penalty which an offender can be made to feel is empty audience rooms and unmarketable books, and visit this penalty on Dr. Herron.'

"In those words is laid bare the full animus of the attack upon Comrade Herron. It is not his supposed 'sin' that frightens the slavish souls of his detractors — it is the message he brings in the written and spoken word that causes fear and alarm among the enemies of the exploited working classes. If Comrade Herron can be ostracised by the public, if those he wishes to reach and rouse to a proper realization of the monstrous conditions existing to-day could be induced to turn away from him with eyes and ears closed to righteousness and reason then his traducers would rest well satisfied.

"But these sages know neither the time nor the people. Comrade Herron will be heard, and the people will listen because the time for him, and such as he, to speak and be heard is now. The people can no more be prevented from hearing the truth of Socialism than can the persecution of Comrade Herron prevent him from speaking it. And his vindication must as surely follow after as it is inevitable that Socialism will triumph against all the obstacles great and small, that may be thrust in its pathway toward victory." (Editorial "The Worker," New York, June 16, 1901.)

Here we have "The Worker" operating its socialist tactics upon evolving "socialist minds."

Surely it were well that the people learn the truth about socialism — my present work is to this end. Having learned it at such a cost of time and zeal in the cause which I idealized as the greatest of great movements, which has turned to ashes in the mouth, I would do my best that the people learn what it truly is with less cost of intellectual effort and less cost of heart's emotion.

It is alleged by the editor of "The Worker" that the press in reporting "Comrade Herron's" divorce proceedings has published "false and malicious statements" about him. We appeal to the reader to judge whether, in view of the facts presented in the foregoing pages, the press has yet given the necessary space to, and analyzation of, the socialist leader's conduct in regard to this matter consistent with the moral education of our citizenship?

Has Mr. Herron been maligned? We say, no! Would "The Worker" have the temerity to deny the facts contained in the report of "The Congregationalist" — or the statement in the letter of Mr. Herron to the "Grinnell Council"? If so we are ready to pick up the gauntlet and do battle on the side of the "Grinnell Council" in the interest of truth and justice.

"The Worker" cannot mislead intelligent men by wholesale insinuations and slander against the Congregational Church; nor against the "Council"; neither against the general public. They are quite the proper persons to "invite an investigation" into the "private affairs" of the public character of divorce, etc., etc. Marriage has a twofold character, it is public or social and it is private or individual. Consequently if marriage be broken it is the right — nay it is the duty which society owes to its present peace and its future welfare to examine into divorce, which because of the hardness of men's hearts has been set up within the civil court. But as enlightened socialists see in this exercise of public duty nothing but the hypocritical and inconsistent . . . pretensions of the corrupt and servile defenders and beneficiaries of the present system " it is quite useless to expect fair play in discussion upon this or any kindred subject. As liberty reads license, to them, so does billings-gate stand for argument.

Neither can "The Worker's" attempt to give this case an economic turn pass current, save with the "socialist mind." The marriage system was not introduced as a part of economic evolution. But it was and it is a part of the Original Design of human society. Therefore neither the "Christless attitude" of the church "towards social problems and their solution" nor "because he (Mr. Herron) has struck bold and deep at the foundations of social injustice " has the institution of marriage any proper connection with the "capitalist system " nor with "wage-slavery."

"The Worker " says Mr. Herron's marriage is "morally correct." We differ — We do not dispute its legality — But we do affirm that the entrance of two women, mother and daughter, into a house as especial family friends; with the result of a visit by the husband with the two women to the holy land; and the later result of the husband's divorce — the desertion of the wife — the fatherless children — and the still later result of the man's marriage with the younger of the women — not to mention the public insults to the dignity and sacredness of the marriage institution — give to Mr. Herron's second marriage a tone quite degraded from the true moral color of marriage as a sacrament.

It were mere folly to prevent the people "from hearing the truth of socialism." It is our determined purpose to see to it that the people have an easier opportunity of "hearing the truth of socialism." Above all, the truth about socialism will show that its economic theories are a rope of sand : And a glimpse of its applied philosophy may be seen in the disruption of the family life of Mr. Herron — and his setting up of a "free family" (notwithstanding the difficulties) along the "socialist way."

Against "The Worker's" slander of the Council — And to offset the standing of the socialist editor's support of the Herron–Rand "Socialist Wedding," we present the following quotations :

"Since the divorce was granted a statement in behalf of the people of Grinnell has been put forth, drafted by Professor Parker of Iowa College, but signed by the mayor of the city, the pastor of the First Congregational Church and a score and more of the leading merchants, bankers, professional men of the community, who are said to indorse it in substance if not in form. This statement in part reads thus:

"What we know of Mr. Herron's life and efforts to induce his wife to ask for a divorce, of the methods understood to have been employed by him to bring it about, of her generosity towards him even now, of the declarations unfavorable to her which seem to us to have originated with him, compels every one here, so far as we know or have learned, to sympathize with her and to deem him a cruel and faithless husband." ("The Congregationalist," May 4, 1901).

"The pastor of the Congregational Church in Grinnell, Rev. E. M. Vittum over his own signature makes the following statement:

"Any statement that he has been persecuted by his church on

account of heresy or socialism is an absolute falsehood. For some time past there have been increasing suspicions as to his moral character, culminating, when a divorce, with custody of the children, was granted Mrs. Herron. The charges against his character will be dealt with by the church, but without haste or excitement. Our church does not believe in lynching."

Rev. Drs. N. D. Hillis and S. D. McConnell of the local clergy, Mr. Rossiter Raymond and Judge Gaynor of the local laity and Rev. Dr. Josiah Strong "were among those who refused to attend the dinner of the Get-to-gether Club of Brooklyn, at which Mr. Herron was to be a guest, and which was finally abandoned on account of the inability of the managers of the club to get speakers who would take their places."

Dr. Hillis, in giving a lengthy interview to the "Brooklyn Eagle" on the break-down of the dinner, said: "My objection to appearing with Mr. Herron was not based upon the vagaries of his intellect, or upon the fact that his thinking seems to me crude, superficial and false in its premises, but upon his deeds, that represent his will and character. I do not wish to be unkind, but there are sins so bald, vulgar, and crass in their persistency, their virulence, that they consume the mantle of charity as a flame a garment."

Rev. Dr. Josiah Strong, who is reported as having visited Grinnell, interviewed Mrs. Herron and carefully investigated the matter, in his letter declining to appear with Mr. Herron, said:

"He and his female accomplice in breaking up a family have committed a crime against the fundamental institutions of society, and have trampled under foot the explicit and unmistakable teachings of Jesus Christ. Their conduct has been despicable beyond the resources of my vocabulary to express, and if all the facts were known these people would not be tolerated in any self-respecting society for an hour."

The socialist estimate of Mr. Herron may be seen from the following quotations. And it is necessary to know that the socialist papers guard closely their columns in the interest of "class conscious" socialists. They alone are to be trusted as the standard bearers, around which to rally the fighting force of their revolutionary principles.

"The Social Democrat" (Haverhill, Mass., May 4, 1901.)

THE MAN HERRON.

From a Sunday Evening lecture given by Rev. Wm. T. Brown, in Plymouth church, Rochester, N. Y."

"After telling of the power of Dr. Herron, whereby he came from the obscurity, a 'little Congregational church in Minnesota,' and 'stirred and electrified the thinking people of this country as no minister has done in the past century,' and of his call to become assistant pastor of a church in Burlington, Iowa. And that 'men of any spiritual sensitiveness were compelled instinctively to recognize the fact that a prophet had appeared among them — a man with a message which the world must hear and reckon with." — He says, "But it was as impossible for Dr. Herron to be supported by any ordinary religious institution, as it was for Jesus to be so supported. Jesus could not have been maintained by any institution of his day and country. They had no use for him, nor he for them. The Burlington church soon discovered they had secured a pastor, the new wine of whose preaching no old bottles of ecclesiasticism could contain. They found that Dr. Herron could not be hampered by the restraints of tradition and custom. And it became evident both to him and to them that a different field must be found for the deliverance of his message.

" . . . his departure from the Burlington church meant his final departure from recognition as a minister. Not a church in the United States or out of it could be found that would tolerate him as its minister. Neither could one be found on the earth that would afford a living support to a man like Jesus of Nazareth.

"But there is a law of adaptation in the universe. Where there is demand there will sooner or later be supply . . . Mrs. Rand felt that this preacher was right — divinely right . . . she had been waiting to devote her wealth to the purpose of changing the system."

"The opportunity had come in the person of Dr. Herron. She had seen he could not be supported by his church, or any other church. She felt that he ought to have a wider hearing and therefore established at her personal expense 'a department to be known as the Department of Applied Christianity,' with Dr. Herron at the head.

"There was in this experience of Dr. Herron a singular likeness to what occurred in the life of Jesus. The only hint we have of the source of personal contribution to the support of Jesus is that which mentions certain women as giving of their means to defray his living expenses while he was preaching in Galilee. When Dr. Herron could no longer hope for support from any source whatever in the propagation of his faith, a consecrated woman alone insured the continuance of his ministry and assured the people of this country the privilege of hearing and reading the message which has made Dr. Herron the greatest prophet of modern times.

"But it was inevitable that, as no church could support or tolerate such a man, so no other institution could. It was only a question of time before he would have to separate himself from all relationship to any sort of institution." Dr. Herron resigned.

"When Dr. Herron gave up his place in the college, he gave up his living. No church, no other college, no institution of any sort can be found that would give him a maintainance . . . Precisely the same thing was true in the case of Jesus. He could get a living as a carpenter perhaps; but after he had begun to preach his revolutionary doctrines it was quite possible that his chances of getting a living at any trade would be slim.

"But the question is whether Jesus had any right to go back to the work of a carpenter after he became conscious of the truth that made him a prophet. That question admits of but one answer. Jesus would have been the most despicable man that ever lived, if, after becoming conscious of the truths he taught, he had not fearlessly and at any cost proclaimed them. Nothing whatever could excuse him from doing that.

"The principle is exactly the same in the case of Dr. Herron. He had no choice but to give utterance to his convictions. The fact that obedience to those convictions might mean sorrow and pain to himself and to others could not weigh an atom."

This blasphemous gush passes so far beyond the bonds of sanity that it is but necessary for a large number of socialists themselves to step just outside of the reeking circle of its psychology to see its wicked undermining of faith in those eternal principles which alone hold the heart of humanity to sweet reasonableness and to honorable judgments. If a clear understanding of the fact that fundamental principles limit rational phenomena within proscribed limits, it would then be possible for socialists themselves to find out the reason why "Dr. Herron could not be hampered by the restraints of tradition and custom." It was not merely the formalities of thought and deed which Dr. Herron attacked, but he assailed the fundamental elements which hold society together as a coherent body. Such an one is a law-breaker — he does not extend the liberties of the people by throwing off the "restraints of tradition and custom," but he enslaves such of the people as follow him — just as he has enslaved himself, for he has locked his own doors upon himself. Therefore "the message" which socialists say makes "Dr. Herron the greatest prophet of modern times" is that same old message which has ever found dancers to its tunes. — But alas for the dancers — they are heavily taxed by their fiddler.

Socialism is an institution! It does not only "tolerate such men," but one may almost say in his own personal organs he is set upon the highest pinnacle of socialist fame — and for what? For breaking the moral law which holds society within its duly progressive course — as the stars are by physical law held to their orbits.

Consider the vulgarity of the running comparison of this sick sweet phrasemonger with Jesus Christ; is it not revolting to good sense. And note that "after becoming conscious of the truths he taught" Jesus would have become the most despicable man who ever lived if he had not allowed women to support him at the task of giving his message — which is assumed to be, because of the earlier period, not quite so great as this of the "modern prophet." All this crass ignorance from men who would scorn an authoritative interpretation of the Bible. — Yet they without apology, set themselves up as being the only sufficient expositors of God's Word. Failing to turn aside religious institutions to their immoral interpretations, these ex-minister socialists are the most pliant servants of his majesty, the mental darkness. They are the most seductive, in speech they turn the power of God's Word to work the downfall of faith, which in some men's breasts burns all too feebly to resist the glitter of the earthly paradise which may be had for a vote.

The unspeakable assumption of the party press in comparing its political leader to Jesus of Nazareth, makes the pen pause. A party leader, too, who had just committed the act of putting away an honorable wife; so plainly in violation of one of the foremost decrees of the Master who had established marriage as a sacrament. Certainly such an outrage upon sober sense ought to meet with the intolerance of every right-minded man — of every man who stands for the integrity of the family within this nation.

It was just at the time that this sentiment was sweeping through the socialist press that the then editor of the "Haverhill Social Democrat" while addressing a public meeting in Boston referred to Dr. Herron as the second Jesus Christ. At the close of the lecture, upon the opening of the discussion which followed, Martha Moore Avery, the author and others declared war upon the current blasphemy within the socialist movement — against the socialist philosophy. It was a sharp turning point from a personal point of view — not very clearly seen at the time, but it progressively came to our minds as the point at which we were confronted with this issue — was the socialism which had animated the minds and hearts and set the tasks of our little group of Boston workers one and the same with the "International Revolutionary Scientific Socialism" of the socialist party? We set to work to test it. And it must be confessed that our zeal in the interest of the wage workers had long prevented our seeing the very patent fact of contradiction, of opposing qualities. The fact of radical disagreement in philosophy had for years been demonstrated by the internal opposition to our work — especially to the work of Martha Moore Avery.

No ! It came at last clearly to view that the socialism of our little band was not the socialism of those loyal adherents to "international revolutionary scientific socialism," not the socialism of those persons who made the mould and of those party members who now hold the mould with which the genuine socialism is stamped. We give over freely and without a shadow of bitterness the name socialism. — Thankful we were that the opposition to us as personal workers was sharp enough and that on the other hand our hostility to their philosophy and practice was strong enough to mark clearly the lines of separation between the two opposing camps.

Martha Moore Avery in opening the discussion referred to, clearly opened up the issue—was this the cause to which she had given so many years of devoted labor? Was it true that the philosophy of Marx was the permanent issue of the socialist movement under the cloak of a political party organized for economic reasons only? If so she would have none of it. Did socialism really stand for the disruption of the home? Did socialism, after all, as had always been asserted by so many, many members, stand committed to atheism as its religious creed? If so she was as ready to give her life work against it as she had heretofore been glad to give her life to it, thinking to promote the industrial wellbeing of the working class in particular and the advancement of society in general.

By turning our attention to the literature circulated to make propaganda these questions were answered. It may justly seem strange that constant workers for the movement knew so little of the movement. But we think it will be clear to the candid mind when the facts are considered. The study of economics had for years taken the attention from off the content of the literature being circulated to make socialist propaganda, and, too, it is easy to confess that we anticipated the advent of men of American breeding in sufficient numbers to swamp the foreign directorship of the party in the United States. And in that way throw off the isms which clung to the party. But this was vain. As we have said the ex-ministers of American birth and culture are the most forceful propagandists of Marxian philosophy. Atheism under their speech wears a mask of religious sentiment over its murky face.

Our Boston School of Political Economy with Martha Moore Avery at its head, as Director had taken a large share of our time and intellectual effort. We had for years been delving into the principles of political economy — and I make free to say that Martha Moore Avery is one of the ablest political economists in the English speaking world. So it was that research into economic principles; and too the assumption that the socialist party was organized for the economic emancipation of the down trodden (which of course we assumed had had the barnacles of European misbeliefs and despotic associations fastened upon it — which it would one day outgrow). This had, despite the constant and fierce friction between us and other influential members of the movement, kept us at work in the socialist party.

Then followed the resolution, offered by the authority at the Massachusetts socialist state convention (1902). These resolutions called for the official sanction only of such speakers as kept their platform utterances clear from attacks upon religion and the church — clear from " free love " and " free family " sentiments. The resolutions did not pass. But a forceful current of vilification did set in against the promoter and the supporters of it. This was more testimony in evidence that the socialist party will not tolerate any interference with the propagation of its philosophy as laid down by its founders and by its leading, its influential propagandists.

Two Socialist Leaders.

In the discussion which followed the presentation of the resolutions, Mrs. Avery and myself were hissed and jeered for bringing up the matter. With a fine display of socialist tactics the author was declared to be unable to bring proof that the current socialist literature was filled with the advocacy of "free love." And with a skillful throwing of dust in the eyes that were just beginning to open to the truth it asserted, that the socialists in Germany, in convention assembled, had declared religion to be a private matter, and that they would do likewise — and that should settle the doubts of those delegates who feared an attack upon the home.

It was then that this book was conceived. The public should be furnished with the avenue through which the facts in the case were easily accessible. The extent of the advocacy of these doctrines amazed us. The boldness with which the literature exhibited its philosophy gave full proof many hundred times over that the socialist dye was sun-proof; it will not wash out nor will it fade.

With the full proof came the conviction that socialism is the devil fish with its fangs tightening about the limbs of our government — with the conviction nothing in conscience was left for those of us who, up to our full opportunity, had placed our lives at the disposal of this cause — those of us who had served this cause as though it were that of the good God — but to turn right about face, cost what it would, and tell the public what it had taken us so long to learn: That socialism is a pest to the life of the world — to the light of the world — to the progress of the world.

William Morris and Ernest Belfort Bax fear that romantic literature will, under the regime of socialism, become extinct for want of tragedies of the heart upon which to hang the tale. In their joint production "Socialism its Growth and Outcome" (page 308) they say:

"As to literature, fiction as it is called, when a peaceful and happy society has been some time afoot, it will probably die out for want of material. The fabulum of the modern novel in its various dressings is mostly provided by the anomalies and futilities of a society of inequality wielded by a conventional false sense of duty, which produces the necessary imbroglio wherewith to embarrass the hero and heroine through the due number of pages."

These socialist leaders need have no fear! The Eleanors and the Averlings would be present by the thousands! They would demonstrate that high degree of heathen bravery — the taking of their own lives, this would supply authors with the tragic heroes of the future — while the Herrons of socialist society will supply fatherless children with which to keep pathos alive in the human heart for some little time. "Free love" and "free families" will give the Morrises and the Baxes the Claras and Dick with which to supply emotional literature with themes — to say nothing of unrequited love if it be not that animalism will have reduced the race to mere "sex fondness" as the basis of union.

Abolition of the State.

WHAT will become of religion? It will die out.
What will become of the monogamic family? It will die out.

What will become of the state? It will die out.

Socialists are aware that religion is the foundation and the salvation of the State — They are aware that the monogamic family is the unit of the state. Hence the destruction of religion and the family is advocated, by them, that the state may come to an end.

Gabriel Deville, a socialist of high standing in the international socialist movement has written a book "The State and Socialism" the socialist estimate of which may be seen in a review of this work and "Socialism, Revolution and Internationalism," of which Mr. Deville is also the author, which appeared in the "Haverhill Social Democrat" (Feb. 16, 1901). Of "Socialism, Revolution and International" it says,

"This booklet we recommend to the public at large and especially to those who use their brains when reading. With such literature in the English language, no man can afford to feed his intellect on the confused articles of capitalistic papers. Gabriel Deville is an authorative writer on Socialism."

We quote from "The State and Socialism" (Gabriel Deville, New York, December 1900).

"The State is the public power of coercion, created and maintained in human societies by their division into classes, and which, having force at its disposal, makes laws and levies taxes."

"For socialists—the existence of the State in a society is bound up with the existence of classes in that society. Hence, this conclusion: before classes came into being there was no state; when classes shall cease to exist there will be no state."

"My thesis is that a social organization is possible without a State, and that the State appears and subsists only in societies divided into classes."

There is so much socialist writing which is vague, so cumbered up with negations and abstractions that the student may be pleased to find a plain statement of their doctrine in relation to this specific subject. Deville has brought out clearly the socialist position regarding the state. Although he says that "Socialist definitions are not arbitrary" one must logically conclude that Mr. Deville's definition is arbitrary for the reason that it is laid down upon a purely arbitrary basis. It is the express mission of socialism to abolish classes, therefore if the state is conditioned upon the existence of classes he is certainly arbitrarily correct in saying "when classes shall cease to exist there will be no state." Of course the question now comes upon the possibility of classes becoming extinct. And this brings up the further question, was there a time when classes did not exist? This definition although arbitrary is negative. It gathers its strength from the assumption that classes are to be destroyed, destroyed by socialists with a "class conscious" programme to be worked out by the use of the political power of that self same state which under their management will become extinct— It certainly takes a "socialist mind" to be satisfied with this intellectual juggling as a substitute for reasoning.

It was the appearance of this book, by Deville, which prompted the author to write the following letter, which was published in the "Haverhill social Democrat" (May 19, 1902). It appeared under the caption "THE STATE."

"THE PAST, PRESENT AND FUTURE."

Innumeral are the works written upon the subject of the State and still confusion reigns. Is it outside the possibibly of man's power to encompass the meaning of the State? No, not if he starts from a reasonable, rational basis.

We suffer from the logic of our friends who, from unsound premise weave a story of the State and the necessity of its being abolished, which, if their premise is accepted, make a very plausible statement.

If one declare that hatchets are the cause of crime and cite their use by Carrie Nation in her property destroying temperance crusade; and the use of one by Storti, in the murder to avenge his sister's honor, one may logically come to the conclusion that the betterment of society will result from the abolition of hatchets. But being rational human beings we know that hatchets are not the cause of crimes, but their use by persons who have subverted them from their function as an aid in advancing civilization to instruments of destruction and death.

This hatchet-logic is employed by many socialists, following the lead of the anarchist school, they say that the State is but the principle of invasion, that it but attacks the rights of others and they therefore declare that the State is but the result of conflicting class interests and that it has existed only since the advent of classes in society: that it is simply a weapon of the ruling class used against the working-class and therefore logically conclude from their false premise that the State ought to be; and that it will be abolished by the accession of socialists to power. One may take care of his enemies, the anarchists, but in the words of the old woman Methodist: "Oh! good Lord, deliver me from my friends!"

As to the statement frequently made that only since the existence of classes has the State been known, I agree, if one speaks upon the broad principle of diversity of gifts and their manifestation, for history knows of no time when classes (differences of human quality) did not exist. But, following the argument of Gabriel Deville in his work on the "State" (translated by Rives Le Monte) who instances the North American Indian tribes and the old gens of Greece and Italy as illustrations of association without class distinction and therefore human relationship co-existant with the non-existence of the State, I must emphatically dissent from his conclusion. They are, rather, most valuable illustrations of primitive democracies, under which a just government existed solely by the consent of the governed. Each and every individual member was both ruler and ruled within these States.

I say that the knowledge of the primitive democratic states, coming to us as it does in the days of our generation is of great inspiration to those who seek to establish a fraternal State, as it is proof that such a State has existed under primitive methods of production; it is the opposite pole from that of the oppressive government of the despotic State, which was also manifested under primitive methods of production.

The successive demonstrations of the principle of the state is mistaken for the state itself. Hence the confusion. . . . I shall say that A State is an association (covering a given area) consciously and unconsciously organized for mutual protection and advantage. State, government and administration are frequently confounded and confused. What is a government? Government is the organic power, the machine to be operated, Theocratic or simply civic, embracing the social relationships, within the confines of a given territory, the tendency of which is to evolve from the paternal (or maternal), coercive to the democratic and administrative. And the administration? Why, the usurped or elective power by which the government is operative.

To those of foreign lands who have never lived within a democratic state, nor been imbued with the spirit of civic freedom manifested at the altitude of that in the United States the socialist talk of abolishing the state may seem good glib logic to guide their intellectual gymnastics with. But one living in a land where men have seen the state evolve from the kings' coercive power to the power of manhood suffrage, where by the exercise of the franchise, once in four years, may be caused a higher manifestation of political organization and of economic opportunity this vapid talk of abolishing the state will one day down. The American Socialists seek not to destroy but to fulfill the possible functions of a democratic state, that up to its greatest capacity it may provide for the equal advantage and enjoyment of all. That it may do what its founders meant it should do, protect life, give liberty and render the pursuit of happiness possible to all.

That the State has been and is used by the "upper classes" to defend and strengthen their power is true; That they through its power have kept the working class in subjection is true. But is this an argument for the abolition of the state? No! a hundred no! It cannot be denied that by the very power of the state the subservient working class may arise from their knees and become themselves the administrators of the state. If in the United Kingdom, today, British subjects are content to remain such: If in Russia the mass-man is content to be terrorized I can but say that masters rule only while those who should be men remain on their knees.

Rather than the timid talk of abolishing that with which the workers have been oppressed, (because of their own ignorance) let us rather be touched with the living fire of freedom as were the American Colonists when they declared that no longer would they be subject to the court of George the third. They arose; broke their chains; emptied the tea in Boston harbor; elevated themselves to a condition, to a state, that to this day manifests the highest degree of civic equality yet attained by man. Ere long — when the working class of the state of the Tzar—the working class of the state of Edward the seventh—the working class of these United States shall decide to arise from their knees, no longer to be the subservient, cringing, sweating, slaving, disinherited wealth producing class, getting but their provender as a beast of burden. When the working class of the world shall have become conscious of their human rights, then there will have been an evolution to that high condition when coercion of man will be unknown and administration of industry engage the power of the state.

Since this article was written a flood of light has elevated the author's understanding. With a fuller knowledge of socialist philosophy, doctrine and practice; with somewhat of an insight into religious principles and the masterful part they play in maintaining civilization, rather than declare that American socialists seek not to destroy but to augment the functions of our democratic state, we freely assert that were socialists to gain the political power they would impregnate society with their philosophies and destroy, if possible, not alone the state but the very foundation of the state. Socialists

are very fond of abolition, of extinction. That which is beyond the comprehension of the materialist mind is fit food for
socialist treason. The family is the first class, therefore it
must die: religion sustains classes, therefore it must die:
The state is the creature of classes, therefore it must die.
While the sober commonsense of the matter is that the order
which allows families to live together is maintained by the
power of the state — and neither the fact itself or the name
by which the fact is known is in danger of being abolished,
the jangling of socialist philosophy to the contrary notwithstanding.

Since writing this article on the state a clearer understanding of socialism has convinced me that it is impossible to
make a distinction in favor of American socialism. The
socialism of America and the socialism of Germany — France
— Italy — England — etc., etc., are one and the same. Socialists seek the establishment of the principles embodied in
the teachings of Marx, Engels, Ferri, Bax, Herron and
hosts of others of international standing. To these teachings
the modern socialist movement is irrevocably committed.

Even though one were to accept the socialist definition of
a state one may, because of the inherent differences in men,
reasonably conclude that as these differences have heretofore
shown themselves in classes, they will continue to do so until
the end of time, therefore the state is a stable institution.
Socialists say the state is a creature of classes — Good! The
classes may pass by. There may be the patrician and the
slaves — the nobles and the villains — the capitalists and the
wage-earners — but the state is the state. Or you may fancy
a socialist state — Oh! I beg pardon, not a state, but — a state
of things — a state of society; a state of any thing, but not —
oh, no — not the state — in which the "class struggle" is
demonstrated by the "administration committee" of the ward,
who have control of the means of production (no, certainly, I
would not say capital now that we are considering a socialist

state. For capital along with the state and a host of other things have all been abolished, long ago) against those who are on the " outs." Or it may be that the "class struggle " is seen in the row between the superintendents and foremen and the workers in the nursing factory, who for a dozen and one reasons may come in conflict and feel like " whipping it into " one another?

Heaven is the only place where differences are elevated into harmonious contrasts — where every act is prompted by aspiration — If heaven came on earth ambition must give place to the doing of things for the glory of God, not for the sake of self gratification. Then and not until then, nor by any other means, will the sore differences amongst men be healed. Difference in quality is natural and will last as long as man is man. Difference in quality is necessary to separate one from the other, but the rasping differences which are created by selfish indifference, from envy, from hate will not yield to a full stomach — nor will the philosophies which socialists say come from a rotund belly better the moral instruction of the race ; and human ambition will see to it in a society surfeited with " sex fondness " that the socialist " class struggle " will fight out its battles on an oozy bed of filth.

The philosophy of socialism logically leads to the introduction of a negative terminology — To a set of arbitrary definitions based upon false assumptions. Gabriel Deville's writings are good specimens of this specious school. He defines capital, wages and the state in negation, that is to say, they are dependent upon passing conditions not grounded upon fundamental principles.

" In order to understand what we mean by the suppression of capital, one must know that capital is for us a character which the means of production have taken on under given, definite social conditions, and which they may lose without affecting their existence in the slightest. It is just the same in the case of the wage-system and wages. The latter term cannot, according to us, be applied to any system of remuneration whatsoever, but only to a mode of remuneration presupposing surplus-labor. It is just the same finally in the case of the word State, which means, in our opinion, a system of social organization which implies necessarily the division of society into classes."

. . . "the future social organization, when antagonistic classes no longer exist, when constraint no longer has to be exercised over some for the benefit of others, will not be a State any more than the means of production will be capital after they shall have lost the power of exploiting the labor of others, or than the future remuneration will be what we call wages when it shall no longer presuppose surplus-labor. These two latter changes will be the result of the suppression of the character of capital which is to-day stamped upon the principal means of production." ("The State and Socialism," Deville.)

The state is the result of economic classes — logically, then, were classes abolished the state dies out.

Capital is the character which the means of production assumes under a given social condition, under capitalism,— logically, when capitalism is abolished, capital no longer exists.

Wages exist only within a system in which surplus-labor is expropriated by the capitalist class from the working class — logically, when the capitalist system shall have been abolished, men will no longer work for wages — wages will be abolished.

If one grant the premise; the definitions, then the socialist conclusions may be granted, readily. But as the premise is false — the definitions false, so consequently, the conclusions are false. — They are useless save as a study of the extremes to which logic may carry the mind when once it is launched upon a sea of irrational speculation — rather than when logic proceeds from the solid rock of reason, of truth.

What is Capital? That which aids a man in the production of wealth. Can a simpler or more primal definition

be presented? If so we shall be pleased to become aware
of it. Can it stand the strain of reason and the test of
logic? Yes, and why? Because it gets at the principle,
the fundamental analysis of the thing. Because it is both
specific and abstract in its application. Because it may be
applied to any form of industrial society. — It holds its own
equally well within the three spheres of industry proper — the
domestic sphere — the civic sphere and the realm of political
economy.

Were socialists to get at the understanding of the fundamental yet simple fact that principles never change — they
were created when God created the universe — that merely
the manifestations of the principle change with the unfold-
ment of the designs which demonstrate the principle, which
are so to speak the physical structure of the principle, they
would abandon their premise; their definitions and their conclusions. In fact it was my study of the fundamental principles of political economy which gave me the key with which
to unlock the falsity of the socialist position and my consequent abandonment of them.

As the principle of capital never changes therefore a
correct definition must hold for all times and under all relationship. The socialist terminology will not hold under
changed economic conditions (they say capital will be abolished under socialism) therefore it is not permanent; not
primal; not fundamental, in a word, it is not scientific.

Capital never changes as an economic principle, what
does change however is the demonstration of the principle —
quite two different propositions. From an evolutionary standpoint what does change is the conditions under which capital
is operated.

Under the conditions, where one man alone forms the
single tools necessary to aid him in procuring wealth, capital
may be called primitive capital. When the free cities were
builded and men associated themselves into guilds — when a

higher form of industrial tools were used in manufacture it were reasonable to refer to the capital then in use, in comparison to primitive capital, as medieval capital. When we enter the era of modern production, where complex machinery requires the united effort of many persons to produce a single commodity — where industrial society is divided into capitalists and wage-earners — it is correct to speak of modern capital. All the while capital has not changed as a principle; it even remains that which aided men in the production of wealth. — Although the conditions under which wealth is produced and consumed have vastly changed there is no need to change our definition. The same principles of analyzation apply with equal force to the family; the church; and the state — in fact to those institutions and to those things which socialists may try but will fail to fathom from their false premise and with their false definitions.

Deville, when writing of wages falls into the same error (the errors of the socialist school) as when attempting the analysis of capital and of the state. He assumes that the term wages can be correctly applied only when speaking of the system of society under which remuneration presupposes "surplus-labor." That is to say wages is a term which rightfully belongs to the prevailing economic system (the capitalist system) which supplies the methods under which capitalists expropriate surplus-time" from the employees.

With the hand of death socialists brush aside the fact that the term wages has been in use centuries before the present industrial order struggled to its feet. Wages is the name of a principle. — When applied to economics it denotes the return in wealth for the human energy, expended upon natural resources, according to an industrial design. This definition will hold when applied to primitive; to medieval, or to modern work — to the work of one lone man or to a collection of men — to any order or class of society. The principle does not change — What does change is the conditions under which wages return to the worker. The return in wealth that man receives for his effort, for the expenditure of his energy, according to an industrial design always was, it is, and it always will be his wages. — For the simple but sufficient reason that principles are eternal.

Social definitions must fail — the race being sane — to get a foothold within the intellectual arena. Where is the common sense in accepting their negative terminology which if adopted will pass with the passing phases of production (just as the phases of the "socialist family" pass and repass — requiring new terms to define its new sensations) when the knowledge of a positive terminology may be had, that will penetrate, for all time, the changing phenomena one may desire to analyze — Eternal principles never die !

If the socialist definition of wages be accepted then one must conclude that the word "wages" did not exist prior to the establishment of the capitalist system. But the fact of the matter is that Marx and other socialist fathers were long-headed enough to see their dilemma. In a blind way they perceived the fact that wages must have some sort of introduction to the evolutionary sphere of industry. This necessity sent them to the ridiculous straits of propping up their theory by asserting that the first economic act is the sex act of procreation — the child being the wealth. That the first economic class division, is the man as the capitalist and the woman as the proletarian. Ye gods ! ye put your servants to strange pranks in the worship of their idols.

The wages of sin is death ! Here the Bible which never makes a mistake between the positive and the negative — never uses 'work' where 'labor' is the word — relates the principle of wages to the moral sphere of man's activity. His physical return if he expend his energy in disruption, is death. Death is the wage which society must receive if it accept the disruption which flows from socialist principles. False bases; false definitions; necessitating false conclusions. The socialist world causing the disruption of the family, the church and the state — would take its wage of Death.

We have seen the socialist assertions that the monogamic form of the family will become extinct. And, too, we have seen that their methods in argument are purely arbitrary. Starting from a premise which has no basis in fact, they coolly proceed to lay down their ultimatum as to its extinction. They assert that economic causes brought the monogamic form of the family into existence and then logically conclude that when the economic conditions radically change that the form of the family will change. Socialists will (so they say) make woman economically free, by giving her an equal opportunity with men to work — and, too, all law, sacred and secular, relating to marriage will be abolished, and so the monogamic family will come to its end.

Socialists adopt the same fatal premise and the same futile reasoning in dealing with the state. We have already seen it in our analysis of Gabriel Deville's postulate upon the state. We now bring forward the definition of Engels and Marx to prove that there is no disagreement among "class conscious" socialists as to the origin or the end of the state.

"The State is simply a product of society at a certain stage of evolution. It is the confession that this society has become hopelessly divided against itself, has entangled itself in irreconcilable contradictions which it is powerless to banish. In order that these contradictions, these classes with conflicting economic interests, may not annihilate themselves and society in a useless struggle, a power becomes necessary that stands apparently above society and has the function of keeping down the conflicts and maintaining "order." And this power, the outgrowth of society, but assuming supremacy over it and becoming more and more divorced from it, is the state." (Page 206).

" The state is the result of the desire to keep down class conflicts. But having arisen amid these conflicts, it is as a rule the state of the most powerful economic class that by force of its economic supremacy becomes also the ruling political class and thus acquires new means of subduing and exploiting the oppressed masses. The antique state was, therefore, the state of the slave owners for the purpose of holding the slaves in check. The feudal state was the organ of the nobility for the oppression of the serfs and dependent farmers. The modern representative state is the tool of the capitalist exploiters of wage labor." (Pages 208-209, "The Origin of the Family, Private Property and the State," by Frederick Engels).

"Economic Determinism" being the premise from which all socialist philosophy proceeds (rather than the perfect design of social order given by God, which is by man progressively demonstrated under the law of evolution) their view of the state is irrational, it is self-contradictory. In substance they say that society is responsible for the individual, and then they declare that the collective will, as expressed by the state, is but an engine of oppression. In parts their argument is directly against their conclusions. In order that classes with conflicting economic interests may not annihilate themselves, society, that is to say the classes themselves, set up a power superior (not to themselves) to the power of any faction of themselves, that order may be preserved. This is simply another way of asserting that the majority rule, while the rights of the minority are protected and that all the people are benefited by living within the commonwealth in safety. That some among the people are better able to guide the ship of state goes without saying to the rational mind — And that power naturally dominates lesser power is a law of nature which also goes without saying to those who can properly weigh differences. Now when all is said and done, this is the very principle which socialists quarrel with. The principle of majority rule is what socialists don't want manifested. What they do want is that the atheistic minority shall dominate and overturn the order of the majority. They themselves have pointed out that there is no order and no safety where the state is not in control. Ah! but, they say, there was a golden time when there were no economic differences. — But as that time is not known save to "socialist minds" it is clear that their ideal freedom means freedom from the restraint of order. Their law is license.

Socialists seem to be unable to distinguish the relative degrees of mass-intelligence which separate the "feudal" or the "antique" state from the "modern representative state." Therefore they fail to see that the state may more perfectly demonstrate the principle of democracy when men in general shall have become more intelligent. It is mere folly to insist that our republican state is a class state. Its administration is in the control of its citizens.

But here is more hatchet-logic:

"The state did not exist from all eternity. There have been societies without it, that had no idea of any state or public power. At a certain stage of economic development, which was of necessity accompanied by a division of society into classes, the state became the inevitable result of this division. We are now rapidly approaching a stage of evolution in production, in which the existence of classes has not only ceased to be a necessity, but becomes a positive fetter on production. Hence these classes must fall as inevitably as they once arose. The state must irrevocably fall with them. The society that is to reorganize production on the basis of a free and equal association of the producers, will transfer the machinery of state where it will then belong: into the Museum of Antiquities by the side of the spinning wheel and the bronze ax." ("The Origin of the Family," pages 211, 212.)

This is brave talk, though it rests on nonsense. Socialists are good at destruction. They talk much of evolution but their favorite process is dissolution.

Like Deville all others follow Marx and Engels in assuming that the monogamic family will become extinct. It must be destroyed! For is it not the unit of the state, and have not the followers of socialism with thundering tones cried out that the state is on its last legs? That there was a time when the state did not exist and the time will soon come round when the socialist party will gain control and choke its life?

To assume that people lived together without a state is to beg the question. The state in one form or another is as old as the race. The regulations of the Gens as pictured by Morgan in his "Ancient Civilization" is as truly a state as was ancient Egypt.

To understand "socialist society" it must be borne in mind that administrative power would be directly related to the production and exchange of wealth. All other departments of human activity would be "free." This may seem a little difficult to other than the "socialist mind;" for although society would be "free" so many things will have been abolished which are now essential to freedom. No liberty of conscience — the rights of parents to give their children religious instruction denied — No homes — children put in the bunks in the barracks — But then society will be "free."

All this is simple however as the reader may see by the following quotation from "Socialism, Utopian and Scientific," by Frederick Engels.

"THE PROLETARIAT SEIZES THE MACHINERY OF THE STATE AND CONVERTS THE MEANS OF PRODUCTION FIRST INTO STATE PROPERTY. But by so doing, it extinguishes itself as proletariat; by so doing it extinguishes all class distinctions and class contrasts; and along with them, the State as such. The society that existed until then, and that moved in class contrasts, needed the State, i. e., an organization of whatever class happened at the time to be the exploiting one, for the purpose of preserving the external conditions under which it carried on production; in other words, for the purpose of forcibly keeping the exploited class down in that condition of subjection — slavery, bondage or vassalage, or wage-labor, which the corresponding mode of production predicated. The State was the official representative of the whole society; it was the constitution of the latter into a visible body; but it was so only in so far as it was the State of that class which itself, at its time, represented the whole society; in antiquity, the State of slave-holding citizens; in the middle ages, the State of the feudal nobility: in our own days, the State of the capitalist class. By at last becoming actually the representative of the whole social body, it renders itself superfluous. Soon as no longer there is any social class to be kept down; soon as, together with class rule and the individual struggle for life, founded in the previous anarchy of production, the conflicts and excesses that issued therefrom have been removed, there is nothing more to be repressed, and rendering necessary a special power of repression — the State. The first act, wherein the State appears as the real representative of the whole body social — the seizure of the means of production in the name of society — is also its last independent act as State. The interference of the State in social relations becomes superfluous in one domain after another, and falls of itself into desuetude. The place of a government over persons is taken by the administration of things and the conduct of the processes of production. The State is not 'abolished' — IT DIES OUT. This is all there is in the phrase about a 'Free State,' both with regard to the just uses to which it is put by agitators, and its scientific insufficiency; this also is all there is in the demand made by so-called anarchists that the State be abolished out of hand."   .

Socialist see things out of their normal proportion — their vision is distorted. It was this fact that caused Engels to prophecy an English revolution for the middle of the last century, which prophetic failure Karl Kautsky, in his life of Engels, tries to smooth over.

"Events which no one could have foreseen were at fault that the prophecy was not fulfilled; above all the June fight of 1848 in Paris and the discovery of the gold fields of California in the same year, which drew across the sea the discontented elements of England and weakened for a time the strength of the labor movement." (Page 7: "Frederick Engels; His Life, His Work and His Writings.")

Engels disposes of the whole matter in a jiffy.

1st. The proletariat gets control of the state. That is,

the socialist parties are voted into political power by the working class.

2nd. They make all the means of production the property of the state. That is, the wholesale confiscation of private capital will take place: or, as Marx puts it, the expropriators are expropriated.

3rd. The state becomes the representative of the whole social body. That is, class lines are eliminated — The "state" which strives to represent the whole social body, is, just now, torn in several parts, with petty jealous factions at work within each part. I wonder if that state will be "representative" of those persons whose property it confiscates?

4th. "The interference of the State in social relations becomes superfluous in one domain after another." That is, marriage, penal and civil law, etc., etc." falls of itself into desuetude.

5th. The state — presto change — renders itself useless.

6th. "The place of a government over persons is taken by the administration of things." Children are included in these "things," for they will become a part of the sex industry.

7th. "The State is not abolished, 'It Dies Out.'"— Aye, and so, too, will the human quality of men die out under such a State."

We have the open acknowledgement that the "Free State" of the socialist is one and the same with that condition which would be the result of the abolition "out of hand" by the anarchists of the present capitalist regime. The difference is this — The socialists are more modern than the anarchists — they are more diplomatic; they will not violently overthrow the state, they will first get political control of the public power and then abolish—no not abolish—they will cause the state to "Die Out." But we may hope that this prophecy like that other of Engels will remain unfulfilled — That other factors will step in and cause the dark clouds of socialism

that now hang over our industrial horizon to clear away —
and then the future Kautsky's may write another apology for
Engels' prediction of the "end of the State."

Meantime the menace of socialism may well arouse all
right minded men to their political duty to the end, that the
state may not, as Gabriel Deville says, be transformed into
"a business administration of affairs" —

"Instead of government there will then be simply a business
administration."

"There will be, instead of persons to be constrained, only
things to be administered." ("The State and Socialism.")

It is imperative that this description of the form of the
future society which socialists contemplate be strictly held in
mind, in order that one may understand the sex relationship
of the ideal socialist society. August Babel — who is by this
time well known to our readers, from quotations from his infamous book, which from cover to cover attacks all religious
doctrines and the integrity of the family — when writing on
the state, says :

"The representatives of the State will have disappeared along
with the State itself — Ministers, parliaments, standing armies,
police and gens-d'armes, law courts, lawyers and public prosecutors,
prisons, rates, taxes, and excises — the entire political apparatus."
("Woman in the Past, Present and Future," page 145.)

This opinion is not merely Babel's ; it is held to by all
socialist authorities — there is no dispute amongst them as to
doctrine upon essentials. We have prided ourselves that at
least two things were sure, death and taxes : But here we
see, that taxes are to go by-the-board. As to death, one
may be sure that if the practice of socialist philosophy does
not kill its promoters ; a society founded upon it would eat out
its own heart.

It is indeed difficult to find anything new in the writings
of socialists who have gathered fame since the days of Marx
and Engels. These two fathers of "modern scientific revolu-

tionary socialism" have very completely covered their ground. Latter writings expand into detail, but their authors are more copyists than originators.

Babel is a prophet! His prediction shows plainly the low level of his mental horizon. It is a fact that materialists hold their gaze so close to the earth that they see only within a small area. And it is equally true that religious light alone gives the proper elevation by which to get a correct perspective of great questions.

This is Babel's prophecy.

"The revolt of the new world against the old has broken out. The stage is crowded with actors, the struggle will be carried on with an amount of intellect such as the world has seen in no strugl gle before and will see in none after. For it will be the last socia-struggle. The 19th century will hardly end before the contest is decided." ("Woman; in the Past, Present and Future.")

And what is the process by which socialists will do away with "Ministers, parliaments, standing armies, police and *gens-d'armes*, law courts, lawyers, public prosecutors, prisons, rates, taxes and excises — the entire apparatus?" We shall let Jean Jaures, the French leader of socialism, answer. "When everybody is an office-holder there will be no. more office-holders." Who would have thought it was so simple! When everybody is a pauper there will be no more paupers.

When every woman is a prostitute there will be no more prostitutes.

When every child is fatherless there will be no more fathers.

When everybody owns the capital there will be no more capital.

When everybody is in power there will be no more power.

"When everybody is an office-holder there will be no more office-holders." It will not require brains, but only well filled stomachs to bring it about.

Jaures is not the only socialist leader who takes this statement seriously. It is used by Vandervelde as a motto in his book, "Collectivism." Deville in "Socialism Revolution and Internationalism." (New York, March, 1901), puts it in this form.

" Under the regime of Socialism, men, all men, will be producers and not office-holders; they will not be office-holders any more than are members of a family who, in order to provide for the satisfaction of the needs of the family, perform severally various functions."

But the fact of the matter is that the "severally various functions" performed, make up the class distinctions. And the socialist row is over this inherent fact of classes. Which it appears are to remain just the same after they have all been abolished. Having seen the whole "political apparatus" abolished, it is but natural, with the prerogative for abolition, that with the accession to political power, the political power itself should be abolished, by the political power "performing its last act." Listen to the father of "modern scientific revolutionary socialism" on this point.

Karl Marx in "The Poverty of Philosophy" (London 1900):
" The working class will substitute, in the course of its development, for the old order of civil society an association which will exclude classes and their antagonism, and there will no longer be political power, properly speaking, since political power is simply the official form of the antagonism in civil society."

One must surely recognize the fact that Marx is logical. There being no classes consequently there will be no society and as there is no society surely there will be no political power. Every one will be satisfied with the superintendents and foremen when once they have been elected, by the last act of the state. For neither Jaures, Deville nor any other "scientific socialist" would, I presume, say that all of their "free men and women" will perform the "severally various functions" in fixed rotation? The man who lives on the hill in the big house and the man who lives in the valley in the little hut, with their stomachs full with the very, very best bread and butter, will both be happy. No party organization is needed to turn the rascals out — So of course "there will no longer be political power."

Civil society will be abolished under socialism? Kindly tell us what will be substituted? Why "free land" a "free family" a "free society." What more does a man want who is knee deep in the philosophy of sex depravity?

It was a fixed opinion with Marx that political power would die out — Here is further testimony from "The Communist Manifesto,"

"When, in the course of development, class distinctions have disappeared and all production has been concentrated in the hands of a vast association of the whole nation, the public power will lose its political character. Political power, properly so called, is merely the organized power of one class for oppressing another."

What a dead level is here, it is flatter and staler than a last month's flap-jack.

Let us hear Babel once more on this subject.

" The expropriation of all the private proprietors of the means of production being effected, society starts on a new basis. The conditions of existence and labor for both sexes, industry, agriculture, traffic, education, marriage, science, art and intercourse— in short, of human life altogether—are changed. The State organization as such gradually loses its foundation. The State is the organization of force for the maintenance of the existing relations of property and social rule. But as the relations of master and servant disappear with the abolition of the present system of property, the political expression for the relationship ceases to have any meaning. The State expires with the expiration of a ruling class, just as religion expires when the belief in supernatural beings or supernatural reasonable powers ceases to exist. Words must represent ideas: if they lose their substance, they no longer correspond to anything.—"Woman in the Past, Present and Future," page 128.

Certainly words must stand for things, but when things are in a hopeless mass of confusion — when ideas start from nowhere and after devious wanderings arrive at the same place — why, then words such as these of Babel fitly stand for the confusion of Babel (I beg the reader's pardon).

We are told in this quotation from Babel what will change and what will die.

The relation of master and servant will expire.

The ruling class will expire.

Religion will expire.

The State will expire.

The sexes will have work on equal terms.

Science and art, in short all the relations of human life will change — after a plan as sure as taxes are now.

Kindly let us turn to Bax. He always has something to say, and he will say it plainly.

"That ultimately civil law must disappear with the last vestiges of modern civilization, no Socialist will refuse to admit. But I still maintain, as before, that one of the first measures of a definitely Socialist administration should be the closing of all courts for the hearing of purely civil causes. Such a measure, which would mean the definite break on the juridical side with the old order, is of too revolutionary a nature to proceed from any other than a revolutionary body, but given such a body, a modern 'Convention' or 'Paris Commune' it could not consistently be refused." ("Outlooks from the New Standpoint," The Curse of Law, page 103-104).

Bax is serious — His doctrine is in strict conformity with socialist teachings — in straight line with Marxian philosophy. Given a modern " convention " (this refers to the French convention of 1798, in which the "soul was abolished") or a "Paris Commune" and socialists may be relied upon to break down all courts of civil law. What would take its place? Why, nothing. "There will be, instead of persons to be constrained, only things to be administered." The socialist argument is, those things will belong to us in common. We shall not have the differences which are seen to-day because of class rule. It is the disputes consequent upon class rule which the civil court adjudicates upon.

Socialists avoid the fact that the greater number of disputes arise over property held in common. The history of the inside working of co-operative and colony schemes plainly marks this tendency.— It would seem that it is not confined to modern experiments. Aristotle furnishes us with the result of his observation, taken over 2,000 years ago.

"This style of legislation wears a good face and an air of philanthropy. No sooner is it heard than it is eagerly embraced, under the expectation of a marvellous love to grow out from it between man and man, especially if the proposer goes on to inveigh against the evils of existing institutions, setting all down to the want of a community of goods. These evils, however, are due, not to the want of a community of property, but to the depravity of human nature. For experience teaches that disputes are far more likely to occur among people who possess property in common and live as partners, than among those who hold their estates in separate tenure. The life proposed appears to be altogether impossible." ("Politics.")

It is truly remarkable to what lengths an abnormal attitude of mind may carry an apparently sane man's conclusions. So little of value is there in "this rotten civilization"—the result of the effort of the race during all the past centuries, that its extinction is thought to be a good thing for mankind. This is clearly set forth by Ernest Belfort Bax, in his "Universal History from a Socialist Standpoint" (page 37):

"Mankind having passed through the fire of the State-world, of Civilization, of history, must come out the stronger and the more perfect. Latterday society redeemed from Civilization will be a higher and a more enduring society than that early society which knew no Civilization. It is towards this world, where Civilization shall have ceased to be, that the socialist of today casts his eyes."

Does not this pass the last ditch of intellectual extravagance? To look forward with longing eyes to a time when civilization shall cease to be, leaves a sane man in no wise short of the conclusion that socialism is idealism run mad. It is this quality of doctrine, propagated with the zeal of fanaticism which makes of the socialist movement, irrational as it is at its base, a formidable foe to civil and religious life. Socialism is the more dangerous to human progress in that its methods are quite in line with the rational procedure of citizens who seek to introduce much needed reforms and also those advance measures necessary to the present social requirements of a progressive state. To be explicit, socialism is an organized political party. It makes its assault upon the state by the use of its constitutional power : and it appeals most strongly to the largest economic class of men within the state — that is to say to the largest body of citizens having the least conflict among themselves relative to industrial interests. Or put it this way, socialism makes its propaganda amongst those men who having the least wealth, have the lesser consciousness of citizenship. Consequently this class of men is most readily converted to the cause. For it is a well known principle that wealth or power brings along with it that self-discipline which leads to conservative action.

Its atheistic basis furnishes socialism with its motive power — with the necessary resistance to the present order. It gives the anti-religious an organization powerful for aggression. It centralizes the hot revolt to present wrongs of the mediocre artists. And its pictures of bounteous wealth stimulate the untrained imagination to strenuous action on its behalf. Socialism is a formidable power and naught but formidable power of a higher quality will prevail against it. No sickly sons of dying faith will stay its oncoming — but robust men who love their country and their God are needed to the fore.

So plainly has J. Sketchley stated the socialist position that we reintroduce this matter from his pen.

The Abolition of the State.

"In every age and in every country the Church and the State have been the great centres of despotism. The Church and the State, the throne and the altar, the priest and the soldier, have ever made war on the people. It is the same to-day. In almost every age efforts have been made to reform the Church, to diminish its power, to free it from corruption. Rivers of blood have been shed, and thousands of martyrs have given up their lives for the purification of the Church. But the Church is still the great engine for enslaving the minds of men, for binding mankind in ignorance and superstition. And the same with the State. For how many generations have not the best of nature's nobles laboured and suffered and died in their endeavours to reform the State. But the State is still supreme. It is still the great centre of despotism, still the seat of centralized tyranny. It still claims unquestioned obedience to its decrees. The State, like the Church, is a relic of barbarism. If we would raise men to dignity, in place of the Church we must have a free and rational system of education. If we would raise man to liberty, in place of the State we must have the free organization of society." ("Our Task To-Day," "The Commonweal," Vol. 4, No. 137).

The underlying motive of the socialist movement is to break down civilization. Therefore the vital points of its life — the family, the state, the church — are assailed with all the poison tipped weapons at its command. But thanks be to God socialists have not the strongest sword. It but remains, first that socialism be seen as it is; and second, that righteous men do right the present wrongs, which so weaken the heart of civilization that a sustained assault upon the state may indeed prove fatal to our country.

The suffrages of the citizens of our country are asked for by the socialist party in the interest of the "free state." This abstract proposition is defined as a condition where

"The interference of the State in social relations becomes superfluous in one domain after another, and falls of itself into desuetude. The place of a government over persons is taken by the administration of things of production."

The process of attaining the end of socialism is both positive and negative — first, to gain the votes — and then with the political power socialists will put their negations into practice.

1st. The relation of master and servant disappears.
2nd. The ruling class expire.
3rd. Classes are abolished.
4th. The proletariat extinguishes itself.
5th. In social relations the state becomes superfluous.
6th. Government over persons is abolished.
7th. Ministers disappear.
8th. Parliaments disappear.
9th. Police disappear.
10th. Standing armies disappear.
11th. Civil law disappears.
12th. Lawyers disappear.
13th. Public prosecutors disappear.
14th. Law courts disappear.
15th. Pensions disappear.
16th. Rates disappear.
17th. Taxes disappear.
18th. Political power disappears.
19th. Office-holders disappear.
20th. The entire political apparatus disappears.
21th. Civil society disappears.
22nd. The Altar is abolished.
23rd. The Throne is abolished.
24th. The Church is abolished.
25th. Religion expires.
26th. Wages are abolished.
27th. Capital is abolished.
28th. The State expires.
29th. Civilization ends.

Trade Unions.

"I want to see the organization of the wage-earners and the organization of the employers, through their respective representatives, meet around the table in the office of the employers or in the office of the union, if you please, or, if that be not agreeable to either, upon neutral ground, there to discuss the questions of wages and hours of labor and conditions of employment and all things consistent with the industrial and commercial success of our country, that shall tend to the uplifting of the human family."

SAMUEL GOMPERS.

BY constantly picturing the misery of the poor : by constantly picturing the greed of the rich : by continual condemnation of all things which meet with dissatisfaction in the mind of the working class, whether the discontent be rational or ridiculous : by unceasing condemnation of the character and the work of those who hold office in the service of the state : by unceasing disapproval of those workmen who hold the offices and so meet the responsibilities of the conflicts of the labor organizations, socialists succeed in making "socialist minds" of the disgruntled. While with their abstract propositions they attract the idealists whose pictures are ephemeral and fall into confusion like a block house when the common sense touch of the actual world is applied to them.

The avenue which affords socialists the best opportunity for propaganda, owing to the uniformity of industrial station held by its membership and because of its democratic spirit — The avenue which affords socialists the best opportunity of making converts is the trade union movement. Without expense they may exploit the time, day by day, from month to month, from year to year, from convention to convention, of the trade unions. Socialists are the sensationalists of the labor movement. They work within the organized crafts for the one only object of compelling the trade unions to support the

323

socialist party. Their advance has been cut off by the wisdom of the greater number of the unionists who take the stand, 1st, that political affiliation with the socialist party or with any other political party would necessarily lead to the disruption of their organization. 2nd. That being an economic organization its first, its prime motive must be to enroll within its ranks men of all political opinions and affiliations, of all races and of all creeds, that the labor cause may present a solid front of undivided power. 3rd. Their position is that unions should apply themselves to the work of bettering the condition of the wage-earners day by day as the opportunities are afforded rather than to turn their energies to the organization of a political party for the capture of the machinery of government, even allowing that the socialist party could work it in the sole interest of the wage-workers were they to capture it.

Trade unions stand for the following civic demands which by petition by the aid of legislative committees, etc., etc., they seek to build in the structure of our state and national law.

DEMANDS OF AMERICAN FEDERATION OF LABOR.

1. Compulsory education.
2. Direct legislation through the initiative and referendum.
3. A legal workday of not more than eight hours.
4. Sanitary inspection of workshop, mine and home.
5. Liability of employers for injury to health, body and life.
6. The abolition of the contract system in all public work.
7. The abolition of the sweating system.
8. The municipal ownership of street cars, water works and gas and electric plants for public distribution of light, heat and power.
9. The nationalization of telegraph, telephone, railroads and mines.
10. The abolition of the monopoly system of land-holding, and substituting therefor a title of occupancy and use only.

11. Repeal all conspiracy and penal laws affecting seamen and other workmen incorporated in the federal and state laws of the United States.

12. The abolition of the monopoly privilege of issuing money and substituting therefor a system of direct issuance to and by the people.

It will clearly appear that the American Federation of Labor stands for the elevation, the perfection, of the life of the industrial masses. That it seeks to bring in industrial peace. But it is well aware that peace amongst men is not a given quantity, which once attained will give permanent satisfaction. The A. F. of L. is not an extremest in philosophy — therefore it is rational in its action. It knows that that which will satisfy men to-day will become unsatisfactory to them in a year or so. Therefore the trade unions from time to time in conformity with the condition of the market, and the prevailing condition of the craft organization, seek to advance its relative standing with the employing class. This they desire to do by peaceful means. By creating a demand for the union label. They would gain, by the numerical strength and by the discipline which loyalty to a cause brings, sufficient economic power to establish reciprocal relationship with the employers of labor upon the principle of justice and good fellowship. By agreements with employers — boards of arbitration and conciliation and other honorable means of settling difficulties are employed by them. Failing by such methods the boycott and the strike are resorted to.

"Trade unions are opportunist in their philosophy and practice. They despise not the day of small things. With the sage Ulysses they may say, 'I am a part of all that I have met.' Contact with tyranny sometimes makes them tyrannical, intolerant treatment sometimes makes them narrow, frank recognition and fair consideration of their claims inspire ir them a conciliatory spirit.

"The trade union ideal is an evolutionary development of the status of the laborer, through collective bargaining and lawful methods, until there shall be fully restored that personal relationship and consideration which has been so largely eliminated from the social equation by modern processes of production."

Religion is a question upon which the trade unions do not assume to pass. The right hand of fellowship is given to any man, any teacher of any religious faith who will aid the unions in advancing the economic standing of the wage earners. Having no philosophical doctrine to draw off the energies in useless disputation it fixes its attention steadfastly upon industrial and economic problems. It may be truly said that trade unions represent the weightiest force in the country which makes for industrial peace.

The progress of the trade union is greatly hampered by the socialists within and without their ranks. This is necessarily so for the reason that socialist ideals are diametrically opposed to the ideals of the trade union. The propaganda of socialism is primarily related to the capture of the powers of government — hence it is political. While the propaganda of the trade union relates strictly to economics. Socialists work upon the trade unionists with the deliberate purpose of making the economic power of the American Federation of Labor subservient to that of the socialist parties. That is to say, their primary object is the complete overturning of the whole industrial order. Holding, as socialists do, that nothing can better the condition of the working class except the establishment of the collective ownership of the means of production and distribution, with its accompaniment, the "free family" and the "free society," they declare that the economic power of the trade unions is unable to effect any real industrial advantage to the working class — hence their determination to capture its numerical strength and convert it into political power — annex it to the socialist parties' power.

Furthermore socialists claim that the economic struggle going on in society is irreconcilable. That the interests of capitalist and laborer are diametrically opposed one to the other. That, consequently, there remains nothing to be done less drastic than the overthrow and abolition of the capitalist class by the working class: therefore the trade unions must be forced to take the socialist position.

The tactics by which the capture of the American Federation of Labor is attempted are the same old socialist tactics (for a leopard does not change his spots) that those of our readers who have been interested to follow us have seen applied to the church and its officials and to individuals. They may now see them applied to the trade unions and its officials, with this difference, the fight is close at hand, the trade unionists are "get-at-ables."

About the year 1889 the socialists, with determination, entered upon their campaign of controlling the trade union movement of this country.

The socialist element within the Central Labor Union of New York City having withdrawn and formed the Central Labor Federation, applied to the American Federation of Labor for a charter. President Gompers of the A. F. of L. rejected the application on the ground that the Socialist Labor Party organization of New York City was affiliated with the Central Labor Federation, that political parties were constitutionally debarred from affiliation with the A. F. of L.

Later the Central Labor Federation of N. Y. city, in 1890, elected Lucian Sanial, a socialist leader, as a possible delegate to the A. F. of L. which was to be held in Detroit. Samuel Gompers had "tumbled to the trick," the socialist political party was not to be grafted upon the trade union movement of this country. After a stormy debate, in which Mr. Sanial was allowed to participate, the convention stood 535 for and 1699 against the admission of the socialist delegate. He (Mr. Sanial) apparently satisfied, returned his thanks for the generous opportunity afforded him by the delegates to argue his case — but upon his return to N. Y. city the Socialist Labor Party declared open war upon the "fakirs" in the "pure and simple trade unions." Time wore on, but still the control of the labor movement of this country was the set purpose of the socialist managers. They had been "boring from within," it was hard work; their hands were sore, and very little progress had been made. They were angry!

Finally, the leaders of the Socialist Labor Party, Daniel DeLeon, Lucian Sanial, Henry Kuhn, Hugo Vogt and others, who then held unquestioned control of the socialist propaganda of this country — and now thoroughly embittered with the officials of the trade unions throughout the country — at their national convention of 1896, held in New York City, launched a new economic organization, affiliated with the S. L. P. and officered by the socialist leaders' chosen men.

The Socialist Trade and Labor Alliance, with hurrah boys, and banners flying, ran up their motto — leave the old wreck, the pure and simple trade union and pull for the shore: it started upon its mission of annihilating the American Federation of Labor.

The socialist leaders declared that their policy of "boring from within" had been a failure because of corrupt leadership — that the pure and simple unions were merely outposts of capitalism — and that the time had arrived to use the "battering ram," the Socialist Trade and Labor Alliance to break in the walls of the "pure and simplers." All sorts of changes were rung upon this term of derision. They were purely economic and so they were purely simple, etc., etc., etc. From that time to this "socialist minds" have battened at their ease upon the flow of slander from the most virile pen of the socialist movement, the force of which is supposed to be great enough to down all arguments.

TRADE UNIONS.

Upon the simple principle of strength in union and contrarywise in disunion weakness : conservative leaders of trade unions have long since been taught by experience that fights between labor organizations are most detrimental to the interests of the working-class — and too, that a conflict is inevitable if there be two organizations of the same craft, in the same community. The main reasons are self evident. There is division of of interests instead of solidarity of interests — the men of the craft are on terms of war with one another, instead of on terms of peace. On the other hand the confidence of the employer is constantly threatened by the necessary dealing with men from two instead of one organization. And when difficulty does arise between employers and employees, then there is a three cornered fight with its vexatious complications added to the necessary details of settlement — this extra conflict is justly laid to the fault at the workmen's door. The general public irritated at the row, with little or no knowledge as to the merits of the case, being confused and so unable to make a judgment as to a just settlement, become habitually disgusted with or indifferent to the whole trade union movement.

Much bitterness was engendered throughout the country, in factory, mine and mill, by the conflicts between the American Federation of Labor's Unions and those of the Socialist Trade and Labor Alliance. The dual unions with their labels soon brought on trouble in different parts of the country — the most marked was fomented in the city of New York; where the Cigarmakers' Pioneer Alliance (S. T. and L. A.) furnished men to take the places of the men of the International Cigarmakers' Union, who were on strike at Davis' cigar factory.

This affair became of national importance — and it proved a boomerang to the socialist leaders. During the years that they had been "boring from within" there was no well grounded reason for the suspicion that these socialist leaders were not good unionists. But during this period the cat came pretty well out of the bag — and socialists found they could neither "bore from within" nor from without with much success.

Many second class leaders finding their influence as socialists within the trade union movement was on the wane; finding that their tirades against the American Federation of Labor leaders were not so well received as they were wont to be — and tiring of a master superior to their collective power, who could not be moved to alter his plan of campaign, though the ships were scuttled; party broils were fomented and at last in '99 a split took place. The larger half had bolted — Leaving the De Leon remnant in control of the old S. L. P., which like the Bourbons had neither learned anything nor had they forgotten anything.

In January, 1900, the bolters held a national convention in Rochester, N. Y., at which time overtures were made to the Debs Social Democracy. Later the union of the two parties was effected. The uniting parties took the name of Socialist party.

With the split of the Socialist Labor Party the sphere of the Socialist Trade and Labor Alliance visibly narrowed. while its troubles visibly increased. The illy defined relation between itself and the Socialist Labor Party gave it constant trouble — not to speak of its external conflicts. Like birds of ill omen it still hovers over the labor movement, flying to any field of trade union battle to gorge upon its prey and to vomit forth its rage with the courage of despair. It is safe to say that there is not in this country to-day a body of men and women who in any cause carry on so slanderous a campaign as this small body, under the leadership of Daniel De Leon, of New York City. They infect the arena of legitimate trade unionism as a pest. Their forte is the challenge: and should one disregard the reputation they have made for vilification of all who differ from them, and accept

330

their offer to debate — a diving suit and one of Sir Humphrey Davy's lamps were necessary to pilot one through the mire— and then one might not prevent asphyxiation from the foul fumes. — These are fully developed "socialist minds" the exact complement of socialist philosophy.

Those socialist party members who have been through the Socialist Trade and Labor Alliance flame of experience and have come out better tacticians are back within the trade union lines, "boring from within." By drawing exaggerated pictures of the prevalent poverty, which God knows is bad enough, — by belittling trade union victories — by throwing discredit upon the work of the trade union leaders they hope to boost socialists up on the ladder of trade union power.

Then there are many socialists who have not the patience to await the result of the attempt to capture the American Federation of Labor by the method of "boring from within." Having no proper conception of the basic necessity of the trade union ; nor of the detailed work it is doing to maintain the standard of American living and the dignity of American workingmen — they consequently regard the subversion of its economic power to the ends of their political scheme as quite proper from a moral standpoint. It was upon this basis of reasoning that the national socialist convention (Indianapolis, 1901) adopted a resolution calling upon "Socialists to join the unions of their respective trades and assist in building up and unifying the trades and labor organizations." If once the real quality of the "socialist mind" is understood, it is not strange — for it was upon this same basis of reasoning — notwithstanding the fair speech of this national resolution — That Eugene V. Debs, ex-priests Thomas McGrady and T. J. Hagerty and others of national reputation in the socialist movement, in June, 1902, launched, at Denver, Colorado, the American Labor Unions, with a socialist platform—The largest union affiliated with this body is the Western Federation of Miners which had previously adopted the socialist principles.

331

The American Federation of Labor gave the socialists at this convention ample opportunity of proving whether or no they were ready to stand by the socialist party declaration in favor of "building up and unifying the trade and labor organizations." The A. F. of L. sent a delegation to this convention, with the request that it abandon the project of organizing a rival national body. — Clearly setting forth that such a course must inevitably bring on local and national conflicts between the American Federation of Labor's unions and the unions of the proposed body.— That as a consequence the cause of the wage-worker would suffer unnecessary injury. The petition of the delegates concluded with an urgent invitation to the assembled unions to join the A. F. of L.

The delegation was answered by Eugene V. Debs, who made an eloquent but irrational address — condemning the A. F. of L. and lauding the project before the convention. He carried the day in the interest of the socialist party. And so began the life of S. T. and L. A. No. 2, under the name of the American Labor Union.

What is the moral weight of a national socialist resolution? Feather light in the scale against an opportunity to annex a body of men to the socialist party. Finding that leaders of socialism had violated the resolution adopted nationally — that they had formed a rival organization to the American Federation of Labor — and desiring to "bore from within" and to bore from without at one and the same time the National Committee of the socialist party firmly grasped both horns of the dilemma by adopting resolutions in which the following paragraphs appear:

"The National Committee of the Socialist Party in annual session assembled, hereby reaffirms the attitude of the party toward the trade-union movement as expressed in the resolution on the subject adopted by the Indianapolis convention of 1901."

"The Socialist Party will continue to give its aid and assistance to the economic struggles of organized labor regardless of the

affiliation of the trade-unions engaged in the struggle, and will take
no sides in any dissensions or strifes within the trade-union movement. The party will also continue to solicit the sympathy and
support of all trade organizations of labor without allowing itself to
be made the ally of any one division of the trade-union movement
as against another."

It will and it won't! First the party's attitude on trade
unions is reaffirmed "we consider it the duty of socialists
to . . . assist in building up and unifying the trades and
labor organizations." But nevertheless as socialists of national power have taken a great opportunity of propagating
socialism by flagrantly violating this mandate by building
up a national organization in direct opposition to the spirit of
unification expressed in the resolution at the national convention; they have acted in strict conformity to the socialist principles of disruption, — the labor movement as a part of civilization must be broken down, before anything can be done
— we must now employ socialist tactics — we "will take no
sides in the dissensions or strife within the trade-union movement." To be sure socialists have created "dissensions" and
"strife." But what of that, the labor movement must be
made subservient to socialist propaganda. To be sure we
use our press and our agitators work for the Socialist party
and the American Labor Union at one and the same time.
But we must not say that we take sides for we want to "bore
from within" the American Federation of Labor conventions
— So we will pass a tactical resolution. We must say that
we will not allow the socialist party "to be made the ally of
any one division of the trade-union movement as against the
other." Then we may, with a bold front — because we have
muddied the waters of understanding — "continue to solicit
the sympathy and support of all trade organizations of labor."

May you? Well, that depends upon the astuteness of
the rank and file of the American Federation of Labor! You
mean to control one and be the ally of the other — notwith-

standing, in the nature of things, each is hostile to the other. Surely you may "solicit the sympathy" of the A. F. of L. but once the membership realize that your trade-union sympathy is as false as your resolution on religion, the end to your "boring from within" will have come — and you will stand in the place in which you belong, by the side of the Socialist Trade and Labor Alliance, No. 2, battering from without.

Fred. W. Long, secretary of the socialist party of Penn., in an official communication replying to a faction of the Socialist Labor Party of that State, expresses, in the most courteous terms possible, the use which socialists make of the trade unions — that is to say, of the A. F. of L. unions. They are merely good recruiting stations.

"Experience has demonstrated the absolute correctness of our position upon the question of the attitude of Socialists toward the trade unions. It is only fair to us who consider the unions as legitimate recruiting stations for Socialism and therefore make constant propaganda among them, that our efforts in this direction shall not be obstructed by any confused or false ideas, on the part of trade-unionists, as to the relation of Socialists toward them. Those who do not agree with us in this matter cannot in good faith come into the party." ("The Worker," Feb. 22, 1903).

The question is, and it will be answered by none other than the American Federation of Labor itself, whether or not the prime service it can render the American workmen is that of becoming "recruiting stations" for a political party whose fundamental principles are absolutely hostile to its own. And contrariwise, the progress socialists make in subverting the power of the A. F. of L. from its original purpose to the control of socialist politicians depends upon its answer to this question.

The organization of the American Labor Union is good proof that the socialists of to-day hold the A. F. of L. in as low esteem as did the socialists of '96. It is the self same experience being made over again — but it begins at a much higher notch of power upon either hand — so the battle will be longer and hotter. Seven years have passed and the S. T. and L. A. No. 1 is reduced to a little rabble of "kickers." By its historic palm S. T. and L. A. No. 2 may, we predict, correctly read its own fortune.

It was, in part, the recognition of the duplicity of the socialist party's conduct regarding the craft organizations, which caused the following resignation to be sent to the socialist officials of the State of Massachusetts.

"Boston, May 21, 1903.

"To the Massachusetts State Committee of the Socialist Party.

"Mr. James F. Carey, chairman.

"Mr. Squire E. Putney, secretary.

"Dear Sirs:—I hereby tender my resignation as a member of the Socialist party. My reasons for doing so are on the following grounds:

"The attitude of the Socialist party towards the trade union is that of using it for political purposes with no regard or respect for its economic advancement. The Socialist American Labor Union which is started in the West is trying with all its power to break down the American Federation of Labor, where officials are termed dupes and fakes. This Western organization is working in the East to break down the power of legitimate trade unions, and it is aided by the Socialists in this vicious work.

"The Socialist press is trying to belittle the work of John Mitchell and the United Mine Workers' organization, whose work has done more for the interest of the workers of America than the Socialist party in the whole time of its existence.

"The American Labor Union and the Western Miners' Federation under the direction of the Socialists declare the coal commission report to be an insult to the honor and dignity of organized labor.

"The Miners' strike and my years' experience as business agent of the Machinists' Union has proved to me, without a shadow of a doubt, that the economic organization is the most effective place to educate and discipline the workmen that they may act intelligently and proceed with order to the conquest of economic justice.

"The trade union movement offers a field large enough for me to use my whole time and energy for some years to come, and it is great enough to hold my utmost loyalty.

"I have sent in my resignation as treasurer of the Boston city committee; also as chairman of Ward 7 ward committee and also as a member of the Boston Socialist Club. I hereby tender my resignation as a member of the Mass. State Committee of the Socialist party.

Yours sincerely,
WILLIAM R. DYER."

The superior officials of the American Federation of Labor have, during all these years, been keenly alive to the necessity of maintaining the integrity of the trade union movement strictly as an economic body — and consequently they have resisted the encroachments upon its integrity by socialists who would overthrow the common-sense procedure for irrational methods in the interest of making socialist propaganda. This successful resistance has given occasion for tirades against such leaders as Samuel Gompers, John Mitchell and many others — and insults to them — Through it all these officers have maintained their due course and have steered the A. F. of L. on her progressive way free from the entangling philosophical or political alliance of the socialist party.

The attitude of these leaders may be seen in the following editorial by Samuel Gompers, who has for twenty years been the president of the American Federation of Labor.

TRADE UNION DEFENDER AGAINST ALL OPPONENTS.

"Take up any issue of a political socialist paper, and the reader will find one or more articles or editorials attacking trade unions and trade unionists. Facts are distorted and perverted in regard to the actions of trade unions.

"Any adverse result of a trade union effort, no matter how

insignificant, is exaggerated into a "crushing defeat; any victory, no matter how materially or morally far-reaching, is belittled and ridiculed.

"As an instance of this, there is not a political socialist paper published which has not declared in so many words that the award rendered by the Anthracite Coal Strike Commission was of little or no advantage to the miners, and therefore, as they put it, the strike was a failure.

"The political socialists' attacks upon, and abuse of, trade unionists are without stint; their motives are always impugned, their honesty attacked, and their activity ridiculed. Let it be known that a man gives his entire attention, study, work, and loyalty to trade unions and trade unionists exclusively, and he is the particular target for the time being of all kinds of socialist vituperation and abuse.

"The labor movement of the country is solidifying in thought and action under the banner of the American Federation of Labor. A few disgruntled men start some little division, such as, for instance, the Western Labor Union, and then the so-called American Labor Union, and the division, though simply an attempted rivalry, insignificant in itself, is coddled and encouraged by the political socialists and their press. All this may seem exceedingly proper to the political socialists, but when an official journal of a trade union, such as the AMERICAN FEDERATIONIST, undertakes to defend the trade union movement against *all* who attack it, whether it be the brutal raving of such members of the Manufacturers' Association, as Kirby or Parry, an open enemy, such as the political socialist De Leon, or other political socialists, pretending friendship but masking behind a cloak of hypocrisy, who subtly try to undermine and destroy the faith of workingmen in their trade union organization, why that is quite another thing.

"To those who antagonize the trade union movement, no matter how they plan their campaign, we say all opponents look alike to us, and the quantity and quality of our counteracting influence in resenting their hostility will be gauged only by the extent of the injury to our movement contemplated by the enemy." (The American "Federationist" June, 1903).

It is certain that "the extent of the injury" contemplated against the trade unions is nothing short of throwing them on the dump heap after the orange (the legitimate opportunity of using them as recruiting stations) has been sucked dry. — There is no shadow of doubt, socialists have as Pres. Gompers and Mr. Dyer say, done all they could to throw discredit upon the conduct of the coal strike — the miners' organization — and the commissioners' report. Of course the reason for this action is simple. If workmen confidently look to the trade unions to solve their difficulties, they will not be "subjects for socialist propaganda."

The miners' strike gave an unequalled opportunity to exploit the "recruiting stations" in the interest of socialist propaganda. The public would listen — general sympathy was aroused. Meetings in the interest of socialism, but advertised as "miners' meetings" brought out large audiences — at which collections for the striking miners were taken. Then with these few thousand dollars, collected chiefly from trade unionists, better opportunities were opened up. These moneys gave socialists entrance into the meetings of the strike region. Well equipped with socialist literature these agitators were able to "feed" the miners upon the stuff well calculated to develop "socialist minds."— All this is simple, it requires only crude manipulation and a little brazen impudence thrown in. For are not the trade unions merely "legitimate recruiting stations for socialism"? Certainly, yes! The point of view is everything! Either the American Federation of Labor is a great organization with an all important work before it or it is a group of non-"class-conscious" men who are really incompetent to advance the interests of the wage-earners.

There was a characteristic display in Boston, of socialist tactics, and of socialist disloyalty to citizenship, during the coal strike. A striking miners' relief committee was organized — composed of citizens, trade unionists and socialists.

Prominent among the workers were Martha Moore Avery, William R. Dyer and the author, who was elected chairman of the committee.

The work of the committee took on much larger proportions than socialists had anticipated, hence its value as a "recruiting station." Wires were immediately laid for its control. The then secretary of the Massachusetts state committee led on the socialist forces. The first move was the attempt to force an invitation to the socialist party to officially participate in the work of the committee. This move Mrs. Martha Moore Avery, William R. Dyer and the Chairman not only refused to aid — on the ground that it was bad faith, for the committee was organized as a citizens' committee, but also took an active part in defeating the proposition. This occasioned the following paragraph in "The Worker" (Oct. 12, 1902):

Referring to the Miners' Relief Committee, he says — "While there are a number of socialists on the committee, yet recognition was afterwards refused the Socialist Party on the ground that the relief work was 'not a political movement.' It may also be added that the principal ones to take this stand are members of the Socialist Party, so the relief committee is not to be blamed if it decided not to recognize the party under the circumstances."

The work of the committee was to climax with a street parade and a mass meeting at which John Mitchell was expected to speak. Upon the proposition to invite the Mayor of Boston to preside upon the occasion, the socialist members upon the committee showed very plainly their contempt of citizenship. A persistent and most vulgar tirade was made both against the government and all its officials. The best argument that was forthcoming against the motion was the silly assertions "I don't want to take off my hat to a man who may shoot me down." "I don't want a capitalist politician to preside at our meeting," etc., etc.

In fully accepting socialist philosophy one loses all sense of citizenship (assuming it once was his), of being an inseparable part of the government, of being bone of its bone and flesh of its flesh. They have no sense of loyalty to our democratic institutions — Their country is so big, so abstract, that it fades out of sight. Socialists cannot understand that a Mayor, a Governor or a President, as chief executive, is but the embodiment of the collective will of all citizens — That although the majority elect these officials, so do the minority have equal rights under the maintenance of government. This view is much too sound to find favor with the distorted facts of their low-browed philosophy.

Socialists cannot understand that prior to an election the mayor was but a candidate for this or that party — but that upon being elected to the office he is forthwith the head of the town. He is the host of the city and may open its doors to guests at his pleasure.

Failing in these two attempts to dominate the committee the socialists withdrew from its work. This was but a demonstration that their activity was not in the interest of the labor movement, but in the interest of socialist propaganda.

It is true as the secretary of the socialist party state committee of Pennsylvania said, socialists consider it legitimate to use the trade unions as "recruiting stations" for socialist propaganda. — Nor do socialist principles forbid the setting up of rival trade organizations. It is but a question of extending socialist energy to the best advantage.

The strike of the miners being over, the socialists, for the time being, having finished their work in the anthracite "recruiting stations," the socialist papers returned to their tactics of destroying the workmen's confidence in the trade union as a possible means of bettering their condition. This was done by belittling and condemning almost everything which the miners' union had done. Adding, always, thas nothing could be done by non-"class-conscious" unions to avail in behalf of the "wage-slaves." — They should instanter vote to "expropriate the expropriators."

Editorials were published, in the "International Socialist Review," "The Worker" and in many other socialist papers, taking the ground that the award of the coal commission was at best nothing to the advantage of the miners. "The Miners' Magazine," official organ of the Western Federation of Miners which forms the backbone of the American Labor Union, declared the report of the coal commission to be "an insult to the honor and dignity of organized labor." The best reason it had to support this extreme opinion was because the commission had not demanded the official recognition of the miners' union. It is not our purpose to discuss this point of the commissioners' award. For just now it is our purpose merely to show that socialist tactics permit of any offence which is calculated to retard the growth, especially of such unions as have socialist rivals in the field.

The president of the socialist miners' union himself steps up in the prisoner's box and furnishes us with clear evidence on this point of socialist tactics. One item of his official report to the Denver Convention (June, 1903,) is in this connection interesting. The socialist miners' president offered "terms of settlement as an ultimatum" to the U. S. Reduction and Refining Co. in settlement of their trouble with the Colorado City Mill and Smeltermen's Union, in which the following proposition appears:

"That in the employment of men of said company there shall be no discrimination between union and non-union men, and that no person shall be discharged because of his membership in any labor organization." ("Miners' Magazine," July, 1903, page 16.)

Consistency is a jewel not to be found in the history of socialist tactics! It is one thing to bluster, to strut, to look fiercely grand in denouncing the other fellow — but quite a horse of another color to meet responsibility with sober thought and action. We have no doubt that he served faithfully and well his union upon this occasion. Furthermore we have no doubt that John Mitchell and the miners' union consider his proposition fitting to the occasion rather than "an insult to the honor and dignity of organized labor." But is it not strange such hostility between expressed sentiment and official act? Ah, no! It is clearly in view — on the one hand the socialist president of the Western Federation of Miners is expending his eloquence in a windy-wordy assault upon John Mitchell and a specific proposition in settlement of the miners' strike — and within socialist circles no possible extravagance in language is subject to rebuke. While on the other hand this same man sobered by the responsibility of trade union power stands squarely in action against his own blatant brag by giving counsel to his men exactly parallel to that given upon this point by the coal commission in its award, in settlement of the miners' strike. So it is with the courage of license, it knows nothing and it fears nothing. Its fool-brave talk crumbles to dust when put to the test in settling every-day affairs amongst men.

The president of the Western Federation of Miners is in such good repute with his fellow socialists and withal such an excellent example of the disruptive influence of socialist philosophy upon men of strength but lacking in self-discipline, that we shall quote his matter against John Mitchell — and the miners' union — which has as little foundation in common sense as his tirade against the coal commission's report.

"Can the leader of this army of men expect to hold his organization intact, when he advises them to continue a policy which offers nothing for the future but strife and destitution, and commends the findings of a board of arbitration selected by the representatives of capital which binds the chains of slavery more securely around his membership and deprives them of even the privilege of appealing to their masters for a period of three years? Bitter, indeed, must have been the hour when the thousands of tried and true union men were informed that the organization for which they had fought was not worthy of recognition. John Mitchell need not be surprised should his membership turn their face to the West, seeking affiliation with organizations which have sent out their message to the world, that as labor produces all wealth, such wealth belongs to the producer thereof. That their mission is not to tighten the bonds which surround the toiler, but the emancipation of the wage slave and the equality of man.

"Trades unions have had a fair trial, and it has been clearly demonstrated that although their ranks have continued to swell from hundreds into millions, we are no nearer to the solution of the industrial problem than we were at the beginning, and even though the name of each and every wage-worker throughout the entire world was enrolled upon the roster of organized labor, under the policy pursued in the past, the conflict between producer and non-producer would still continue." ("The Social Democratic Herald," June 6, 1903.)

This is but one of the frequent displays of socialist tactics. If resentment and disgust at alleged incompetency both of the American Federation of Labor, its local unions and its leaders, great and small, can be kept up in a constant flow: why then, "socialist's minds" may be evolved out of trade unionists.

Trade unions have been tried, forsooth. The labor leaders themselves affirm that they are just entering upon the initial stage of organization and power. Less than half a century is indeed a short time to adjust the standards of living of the working class to the vast changes that have taken and are constantly taking place in the methods of the production and exchange of wealth. — If nothing whatever were said of adjusting the equitable return to the owner of the capital in relation to that of the workmen in his employment. To say that "trade unions have had a fair trial" and that they have proved incompetent to bring about the result for which they were designed, is as short-sighted as to affirm that although if a farmer should thin out his beet crop and sell the tender plants for beet greens, that were the crop fully grown it would yield him no further return for his work. As a matter of fact it requires but little knowledge of trade union data to state with certainty that an advance in wages; a reduction in hours and also improved conditions of labor are, thus far, results to be set down to the credit of trade union effort. And as union-soldarity is the real back-bone of the trade union power, it is certain that those men who split the ranks of labor, and cry "no good of unions," are not the friends of the working class — however ardent their enthusiasm for making an ideal state, by votes, right off quick, in a minute. Social-ist tactics greatly aggravate the surface of the labor move-ment — big talk is attractive but irresponsible, it is deeds that count. And after long runs it has been proven that such men as John Mitchell stand the strain and are able with sane phil-osophy and rational methods to move forward towards the establishment of industrial justice. — While at the same time a much higher order of economic society is being progres-sively erected.

As to the prospects of the trade unionists unquestionably they are good as the subjoined report of the secretary will show.

"WASHINGTON, D. C., July 4, 1903.

"The American Federation of Labor, through its organizers, is doing yeoman service, by organizing locals for international unions, forming unions of crafts and callings that in years past have refused to organize. International organizations of such crafts and callings must be formed in the near future.

"The following table for comparison will furnish you with some little idea of the growth of the American Federation of Labor during the past (6) years:

	1897.	1903.
Internationals	55	110
Central bodies	51	573
State branches	10	28
Local Trade and Federal Labor Unions	444	2,214
Totals	560	2,925

"Following is a table showing the average paid membership of the American Federation of Labor, commencing with 1897 and ending in 1902. The fiscal year of 1903 does not terminate until September 30th, hence, the membership total is subject to change through reports from the Internationals during the next two months:

1897	265,600
1898	279,000
1899	350,400
1900	550,300
1901	789,500
1902	1,025,300
1903	1,457,593

"It is generally understood that the Brick Layers' and Masons' International Union will affiliate with the American Federation of Labor; if so, that will be an addition of 80,000.

"In 1897 the income for twelve months was $18,600. During the first nine months of this fiscal year ending July 1st, the income amounted to $173,700.11. A marked increase in unions and membership, and a remarkable increase in funds.

"There is now $55,894.50 in the defense fund.

"There are in the field at the present time thirty-six paid organizers who are devoting all their time to the work of settling grievances and organizing unorganized wage-workers. Besides these, we have over 1,100 district organizers.

"The outlook is very satisfactory. The Internationals are making rapid headway. The general success of the labor movement along the lines of organization has been phenomenal.

"The employers are awakening to the fact that organized labor is truly a power, and, fearful of what is sure to follow, that is, a pronounced desire for shorter hours and increased scale of wages, they are organizing for the purpose of resisting the efforts of the trade unions to shorten hours and increase wages. The employers' efforts will be futile. The constant vigilance of the officers and members of all unions affiliated with the American Federation of Labor will more than offset their hostility, and the great labor movement will steadily march forward.   Yours fraternally,

"(Signed)   FRANK MORRISON,
                            "Secretary,
                  "American Federation of Labor."

345

Socialists do not trouble themselves with the relation of facts to facts. Abstractions are much more pliable upon the agitator's tongue. It is vastly easier to shout liberty, equality and fraternity than to do the patient and heroic deeds required to emplant those great principles within the organizations and the relations which make up the sum total of civil society. One may quickly sweep the deck clean with the abstract statement "that although their ranks (the trade unions) continue to swell from hundreds into millions, we are no nearer to the solution of the industrial problem than we were at the beginning." But the facts are here just the same — just the same has the work of President Gompers and other labor leaders told upon the American public — just the same the great fact stands out that the President of these United States has called upon the officials of the trade unions to state to him, the nation's chief, their side of the case in the presence of their employers who had refused to treat with them. "No nearer the solution of the industrial problem" when the power of the nation is invoked that justice may be done unto the coal miners by their employers? "No nearer the solution of the industrial problem" when the United States has deemed it for the public weal that a commission be established to inquire into and make recommendations of settlement upon a matter of grievance by wage earners against powerful corporations? "No nearer the solution of industrial problems" when with trade union power against capitalist power a truce of three years is entered upon? Entered upon in response to the solicitations of the nation in its own behalf, that is to say, in the interest of the downtrodden, equally with the interest of the well-to-do and the rich. If no advance has been made towards the solution of the industrial problem by the trade unions, whence comes this power of the miners to resist to some degree the oppression of their rapacious employers? What power have miners other than that of a union front to enlist the national arm in its cause?

TRADE UNIONS.

Socialists may employ sophistry instead of honest argument, it will not avail in the face of the facts, to prove that trade unions are "no good." They may throw volumes of cold water — and statements like the following may dampen trade union effort, somewhat, but they are soon seen to be weak kneed when made to stand up to the common sense in the matter. "The findings of a board of arbitration . . . which binds the chains of slavery more securely around his membership and deprives them of even the privilege of appealing to their masters for a period of three years," is the best thing that the president of the Western Federation of Miners in his official report to the socialist miners, so late as June, 1903, has to say of John Mitchell's work. Surely the fever heat of passing jealousy may well have had time to cool — and it must therefore be taken for that which it is, the determined purpose to foist upon the trade union movement the claims of the socialist party. No lesser interpretation can adequately explain the aggressive and slanderous attacks of socialists upon the trade union movement. Socialist hostility is grounded merely in the fact that trade union leaders will not give over, bag and baggage, the American Federation of Labor to the control of socialist party politicians — that they maintain their due course as an economic organization, advancing wages, shortening hours and improving conditions, despite the resistance set up by socialists. Of course every victory won takes the edge off their calamity howl, therefore it must become louder to have the same effect.

"The Socialist Standard" (Pittsburg, Pa., May 23rd, 1903) referring to the officials of the A. F. of L. says editorially:

"We notice that the Chicago Socialist takes the measure of Mr. Theodore Shaffer pretty accurately and it is altogether certain that before the Socialist Party gets through coquetting with impure and simpledom, they will discover that there are many others. Labor Fakirs are the curse of trades unionism from Gompers down, and including the much lauded Mitchell, and the sooner this is understood the better for the working class."

In an issue of "The Socialist," Seattle, Washington, there was recently published a full page cartoon — The naked body of a workman was exposed, covered with flies, mosquitoes and bugs of all sorts — each one with the face of an alleged enemy of the workman. There were the faces of Mr. Parry, Mr. Baer, etc., etc., together with Samuel Gompers, and other honored and trusted trade-union leaders, represented as sucking the life blood of the working class. There was no word of rebuke nor of caution in all the socialist press upon this contemptuous linking together of Mr. Parry and Mr. Gompers as oppressors of the working class.

When policy does not counsel otherwise the following editorial in "The People's Press" (Chicago, January 31, 1903), may be taken as a sample of their "honest" opinion:

A Socialist contributor to "The People's Press" of Albany, Ore., says:

"The labor unions are coming our way. Most of them are now with us, and the remaining ones will soon come, if we are true to ourselves and to the struggle of the producing class for simple justice."

"Bro. 'Rip Van Winkle' must have been asleep for a great many years, or must have cobwebs on the brain; for if he had read the proceedings of the late Miners' Convention — aye! the proceedings of any labor Convention — he could have seen that every Socialist proposition that was brought out by Socialist comrades, was killed — yes, killed! even before it had a chance to be debated!

"Labor Unions with Socialists? Rot! The whole American Federation of Labor, from Sammy Gompers and Mitchell down, are against Socialism! These are historical facts: Gompers fought and defeated Socialism in the last A. F. of L. Convention; in New Orleans; the Pope's 'loyal son,' Mitchell, and 'his holy water sprinkled' assistants, last week in the Convention of the United Mine Workers of America, defeated all resolutions in favor of International Socialism, even 'voting down' a proposition favoring public ownership and operation of the mines for the benefit of all the people. Under Socialism, these labor Judases would be out earning a living in the sweat of their own brows, instead of living, *like capitalists and priests, on the sweat of the fool working class !* No, Comrades, the labor unions are not with us! They are with the priests, and on the side of their masters and oppressors."

By ridicule, condemnation of sophistical argument every effort to establish industrial peace is hampered by socialists, — and every achievement sneered at and belittled.

" The Chicago Socialist" (July 18, 1903) has this to say :

"Peace, Peace, again Peace, Peace." At this time when John Mitchell of the mine workers and any number of miner labor leaders who desire to obtain prominence by securing praise from the capitalist press by talking nonsense about peace and conciliation between capital and labor."

It is the duty of socialists to come to the fore and cry, "I told you so, peace is impossible." Ah! ahem, it is impossible unless you good fellows of the trade-unions vote us socialist politicians into power — then we will have peace — we will destroy the state which we want you to put into our hands — we will destroy the family, it is no good anyhow because it is founded upon "property rights" and we want "free love" to found "free families," so that the "useless wading through the mire of the divorce court" will be over once for all — we will abolish religion and a whole host of other things necessary to civilization — then and not until then will the working class have peace. — Just imagine the "peace" which would attend such a condition as the socialists picture, the confusion of Babel would not be a circumstance to its discords.

"There can never be any reconciliation between capital and labor," hence the socialist revolution must come — vote it in ! say the socialists.

The trade-unionists take the opposite view, they declare that "reconciliation" may be established between workmen and their employers; through mutual trade agreements entered into between trade-unions' and employers' organizations. Socialists hold up to view the co-operative ownership of capital and the establishment of the "free family" as the necessary revolution by which to usher in industrial peace — While unionists deal with immediate problems, on the principle of progressive movement towards the establishment of equitable industrial relationships — one has envy and gush to stand on, and the other the rock of common-sense. Unionists work upon the principle that honest service on the one hand and honest remuneration on the other is the basis of industrial peace — and that mutual education as to their respective rights and duties will aid greatly in settling industrial conflicts. All this is too prosaic for the uncontrolled fire of the socialist — when the bottom of his philosophy is reached it is grounded in the belief that "class hatred . . . is the only moral incentive" of the working class. We quote from the "Condition of the Working Class in England" by Frederick Engels (page 237) :

"They 'the socialists' understand, it is true, why the workingman is resentful against the bourgeois, but regard as unfruitful this class hatred, which is, after all, the only moral incentive by which the worker can be brought nearer the goal."

An explanation, which is not given, as to how that which is unfruitful can bring a cause nearer its goal, would, at least, be interesting as a study of intellectual somersaults. However it but takes the "socialist mind" to be satisfied with an affirmation and a denial which is grounded upon one and the same premise.

The irrational (we hope we may say foreign without offence) spirit of socialism is nowhere better portrayed than when it confronts the dignities and duties of citizenship. It is certainly logical, if neither rational nor reasonable, if the power of the state is valued merely as a weapon with which to destroy the state, the family, religion, etc., etc., that no loyalty to no love for one's country should be felt. Hence it is that in affairs of government no socialist, no "scientific socialist" is in sympathy a citizen, he is but a political guerrilla — he seizes the arms of the state not in its defence, but only to overpower it. We give side by side the opposing positions of the trade unions and the socialist party as to the state militia. These two official statements sufficiently explain the rational attitude of the one and the irrationality of the other, coupled with its duplicity, for the intent is to make it appear that trade unions are working side by side with the socialist party in this matter.

"The resignation of Charles Stevenson, formerly a member of the Socialist Town Committee of Clinton, Mass., was asked by that body on account of his membership in the state militia. The letter of the committee read, in part: 'It is the unanimous opinion of your associates on the Socialist Town Committee that your action in joining the militia is in violation of the spirit and aim of the great world-wide Socialist movement (of which the Socialist Party of Clinton is an integral part), which stands for the emancipation of the race from capitalistic exploitation, and in every way opposes the existing spirit of militarism now fostered and kept alive by the capitalist class for the sole purpose of further enslaving the workers. . . . . The present structure of government is the creation of the ruling class. That being so, the militia is part of the equipment of capitalist society. . . . Your membership on the Socialist Town Committee is not desired by the other mem-

"J. J. H., *N. Y.* — Yes, a member of the state militia can be seated in a trades council. In fact, the matter is so obvious that it ought not be open for discussion at all.

"A man who is a wage earner and honorably working at his trade or calling to support himself and those dependent upon him, has not only the right to become a citizen soldier, but that right must be unquestioned.

"The militia, i. e., the citizen soldiery of the several states in our country, supplies what otherwise might take its place — a large standing army.

"The difference between the citizen soldiery of the United States and the large standing armies of many European countries is the difference between a republic and a monarchy — it is the difference between the conceptions of liberty and tyranny.

"While organized labor stands against the arbitrament of international or internal disputes by force of arms, yet we must realize we have not yet reached

bers thereof, and by vote of the committee your resignation is asked for.' The capitalist press is wildly excited about Socialist and trade-union opposition as usual when they see that the working class is beginning to open its eyes to its own interests." —"The Worker," August 16th, 1903.

the millennium; that in the age in which we live we have not the choice between armed force and absolute disarmament, but the alternative of a large standing army and a small one supplemented by a volunteer citizen soldiery — the militia of our several states.

" With this both wisdom and policy, as well as principle, should warrant our trade unions in not taking any cognizance of the matter at all, allowing each member to follow the bent of his own inclinations, insisting only that he shall be a wage earner, a faithful member of his union, and true to the cause of labor — the cause of humanity.—Ed. —"The American Federationist," August, 1903.

Another point of vital issue between the unionists and the socialists is in regard to the right of men to own and operate property as capital. Socialists claim that capitalists compose a "robber class" and they advocate the confiscation of capital as a just act. Trade unionists stand for the natural and also the legal right of men to hold such wealth and to operate it, at their pleasure, as capital as one shall have become legally possessed of.

We do not deem it necessary to supply data in proof of the trade unions' position for it is the normal one, that is, it is conceded by all save socialists that the constitutional right of holding property and of being protected in one's holdings is based upon the inherent, the moral, the God given right — given alike to all men. But the position so subversive of all civil law as that taken by socialists does not require data to convince the thinking man that so bold an assault upon the foundation of civil life is contemplated by a political party. Upon this point of Socialist philosophy, Marx, the father of "modern revolutionary scientific socialism" is not silent. The Communist Manifesto clearly enunciates the point and moreover it is as clearly put forth that this point of property in capital, in socialist philosophy, involves another of still greater importance — that of the monogamic family, which is, according to socialist doctrine founded upon property. Therefore the fall of one involves the fall of the other.

The classic literature, the propaganda pamphlets, the "cart-tail orators" and the lecturers, all use the same language, set for them by the Manifesto — "The expropriators must be expropriated;" capitalists are the "robber class," they have no legitimate right to the capital they hold. Capital is the surplus-value taken by the wage-system from the working class. Capital is merely unpaid wages, and many other like phrases fill the socialist press and are in constant use upon their platform. "The Socialist" published by the Socialist Educational Union of Seattle, Washington (June 21, 1903), says: "While an official declaration is lacking all understanding socialists must concede that the socialist theory of political economy and the Socialist conception of justice lead to that which is confiscation." The article then proceeds with the usual socialist argument in justification of their position — which is, that two hostile classes exist in society — that the capitalist "wrings" from the other through rent, interest and profits and basically by a "system which recognizes the right of one man to sit upon the back of another." This condition of affairs must be abolished. The article goes on to say that socialists do not stand for "government ownership" but for the whole industrial capital of the nation to be "democratically administered." This follows:

"We do not believe in recompensing the present possessors *because to do so would be to deprive the producers of a part of the fruits of their labor; a thing which is abhorrent to the socialist theory of right and justice.* Since confiscation is necessary to stop the infamous practices under which the masses are sweating blood, we stand for confiscation. . . . We stand for what we know to be right, regardless of the feelings of those who would sacrifice principles to expediency."

The semblance of argument is then abandoned for that grea er freedom of expression namely, condemnation of existing wrongs, which when viewed through the spectacles of socialist philosophy are seen in exaggerated proportions as though to silence all opposition the regulation negative defense of socialism is resorted to ; we quote :

"To those who think confiscation wrong we reply that nothing human ingenuity can devise could be more wrong than the system we are at present upholding and maintaining."

"Father" Thomas J. Hagerty, who is one of the western leaders — an organizer of the American Labor Union and the socialist party in the "A. L. U. Journal" and in the "Social Democratic Herald," Milwaukee, Wis., (March 14th, 1903,) says :

"Socialism denies the lawfulness of the present ownership on the ground that no length of time will justify an injustice or establish a stolen title.

"Since no one man has produced absolutely independently of his fellowmen any of the socially material or intellectual commodities of civilization, no one man or set of men have the right to their exclusive ownership and exploitation. If we are to make compensation to the present owners of the machinery of production and distribution, we must acknowledge that they hold just titles thereunto, and that the proletariat can acquire a rightful possession thereof only by being again exploited. That is to say that the workers must pay out of each day's labor a certain percentage to the Capitalist class; or, in other words, the people would become simply a general manager of industries in the modified interests of the ruling class. This would, beyond doubt, admirably suit the *Hearst Party* and the wild advocates of *State* socialism."

Speaking of the railroads the "Father" says :

"Socialism means to take them into a collective ownership absolutely without compensation of any kind from the present usurpers thereof, just as the federal army freed the chattel slaves of the South without paying a cent to their masters."

This is a favorite reference with socialists, and it is extremely seductive to the untrained mind — and to the enthusiast whose patriotism is aroused, only to be soured by further socialist contact. A better understanding could be had by the general public if it were well understood that socialism is a declaration of war not only against the capitalists but against society itself. For it is not less than this that the socialist party aims at. Not until recently have men become awakened to the danger of this lawless sentiment gaining political ascendency in our country — Perhaps the greatest source of danger lies in the fact that a large number of the most active workers in the socialist party are not themselves "class conscious." And as the socialist tactics foster double dealing the party machine may make use of such persons so long as they are not clearly acquainted with the issues or strong enough to set the tide against socialist doctrine within the ranks — in a word, so long as they are safe, they may make propaganda. "Oh come in, you will learn what socialism is later." Yes, certainly that is the reason for a continual influx of men and women of generous spirit, idealists not materialists in the proper sense, who aid greatly a work in which they would not engage did they clearly understand its import — We may say in passing this is the cause in great part of the confusion as to what the doctrine of socialism really is. Confusion as to whether one holds to religious idealism or whether it is a bread and butter movement — While all the time the "class conscious" leaders are perfectly well aware that the destruction of the state, the church, of the family and religion is the end and aim of the socialist movement. It seems to us that a simple but critical analysis of socialism is the best guard against this phase of the danger. Hence, this is one reason for issuing this book.

Another real danger from socialistic encroachments upon

rational standards lies in the fact of poverty, of miserable living in the midst of super-abundance. Socialism stalks abroad with its ulcers covered with a fine robe spun of deceit, and by brilliant oration and sick sweet sympathy it seduces men into believing that it holds the patent remedy for the woeful lack of justice in the economic world, which, after all is said and done, lies at the bottom of man's indifference to his brother man. The economic injustice is being adjusted by the trade unions. It is progressively securing the equity so necessary to the peace of the industrial world. But it is beyond the province of labor organizations to compel that human love which alone may manifest in acts of mutual helpfulness — in acts of wholesome charity which endureth all things and stinteth not the hand of mercy. This danger in our civilization must be met and passed by a fuller obedience to religious principles. It is this lack of justice — this want of mercy so vulgarly apparent in the civic and industrial world which battens the ribs of the socialist camp with raw recruits. The public must seek means of avoiding the menace of socialism from two sources. Trade unions may be sustained in their effort to progressively advance wages upon the rate of profits; shorten the hours, and so afford a higher standard of culture to the workmen and generally advance the conditions under which men do the work of the world. But behind this effort there must lie the human motive, that spirit which in honor prefereth one another — A sense of obligation must take possession of the hearts of the rich if they would aid in purifying the life of the people that they may not fall a prey to the socialist vulture, which "has no use for morals."

But we do not mean to stray too far away from our point of confiscation — only far enough to show that however lacking socialism is in solid ground to rest upon, it is logical in its programme of destruction. That its declarations regarding confiscation rest back upon the denial of the right to operate wealth as capital — and upon its postulate that

356

private property ushered in the monogamic form of the family as a result of that blind force which stands behind progress.

"The Worker" (New York, July 5, 1903), in its leading editorial, says, on the subject of "Confiscation,"

" It is conceivable that, if the capitalists have the sense to bow to the popular will as expressed at the ballot-box, the working people, more generous in the exercise of power than the capitalists have been, might grant them some special concessions in consideration of their quiet submission to the new social order. That is conceivable. We do not know whether it is probable. Judging from past history, it seems rather more probable that the capitalist class, which talks large about law and order now that it makes law and maintains order to suit itself, will, once the political power is voted out of its hands, throw law and order to the winds and by foolish attempts at reactionary conspiracy and insurrection forfeit all chance of lenient treatment.

" But, however that may be, if any such concessions are made to the dispossessed exploiters, it will assuredly not be as a measure of justice, but as a measure of generosity. They have no claims against us. We have incalculable claims against them. It is not for them to raise the question of compensation.

" Compensation? Who are they, the drones of society, to talk to us, the disinherited, of compensation when we resolve to enter into possession of that which is our own? They owe us all that they have, all that they are. It is a bitter debt of wrong that we owe them. Let them not talk of repayment."

Hundreds of further authoritative statements on the question of the confiscation of capital could easily be produced, substantiating the claim that socialism is an organized attempt to gain the political power for the purpose of committing the most stupendous robbery the world has ever seen, under the guise of legality. It is amazing, the specious arguments that these Sir Knights of "scientific socialism" pull over the face of their proposed gigantic theft. Socialist politicians, even in the embryo, are drunk with the prospect

357

of controlling, ah! no, of administering the vast mass of private capital employed in the processes of industry, commerce and finance. They are so thoroughly "over seas" that they even think themselves sober, even virtuous, when they gravely talk of generosity to those they contemplate robbing. Socialism quaffs at the bowl of wrath and mistakes the goblins of its dream for modern men and women.

We are now arrived at the last point of opposition in principle and in methods of trade unionism to socialism, which it is our purpose to take up at this time. Here one may find the same quality of sanity which characterizes the trade union position as in those of our previous analyses — While on the other hand the same spirit of irreconcilability is taken as is native to socialist philosophy — It will have none of nothing! It is thoroughly negative and it mistakes its aggressiveness for positiveness — It is always "*agin* the government." With an assurance born of ignorance and a few ambiguous phrases dubbed as science, socialism wears a chip upon its shoulder against all comers in the economic field, where it must be confessed the general lack of knowledge upon the fundamental principles of economic phenomena allows the socialist strut to become somewhat impressive.

Socialists scorn the trade union motto, a fair day's pay for a fair day's work. They declare that nothing less than the "full product" of a man's toil should satisfy him. This sounds well as an abstract proposition of justice — And we should certainly agree that trade unionists were well credited as cowards if they declare for less. But an abstract principle is not a standard, for it is of necessity that upon which the standard rests. It is the dinning of justice, justice, justice in men's ears with no comprehension of the proportions which the perfect principle of justice must assume relative to the affairs of men that works the mischief with brilliant minds of shaky morals. Men should receive the "full product" of their toil? Very well! What shall be done to bring about this state of affairs? For we shall assume that men operating capitals and men working for capitalists are now generally receiving inequitable shares of the wealth produced. That is to say, wages are too low relative to the profits accumulated.

To be sure, this is very simple, exceedingly so, vote the socialist party into power and we will give each man the "full value" of his labor by the establishment of the collective ownership of capital. Ah! yes, — the "full value"— You see, not the "full product" but the "full value" will be given — Let me see — the value? Yes, the value. Why, of course, this is the science of socialism, one must know the economics of socialism to understand the movement.

I see that your proposition of giving to each worker the "full value" of his product involves the knowledge of what value is as a distinct proposition from the "full product" which a man produces. It is deep ground and to cover it one must know wages as a principle as distinct from the wages system which is the application of wages to the present stage of industrial development.

Wage-slaves only get a part of their product, the capitalists on their backs get the largest half. Wages? — what are wages anyhow? Why, — wages? Of course wages is what a man gets for his labor, his "surplus-labor" is what the capitalist gets for nothing. A most stupendous robbery! the thieves! All they think of the working class is to squeeze the life blood out of them. Nothing but socialism is of any use — We must have the social revolution — we must abolish this awful system — we must abolish the wages-system. Then we shall have no wages — everybody will be a capitalist, although we will abolish capital and leave only the means of production. Oh! really the way out of the difficulty is sweet simplicity itself, socialism is.

But Mr. Socialist, I know very well that wages as an abstract term is the return in wealth for a man's economic effort — but as all abstract principles must be brought down to relative applications, so of course, if one would rationally view wages he must deal with specific applications of the general principles — and I must defend the trade union motto on the ground that it is strictly in accord with common sense. It combines in popular speech the elements of justice and morality. That is to say it gives expression to correct judgments as related to the volume of value deposited by a day's labor together with an expression of the honest, the moral, element of square dealing between man and man. I must therefore defend the trade union motto as being strictly scientific — despite your bluster, sir. Both your proposition to give each man his "full value" and the motto of the trade unions rest upon the same economic principles, — but whereas you have stated your position in a glorious abstraction — if I may be pardoned, bitten off more than your socialist jaws can chew, the trade unionists have in their motto reduced the abstract principle to its concrete form — to the differing economic relationships in the common sense world of every day affairs. But, Mr. Socialist, you shall not escape so readily as to leave the question at the fever heat of imagination. Your blatant confidence in your own ignorance will not serve you on this occasion. We will bring you to the touchstone. And we will show that if your abstractions, your glaring theories, are probed to the quick, your vagueness is all the foundation there is to be found for your vaingloriousness to rest upon. To be specific, Mr. Socialist, we shall examine your economic ground and bring your boastful "science" to its knees. You would give each man his "full value" (after the revolution) — good! So, too, would "a fair day's pay for a fair day's work give to each man his full value, but before the revolution — without a revolution in the "system." And this too notwithstanding the fact that you have nothing but contempt and ridicule for trade unions as a means of solving the industrial problems confronting the American people — Although you do value them as "recruiting stations" for socialism.

Oh! but one can't deal fairly with the robber class. Every capitalist is a robber, although he himself personally · is not to blame for it, it is the system which makes him so. He exploits the workingmen — he appropriates the surplus values to his own uses. — The whole system is rotten, it can't stand five years longer — Wilshire says so.

So, too, did Marx and Babel and many other socialists prophecy that capitalism would fall ere this — but despite the prophecies of socialists and second adventists the world still moves on its due course. And too it were better to be a little cooler, Mr. Socialist, for I have you at long range where I can keep you under fire — and this is, to tell you the whole truth, but the first gun on the skirmish line — I merely mean to introduce the battle on economic ground — to declare the war which I am confident will last longer than the years allowed in your prophecy for the end of capitalism. But to the issue — you declare that each man should receive the "full value" of his toil. So do trade unionists. The difference is you put forth a vague abstraction — while they put forth a practical proposition. You attempt to work out of your own reach — while they work with what there is to do with, close at hand. They take the steps which lead on their journey's way. You would put on the seven leagued boots which like the darkey's coat, you fit too soon. In a word, trade unionists have a workable, a possible programme; while you have an irrational, an impossible programme.

As men work together, and must work together, under the law of that Great Design which the good God impressed upon the human race, each man and all men perforce sustain economic relationships. Under the law of justice each man should receive his relative share of the value deposited by him in the wealth created and in the services rendered. Pardon me, you will not, Mr. Socialist, be allowed (for I know

361

your tactics full well) to run off at a tangent and inveigh against the capitalist system — for denunciation does not solve problems as you so often seem to think. If it were that men must now begin at the very beginning a super-human effort would be required to approach the task of clas-sifying so vast a phenomena as that which makes up the eco-nomic division of man's activities. But as the race has been sane centuries before socialists were "class conscious," long ago there have been interwoven into the fabric of industrial society those eternal principles which are in no danger what-ever from socialist assault upon them (however much our in-stitutions are endangered) for the simple but sufficient reason that they are eternal — that is, unlike the human institutions which may come and go, eternal principles are above the creative design of man. Man may obey them or he may dis-obey them, but he cannot abolish them, as foolish men in their folly fondly believe.

Long ago — but not before men were sinners — wise men embodied the principle of justice in the relationships of men. Values were measured, that wealth might be equitably exchanged, and that a man mightest receive his just hire. But were the values Perfectly measured? Certainly not — for the work of the hand of God alone is Perfect, if measured by the Perfect standard. However, from a human stand-point progressively perfect measures of values as standards of price have been erected. Now here is a point — which you, Mr. Socialist, who are wont to talk so profusely of value would do well to note. Values were never, in all the world, measured without being measured by value — by the unit of value — by value in independent form — by money. And whereas money was and is created by society — by the state — value is created by individuals — by all those persons who apply their energies to the production of wealth — to the ser-vices necessary to the economic sphere. Value, economic value, infers within that division (we may say fluid division) of the economic world which pertains to the exchange sphere, and to that department of economics alone. So before one may have a workable knowledge of the laws which govern the giving and the receiving of "a fair day's pay for a fair day's work," he must with intellectual precision be able to separate the economic sphere into three clear cut divisions. The sphere of domestic economy must stand as distinct as one line of a triangle from the other two; and the sphere of civil, of governmental economy may be likened to the second line of the triangle which is sharply distinct from the first and the third lines which make up the triangle. While political economy proper, the sphere of exchange, is not to be confounded, if science is maintained, with either of the other two parts which make up the general whole of economic life. We shall now ask a question. How may economic values be measured so that a man may receive his just share of the value which he has deposited within the exchange sphere of wealth? Mr. Socialist, you will kindly answer.

Why, under the coöperative commonwealth, where of course the ward committees will administer the industries — and let the people do as they please, for we will not tolerate any interference with the personal liberties of anybody. The curse of all times is that there have been laws to compel men to do what they didn't want to do — we insist upon "freedom" you know. Oh we shall all be rich and happy under socialism. — Why! then women will be free to work on equal terms with men. Free love will make the family free; and the free family will make men free. Socialist freedom will be beyond the wildest dream of man. After the state and religion and all authority and restraint of all kinds have been abolished there will be nothing left to prevent liberty to all. Men and women will be free to live out the noble life there is in them. They will be free——

Mr. Socialist, will you be so good as to come back to the question? We are sufficiently acquainted with your philosophy to know that we should write slavery and licence where you write freedom and liberty. For a man cannot run counter to the moral law, however glibly he may talk about it, without enslaving himself. — Permit me, the question is, what is your proposition for measuring value?

Under the coöperative commonwealth — but of course I can't make cook shop receipts for the future society. For a free society will certainly know much better what it wants than any socialist to-day could tell them. That force called progress will turn things over — it will bring on the revolution. Then the capitalists will have to get down from the backs of the working class, my class. Oh! they are class conscious enough — they know well enough how to grind the face of the poor — to keep the children in ignorance by working in the factory before they are old enough to go to school. — Socialism will give their children a chance to go to work and earn an honest living. — We will ——

Pardon me — we are quite keenly alive to the sins committed upon innocent children and we yield to no man, up to our capacity, in our sympathy for those who are deprived of comfortable homes and educational advantages. However, it illy suits the complexion of your philosophy, Mr. Socialist, to talk in defence of children. Under your proposed regime there would be no homes of any kind — and we are confident that millions will testify to the fact that homes of poverty have been homes of happiness. — And as for education, your atheist schools would deprive children of that most necessary department of education. For you explicitly state that a "free society" would not permit the brains of children to become dulled by the teaching of religious superstitions. We are not discussing miseries or the education of children, but a question which requires something more than the flow of the heart's emotion. This is head work not heart work. If a surgeon were to let his eyes overflow with tears at the suffering of his patient, he would be unable to give him the much needed service of professional skill. Will you tell me how you propose to measure value?

We shall have no use for money; the money sharks have had it all their own way long enough. There will be no more of turning men, women and children — infants in arms — out on the street in the snow and sleet. No more ——

But, sir, I must insist that you come to the point — diffuseness is a very poor substitute for sticking to the point in an argument — a point which I insist shall not be glossed over. Your scorn for the trade unions as a pure and simple organization has a very poor edge to it — it turns away from the core of the question at issue between you. How do you propose to measure value if not with money? For upon the right of individual ownership of property rests the exchange of property — and upon the exchange of wealth rests the necessity for money and the consequent evolution of money. Now if you say one may own wealth but not capital, you deny the essential element of private property, namely the right to use one's own. — We are frank to say that the philosophy of socialism loves the working class merely as a bargain to gain its political power. And it is an exceedingly funny episode in your history, the quarrel of Leibknecht and Marx over the fact of a workingmens' party which had no workingmen in it.

Yes, I see what you mean — A man is entitled to all he produces. His labor-time will tell what his share is. He will be given a labor check and he can exchange it for a beefsteak or a new shirt as he chooses.

I thank you, Mr. Socialist, you have at last, though reluctantly, put yourself on record. You will have "labor checks." You have had little to say on the subject of money all these years that you have been making propaganda amongst the radicals, but "labor checks" are "fetching." They are so simple! So easy to understand. Your ward committee who administers the industries (but, oh! no, I understand you, you say there will be no politicians under socialism. For the very good reason that all will be politicians — yes, of course some men will be higher in rank — they will be on the administration committee — but then that is nothing for all will have liberty, equality and fraternity all the same). We say your ward committee will keep the time and as "labor checks" are not money one man's time will stand equally as against another's in whatever craft or profession. Surely there will be no disputes as to the justice of the exchange — for has not each man a right to his life and his liberty and his pursuit of happiness. It is the system — it is capitalism which makes men bad. Yes, certainly, Mr. Socialist, you see I know all your — I beg pardon of common sense — arguments. If values are to exchange equitably for values it is necessary to get at the substance of value. To know what value is in its essence. Positively it is not labor time as against labor time irrespective of the quality of the work. Degrees of quality count as well as numbers of hours. Therefore one hour's work requiring a high degree of skill is not equal to one hour of work of a lesser degree of skill. — For the simple reason that a higher rate of intelligence was expended in the one case than in the other. — The work ran at a higher pressure so to speak. — Therefore the labor deposit was larger in volume, it weighed more. It is clear that value, or if you please the human labor crystalized within wealth proper, or within an economic service must be the result of that which is twofold in its nature, namely, time as fixed by hours and the specific quality of the work. Consequently, that equity may prevail, that a man may, to put it abstractly receive the full value of his product or to put it concretely, when applied to the wage-earner, get a fair day's pay for a fair day's work, the specific portion due a man must be determined upon the twofold principle of time and quality. This is the precise service which money renders. Being value itself, being value in independent form, its unit becomes the measure of value and so consequently the standard of price. This is the stumbling block over which socialists fall when they declare for the labor check as a substitute for money. Therefore it is not " labor time," but time plus quality of work which forms the essence of value, while money forms the independent substance of value. Therefore it is that the motto of trade unionists is rational. It deals with concrete realities — with relative relationship in the industrial world. Not with an abstraction which to be rational must first be worked down to a practical standard. Socialists discard one half the basis necessary to the understanding of value. —When they talk of "time checks" they gloss over or utterly ignore the principle of intensity as related to differing designs for producing wealth. — They deny those higher degrees of intelligence which are necessary to the higher grades of work. Their economic theory reduces all men to the same dead level of mediocrity. This being impossible because the Original Design gives each individual a character and capacity peculiar to himself. The fact that socialists declare for "labor checks" is proof that their propaganda is non-intelligent — non-scientific and non-moral — or rather because no body of persons are able to escape human responsibility, however stoutly they may deny it, the purely economic part of their propaganda is immoral, intellectually; that is to say, it is inethical.

Now Mr. Socialist, as you have the temerity to ask for the suffrages of our countrymen — especially do you appeal to those citizens who are members of trade unions — standing on trade union ground we challenge you to a defense of your position in opposition to that expressed in their motto " a fair day's pay for a fair day's work " — we declare it to be strictly equitable.

The American Labor Union is organized as the "battering ram" to besiege, and to conquer, the American Federation of Labor, to the end of annexing this great economic organization to the tail of the socialist party kite. And here is a pen picture of the ease with which it is to be done. The letter is from an ex-priest who is a socialist and an American Labor Union leader. It was printed in the "Advance," Aug. 16, 1902. "Bellevue, Ky., Aug. 1, 1902. Picnic Committee, Alameda County Socialists.

" The action of the late convention at Denver has changed the tide of battle and has given a new impulse and a new phase to the movement (the socialist movement). In a few years — perhaps in one or two, and certainly not more than three — the American Labor Union will absorb the American Federation of Labor, and the masses will march to the polls under the banner of Socialism."

(Signed)   T. McGRADY.

There are two more years in which to fulfill the prophecy — Socialists are battering from without and boring from within — for many are still intent on the capture of the American Federation of Labor by the peaceful means of shelving the time tried and true officials and of elevating to their places "class conscious socialists. It is found somewhat difficult to name one to walk in the shoes of President Gompers, but the ascendant to the place of the Secretary (Mr. Morrison) is already found, even the author is able to give his name.

If the downfall of the A. F. of L. should become a matter of history — which I have no fear will be the case — it is certain that the trade union movement cannot hold the respect which it has gradually forced from a reluctant public opinion by its years of hard and intelligent work. And it is equally certain that were so disastrous a fate to befall the A. F. of L. its best support, those great masses of men who stand for the moral principles which are the bulwark of the family, the church and the state would stand from under and let it sink to its death. The trade union that declares for socialism must be met on the same ground as socialist parties

368

are met — they must be recognized as the enemies of society — whipped off the political arena.

Fear not! Such men as Samuel Gompers and John Mitchell stand as good security against so dread a fate. They are too well versed in the principles of socialism not to heed the danger — they are too well acquainted with socialist tactics not to understand their modes of attack — the American Federation of Labor is too strong in honor and in purpose of integrity to sink to a lower place. Its prospects are bright and its face is squarely set towards the right.

———

"Now I have stated what I considered necessary to be said on these points. It is sufficient to serve as a picture of a stranger who knocks at your door, and whether you admit him friendly or dismiss him unheard, he is prepared for both, and must be contented with either."

———

Addenda.

REGARDING socialism as a menace to civil society the author has sent this book out upon its mission of education as to what socialism really is. As the contest promises to be long and as this book is expected merely to open up the question a Magazine has been started within which from month to month the special questions within this field will be dealt with. The author would recommend that those persons who care to see the propaganda of socialism in all the various departments, its political, economic, sociological, philosophical, and theological, analyzed by able critics of this world wide movement, that they seek information from the "Wage Worker," — 133 Summer Street, Boston, Massachusetts.

Socialist Authorities Quoted.